Michael Ramsey

The
Gospel
and the
Catholic
Church

ἱερουργοῦντα τὸ εὐαγγελίον τοῦ Θεοῦ

—Rom.15.16

Foreword by Geoffrey Rowell
Chaplain of Keble College, Oxford

First published 1936 by Longmans, Green and Co., London
Second edition published 1956 by Longmans, Green and Co.

This new impression of the second edition, with new Foreword by
Geoffrey Rowell, published in Great Britain in 1990 by SPCK, Holy
Trinity Church, Marylebone Road, London NW1 4DU

British Library Cataloguing in Publication data
Ramsey, Michael, *1904 – 1988*
   The gospel and the Catholic Church, — 2nd ed.
   1. Catholic Church. Relations with Anglican Communion
   I. Title
   282

   ISBN 0-281-04469-4

Printed in the United States of America

FOREWORD

IN 1936, when the young Michael Ramsey was Sub-Warden of Lincoln Theological College, the first edition of *The Gospel and the Catholic Church* was published. As Ramsey wrote in the Preface, his intention was to expound the nature of the Church 'as a part of the Gospel of Christ crucified'—a theme to which he had been led 'both by the New Testament and by many discussions of the problem of the reunion of Christendom' (p. vi). Such a theme was in line with St Paul's comment in Romans 15.16, quoted on the title page, concerning his calling 'to be a minister of Christ Jesus...in the priestly service of the gospel of God.'

As a student at Cambridge Michael Ramsey had been influenced by Sir Edwyn Hoskyns. He wrote of this in the foreword he contributed to the posthumous work of Hoskyns and Davey, *Crucifixion—Resurrection*:

> Hoskyns had a remarkable influence, and I was one of those who as a young student came under his spell...though I never became an uncritical devotee.... It was exciting to follow him as in his lectures he traced the religious experience of the early church, the relation of the experience to the events from which it sprang, and the interpretation of both events and experience in theological terms.[1]

The theme of religious experience and its relation to doctrine and the life of the Church was an important one for the Anglican 'Liberal Catholicism' of Cambridge, which in 1926 had produced *Essays Catholic and Critical*. In that volume Wilfred Knox wrote that Christian experience was 'the apprehension of God through the person of Christ...vouchsafed to all Christians who in any way attempt to live up to the standard of their profession.' Christian doctrine and Christian devotion were inextricably linked. The truth of the Catholic faith was 'guaranteed more by its intrinsic value as proved by past experience than by the oracular infallibility of certain isolated definitions.'[2] In another

---

1 E. C. Hoskyns & N. Davey: *Crucifixion—Resurrection: The Pattern of Theology and Ethics in the New Testament* (ed. G. Wakefield), 1981, p. xi.
2 E. G. Selwyn (ed.): *Essays Catholic And Critical*, 1926, pp. 104, 114.

essay Hoskyns wrote on 'The Christ of the Synoptic Gospels,' concluding that 'the New Testament is one book, not merely because certain documents have been collected together by ecclesiastical authority or by common Christian usage, but because it presumes an underlying unity of faith and experience.' 'The characteristic features of Catholic piety have their origin in our Lord's interpretation of His own Person and of the significance of His disciples for the world.'[3] It was this essay which convinced Michael Ramsey of 'the continuity between the historical Jesus and the Christ of apostolic faith.'[4] In his *Cambridge Sermons* Hoskyns commented 'how rarely the word Christian occurs in the New Testament compared with the word Church...as men of His *Ecclesia*, we possess the word and wisdom of God; we share in the worship of God in spirit and in truth....We are...confident that the revelation of God, I will not say *stands* in the Bible, in the sacraments, in the creeds and in the Christ, but occurs, acts, is energetic and effective through them.'[5]

It was with similar convictions that Michael Ramsey began his exploration of the nature of the Church by pointing to the theme of crucifixion—resurrection. 'S.Peter, S.Paul and S.John show plainly that the meaning and ground of the Church are seen in the death and resurrection of Jesus and in the mysterious sharing of the disciples in these happenings' (p. 6). The early chapters of the book are a powerful recall to the Christian living out of cross and resurrection that is needed no less today than when it was first written. Only when that foundation has been firmly laid can the nature of the church's unity be explored, and the place in that unity of church order, episcopacy, worship, liturgy and creed be established. There is a concern to overcome the endemic individualism of much Western Christianity in both Protestant and Catholic forms, and to recover the sense of the organic life of the Church as the Body of Christ. Ramsey was appreciative of Gabriel Hebert's book *Liturgy and Society*, and shared with Hebert an indebtedness to F D.Maurice

---

3 *Ibid.*, p. 175.
4 Hoskyns & Davey, p. xi.
5 *Ibid.*, p. 53.

on the one hand and an awareness of the nascent Liturgical Movement on the Continent. His theology is a prayed theology and a corporate theology. In some of what Ramsey writes the influence of the work of the Belgian Jesuit Emil Mersch on the 'Mystical Body of Christ' is apparent.

Hebert reviewed Ramsey's book in *Theology*, stressing how Gospel and Church belong together in the New Testament, and how one root cause of Christian division has been the 'failure to see any intimate organic connection between the Gospel and the outward order of the Church.' He welcomed wholeheartedly Ramsey's insistence that for 'the Christians of the apostolic age, the facts of the death and resurrection of Christ were at once external facts belonging to history, and internal facts ever renewed in their own experience.'

> They themselves had died and been raised with Christ; they had been 'buried with Him by baptism unto death,' and they were 'risen with Christ' to a new life, a life of incorporation into His Body, as members of Him and thereby members of one another. They had died to the old self-centered life, they had received a share in a new life of *koinonia*. These are the two poles around which the New Testament conception of the Church revolves—the death and the *koinonia*.[6]

It is this emphasis that makes baptism and eucharist constitutive of the Church. It is this which is embodied and expressed in the apostolate and the creeds.

Michael Ramsey wished to recall both Evangelicals dismissive of church order, and legalistic Catholics to a truly catholic awareness of the continuity and interdependence of the Gospel and Church order. He sought to present the Episcopate as the continuity of apostolic ministry in the church, which is 'built upon the foundation of the apostles and prophets.' He wished such an understanding of the episcopate to be a contribution to Christian unity, which itself was inseparable from 'the growth within every part of the Church of the truths of the Body and the

---

6 *Theology*, Vol. xxxii, May 1936, No. 191, pp. 307-9.

Passion, no less than of the "outward marks" which express those truths.' 'The unification of outer order can never move faster than the recovery of inward life' (p. 222). In that quest for the holiness which is inseparable from the quest for unity both the witness of catholic Christendom and of the Reformers (most notably Martin Luther) had an essential part to play. As Archbishop of Canterbury Michael Ramsey's own involvement with the quest for both unity and holiness was undoubted, and it was fitting that among the gifts he presented to Pope Paul VI when he visited him in Rome in 1966 and initiated with the Pope the ARCIC conversations on the basis of the 'Holy Scriptures and the ancient common traditions', was a copy of *The Gospel and the Catholic Church*. The short but prophetic appendix on 'The See of Rome and Unity' might be viewed as a working text both for ARCIC's observations on universal primacy and Archbishop Runcie's comments during his 1989 visit to Rome.

> It seems possible that in the reunited Church of the future there may be a special place for a *"primus-inter-pares"* as an organ of unity and authority. Peter will be needed as well as Paul and Apollos, and like them he will be chastened and repentant.... A primacy should depend upon and express the organic authority of the Body; and the discovery of its precise functions will come not by discussion of the Petrine claims in isolation but by the recovery everywhere of the Body's organic life, with its Bishops, presbyters and people. In this Body Peter will find his due place, and is hastened not by the pursuit of 'the Papal controversy' but by the quiet growth of the organic life of every part of Christendom (pp.227-8).

The Gospel and the Catholic Church was republished in 1956, twenty years after it originally appeared. As Michael Ramsey acknowledged in his Preface, since the time of its first appearance a host of new questions had arisen in a world and a Church greatly changed. He made a few minor changes by removing some references to earlier controversies and by adding some additional notes, but he believed his general thesis still stood and the book was widely welcomed. It is this second edition which is reprinted here. This new publication is likewise a result of a conviction that, despite circumstances that are further changed since 1956, it remains a classic theological work which repays careful study as a profound exposition of that reformed Catholicism to which Anglicanism at its best has borne witness. Here is a revealed theology, a biblical theology and a theology rooted in prayer—and we have need of all these in an age of relativism and change. The doctrine of the church is once more at the centre of much Anglican discussion and reflection in times when Anglicans are facing sharp questions about authority, ministry and unity, and where the different answers given to those questions spring from different perceptions of the Church and threaten to create new divisions. Whether or not one agrees with the recent contention of Paul Avis that an Anglican ecclesiology can 'no longer be drawn from the writings of English divines from Richard Hooker to Michael Ramsey,'[7] there is no doubt that to 'read, mark, learn and inwardly digest' *The Gospel and the Catholic Church* will at least ensure that the debate is both deeper and more informed. In a generation when many Anglicans, both ordained and lay, have come into the Church from outside there is much to be learnt from the exposition of Catholic ecclesiology by an Anglican who himself came from a Congregationalist background, was rooted in Scripture, and drank deeply at the wells of the theology of the Fathers and of Orthodox spirituality. All concerned with the identity of Anglicanism can still learn much of the temper of Anglican theology and its ecclesial character from this seminal book by an archbishop who, with all his much-loved eccentricities, was one of the spiritual leaders of this century.

November, 1989

Geoffrey Rowell,
Keble College, Oxford.

---

7 P. Avis: *Anglicanism and the Christian Church: Theological Resources in Historical Perspective*, 1989, p. xviii. Avis, while appreciative of Ramsey's positive evaluation of the Reformers, is critical of his advocacy of the 'apostolic paradigm' of the Church. 'The doctrines of ministerial priesthood and apostolic succession do not sit happily together.' (p.172, cf. 306-7).

PREFACE TO THE FIRST EDITION

THE underlying conviction of this book is that the meaning of the Christian Church becomes most clear when it is studied in terms of the Death and Resurrection of Jesus Christ. The author attempts to apply this conviction to some of the problems concerning the doctrine of the Church. What is the nature of Christian fellowship in contrast with other ideas of unity amongst men? Is Episcopacy merely a convenient form of Church government, or has it some deeper meaning in the Gospel of God? These are among the questions which this book discusses, by expounding the Church as a part of the Gospel of Christ crucified.

The author has been led to this line of approach both by the New Testament and by many discussions of the problem of the reunion of Christendom.

(1) The study of the New Testament points to the Death and Resurrection of the Messiah as the central theme of the Gospels and Epistles, and shows that these events were intelligible only to those who shared in them by a more than metaphorical dying and rising again with Christ. It is the contention of this book that in this dying and rising again the very meaning of the Church is found, and that the Church's outward order expresses its inward meaning by representing the dependence of the members upon the one Body, wherein they die to self. The doctrine of the Church is thus found to be included within the Christian's knowledge of Christ crucified.

(2) Discussions on reunion often seem to lead straight to a deadlock. The adherents of one tradition use language about the divinely ordered constitution of the Church and about regular channels of grace. The adherents of another

tradition appeal to the Gospel and to the general body of the redeemed, which can use order and constitutions but which can never be determined by them.   The differences lie deep—and a fresh line of approach seems needed, namely, to study the Church's order not in institutionalist terms but in terms of the Gospel, and to ask (to give but one example) whether Episcopacy tells of some aspect of the Gospel which would lack expression if Episcopacy were to be abandoned. Thinking along these lines, the author reached the conclusion that the structure of the Catholic Church has great significance in the Gospel of God, and that Apostolic succession is important on account of its *evangelical* meaning.

The plan of the book is as follows.   In *Part I* the relation between the Messiah and the Church in the New Testament is examined, and it is argued that the main structure of Catholicism springs directly from the Messianic Gospel. In *Part II* the main phases of Christian history and the problem of reunion are brought into relation to those facts about the Gospel and the Church which the study of origins has disclosed.

The reader will notice that the size and scope of the two Parts are different.   Thus in Part I there is a thorough and detailed inquiry into the primitive meaning of the Church.   In Part II a similar attempt at thoroughness is impossible—so vast is the field—but a number of historical applications of the fundamentals are carefully made, in the hope that the reader who accepts these fundamentals may make similar applications to the situation which concerns him most.   For, if the Church's meaning lies in its fulfilment of the sufferings of Christ, then every part of its history is intelligible in terms of the Passion.   The right interpretation of the Church's task, in this present as in every age, will begin with the Biblical study of the Death and Resurrection of the Messiah, wherein the meaning of the Church is contained.

PREFACE TO THE SECOND EDITION

THE call for a re-issue of this book some twenty years after its original publication suggests that its thesis still claims a hearing. The book was written at a time when the impact of the revival of biblical theology upon the doctrine of the Church was first being strongly felt in this country, and it was itself an outcome of that impact. Since then a host of new questions has arisen in a world and a Church greatly changed. But rather than add to the length of the book by drawing out fresh contemporary applications, I have revised it simply by removing some passages concerned with controversies of twenty years ago (particularly in the last chapter) and by adding some Additional Notes of a corrective kind. I have followed this course in the hope that readers will be able to draw their own applications and will welcome the exposition of the main theme as it stands.

September, 1955   MICHAEL DUNELM

CONTENTS

PART I

CHAPTER I

CHAPTER II

CHAPTER III

CONTENTS

CHAPTER VII

CHAPTER VIII

CHAPTER XI

(*i*) The Western Church achieved vast successes, but it presented a maimed Catholicism. (*a*) The Papacy crushes out the true meaning of the Bishops; (*b*) the severance of East and West brings loss to both; (*c*) legalism; (*d*) decline in the organic sense of the Body; (*e*) underlying perversions of the Gospel. Recovery of the deeper doctrine of the Church could come only through recovery of the Gospel. Crisis of the Reformation.

The Counter Reformation, for all its fruits, failed to recover the doctrine of the one Body effectively, since (*a*) it led on to modern Papalism, (*b*) its characteristic piety was individualistic. Latinism is thus but a partial and sometimes a divisive element in Catholicism.

(*ii*) Yet the outward divisions and perversions have not prevented the continuance of the inward life of the Catholic Church in the unbreakable unity of the one race. The essence of Catholicism to be sought in the underlying fact of Corpus Christi, as seen (*a*) in the Liturgy and the liturgical movement, (*b*) in the renewal of contact with the East and the Eastern view of $\sigma\hat{\omega}\mu\alpha$, (*c*) in the Gospel whence the meaning of Catholicism is derived.

CHAPTER XII

(*i*) In Luther and Calvin the revival of the Gospel brought with it the revival of the corporate idea of the Church. But the revival failed to sustain itself, because the Reformers failed to see the primitive relation between the Gospel and Church order. *Luther* restored not only the Pauline sense of justification, but also the Pauline doctrine of the Body. Yet Lutheranism lapsed into individualism owing to (*a*) a false antithesis between inward and outward, (*b*) failure to see the meaning of the Apostle and the Bishop as organs of one historic and visible Church. *Calvin* also revived a deep churchmanship, but he too missed the meaning of the Apostles, and "levelled" the Bishop and the presbyter. Hence the return to the Pauline Gospel was incomplete.

(*ii*) Through missing an important element in Pauline Christianity, Protestantism has again and again fallen into subjective tendencies quite at variance with its original supernaturalism. Examples from (*a*) worship, (*b*) piety, (*c*) use of scripture. The need to ask whether Church order has not a vital connexion with the Gospel of God.

CONTENTS

CHAPTER XIII

CHAPTER XIV

APPENDICES

PART I

CHAPTER I

The Church and the Passion

Throughout the centuries the Church of God has had both its devoted adherents, who would die for it, and its persecutors, who have sought to destroy it. Thus, both in love and in hatred, men have reckoned with it seriously, and have been compelled to think out their attitude towards it. But at the present time there is a very different mood widespread, one of apathy and bewilderment which asks, "What is this strange thing, the Christian Church? Whatever can it mean? What relation have its services, its hierarchy, its dogmas, its archaic and beautiful language, to the daily troubles of mankind?" This bewilderment leads many to pass the Church by, since it seems to do and say so little about the things which matter supremely—world peace, social reform, the economic tangle. "And is not the Church itself divided and beset with controversy?" Surrounded by men and women too apathetic even to be hostile, the Christians are driven to think out where the relevance of the Church really lies.

There are many, therefore, within the Church who believe that its relevance must be found in its ability to take a lead in social and international policies, and who would meet the situation by attempts to make the Church " up to date " and " broad-minded " and " progressive " in the cause of peace and economic reform. The Church in their view must bestir itself to provide such remedies as thoughtful men outside the Church demand, and to answer the questions which such men are asking ; and if it fails to do this it remains a scandal, ignored by this generation.

But the New Testament suggests that the right answer begins at a very different point. For the relevance of the Church of the Apostles consisted not in the provision of outward peace for the nations, nor in the direct removal of social distress, nor yet in any outward beauty of the Church itself, but in pointing to the death of Jesus the Messiah, and to the deeper issues of sin and judgement—sin in which the Christians had shared, judgement under which they stood together with the rest of mankind. In all this the Church was scandalous and unintelligible to men, but by all this and by nothing else it was relevant to their deepest needs.

For the relevance of the Church can never be any easier than was the relevance of the Messiah. He provoked questionings and doubts among many of the wisest and holiest of His race. He perplexed those who looked to Him as a national leader, as a reformer, a prophet, a teacher and a healer, and even as Messiah; for He abandoned His useful and intelligible works in Galilee in order to bring God's Kingdom by dying on the Cross. " There was no beauty in him that we should desire him." And the life beset by the " whys ? " and the " wherefores ? " of good and sensible men ended with the terrible question-mark of the cry of desolation from the Cross, " My God, My God, why hast thou forsaken me ? " So ended His earthly life, but in the manner of its end and in the " why ? " uttered on Calvary, there was present the power of God ; for Jesus knew whence He came and whither He was going. His Church on earth is scandalous, with the question-marks set against it by bewildered men and with the question-mark of Calvary at the centre of its teaching ; yet precisely there is the power of God found, if only the Christians know whence they come and whither they go. They are sent to be the place where the Passion of Jesus Christ is known and where witness is borne to the Resurrection from the dead. Hence the philanthropist, the reformer, the broad-minded modern man can never understand, in terms of their own ideals, what the Church is or what it means. Of course it is scandalous, of course it is formed of sinners whose sinfulness is exposed by the light of the Cross, of course there is an awful question-mark at its centre. These things must needs be, if it is the Body of Christ crucified and risen from the dead.

Thus the first need of the Christians, in face of the apathy and the bewilderment about the Church, is to know and to be able to say plainly what the Church really *is*. This does not mean to know and to say what the Church *ought* to be, as, for instance, that it ought to be full of love and peace and to shower blessings on mankind, and that it will soon be doing this through a new energy of the Holy Spirit. " It doth not yet appear what we shall be." Before the Christians can say these things about what the Church ought to be, their first need is to say what the Church is, here and now amid its own failures and the questionings of the bewildered. Looking at it now, with its inconsistencies and its perversions and its want of perfection, we must ask what is the real meaning of it just as it is. As the eye gazes upon it, it sees—the Passion of Jesus Christ. And the eye of faith sees further—the power of Almighty God. The Christians will not try to answer the philanthropist and the reformer by meeting them on their own terms and by hiding the scandalous Gospel. They will say plainly what the Church of God is, and whither it points. Philanthropies point to the conditions of men's lives, the Church points to the deeper problem of man himself.

This book is written as a study of the Church, and its doctrine, and unity and structure, in terms of the Gospel of Christ crucified and risen. In the light of this Gospel the meaning of the Church will be examined. It seems that both the theologian, and the worker for Christian reunion, and the philanthropist are compelled towards this line of approach.

(1) The *theologian* is forced by the New Testament to study the Church in this way. The Church has often been expounded as the " extension of the Incarnation," and in these terms some classical teaching about the Church has

been given. But the New Testament takes us deeper than this. It shows us how the disciples knew themselves to be the refounded Israel of God through being partakers in the Messiah's death. The prediction by Jesus of His death had bewildered them ; and in answer to their bewilderment He taught them that they would not understand the death except by sharing in it. The language in the Gospels about following Christ in His Passion,

" if any man would come after me, let him deny himself, and take up his cross, and follow me " (Mark 8³⁴),

" are ye able to drink the cup that I drink, or to be baptized with the baptism that I am baptized with ? " (Mark 10³⁸),

" take ye : this is my body " (Mark 14²²),

is answered by the language in the Epistles about dying and rising with Christ,

" always bearing about in the body the dying of Jesus, that the life also of Jesus may be manifested in our body " (2 Cor. 4¹⁰).

S. Peter, S. Paul and S. John show plainly that the meaning and ground of the Church are seen in the death and resurrection of Jesus and in the mysterious sharing of the disciples in these happenings. It is a Church, because " Christ loved the church, and gave himself up for it." (Eph. 5²⁵.) It is a temple, because " the stone which the builders rejected, the same was made the head of the corner." (1 Pet. 2⁷.) It is a body, because " he hath reconciled us in the body of his flesh through death." (Col. 1²¹⁻²².) It is universal, because " ye that once were far off are made nigh in the blood of Christ." (Eph. 2¹³.) Its worship is the proclaiming of " the Lord's death till he come." (1 Cor. 11²⁶.) Before ever the Apostles realized the full doctrine of the Incarnation or thought of the Church in terms of it, they knew the Church through knowing the Lord's death and resurrection. Thus, while it is true that the Church is founded upon the Word-made-flesh, it is true only because the Word was identified with men right down to the point of death, and enabled men to find unity through a veritable death to self.

The doctrine of the Church, and its order, ministry and sacraments will in these pages be expounded not primarily in terms of an institution founded by Christ, but in terms of Christ's death and resurrection of which the one Body, with its life and its order, is the expression.

(2) The movement towards the *reunion* of Christendom is also compelled to see its problems in close connexion with the Passion. Before he passes on to his schemes of reconciliation, the Christian is compelled to pause and ask what the present fact of disunity means. Why is it ? And he will not simply say that it is wrong, and flee from it in the quest of new visions and ideals and policies ; he will pause again and dwell upon the facts, just as they are. In them is the Passion of Jesus ; and in them already the power of God. Both divisions and unity remind us of the death and resurrection of Jesus. Division severs His body : but unity means the one Body, in which every member and every local community dies to self in its utter dependence upon the whole, the structure of the Body thereby setting forth the dying and rising with Christ. And if the problems about schism and reunion mean dying and rising with Christ, they will not be solved through easy humanistic ideas of fellowship and brotherhood, but by the hard road of the Cross.

When reunion has been discussed, there has often seemed to be an *impasse* between two types of Christianity. On the one hand, there is the Catholic tradition which thinks of the Church as a divine institution, the gift of God to man, and which emphasizes outward order and continuity and the validity of its ministry and sacraments. To the exponents of this tradition, unity is inconceivable apart from the historic structure of the Church. On the other hand, there is the Evangelical tradition which sees the divine gift not in the institution but in the Gospel of God, and which thinks less of Church order than of the Word of God and of justification by faith. This tradition indeed emphasizes the divine society of the redeemed, but it finds it hard to understand the Catholic's thought and language about order and validity and his insistence upon the historic Episcopate. The two traditions puzzle one another. The one seems legalistic ; the other seems individualistic. To the one " intercommunion " is meaningless without unity of outward order ; to the other " intercommunion " seems the one sensible and Christian way towards unity. And thus the debates between the two traditions are often wearisome and fruitless.

A fresh line of approach seems needed. Those who cherish the Catholic Church and its historic order need to expound its meaning not in legalistic and institutionalist language, but in evangelical language as the expression of the Gospel of God. In these pages Church order, with its Episcopate, Creeds and Liturgy, will be studied in terms of the Gospel. It will be asked, for instance, what truth about the Gospel of God does the Episcopate, by its place in the one Body, declare ? And what truth about the Gospel is obscured if the Episcopate is lacking or is perverted ? If the historic structure of the Church sets forth the Gospel, it has indeed a meaning which the Evangelical Christian will understand, and it may be possible to show that reunion without that structure will impair that very Gospel which the Evangelical Christian cherishes.

(3) The *philanthropist*, outside or inside the Christian Church, is also confronted with the death of the Messiah. He longs passionately for the mitigation of the economic sufferings of mankind and for an effective international spirit. His longing is after the obedience of Christ, for he knows that Christ healed the sick and the possessed, and fed the bodies of men, and he looks to the Church to do the same. But as Jesus in the midst of His works of healing and feeding was moving towards death, so also is His Church. For the Church exists for something deeper than philanthropy and reform, namely to teach men to die to self and to trust in a Resurrection to a new life which, because it spans both this world and another world, can

never be wholly understood here, and must always puzzle this world's idealists. Hence, as the Body of Christ crucified and risen, the Church points men to a unity and a peace which men generally neither understand nor desire.

Thus the Church is pointing beyond theology, beyond reunion-schemes, beyond philanthropies, to the death of the Messiah. It leads the theologian, the church-statesman, the philanthropist, and itself also, to the Cross. The dying is a stern reality; theologian, reunionist, philanthropist learn that their work and their ideal is, in itself and of itself, nothing. But all that is lost is found; and the Cross is the place where the theology of the Church has its meaning, where the unity of the Church is a deep and present reality, and where the Church is already showing the peace of God and the bread from heaven to the nations of mankind. The Jews stumbled at the death and resurrection, and hence they never knew the Church to be the Body of the Christ. The disciples knew it, only when He had died and was risen from the dead.

"Forty and six years was this temple in building, and wilt thou raise it up in three days?

"But he spake of the temple of His body." (John $2^{20.}$)

CHAPTER II

ONE DIED FOR ALL

I

THE Passion of Jesus and the Church of God are themes central and inseparable in the New Testament. But neither is intelligible apart from the Old Testament; for Jesus died that the scriptures might be fulfilled, and the Church which He claimed as His own was the ancient Israel of God. The Old Testament has both its Church and its Passion, and Christ is the fulfilment of both.

The Old Testament itself confronts us with God's method of bringing unity to the human race beset with the disorder of sin. He chooses a nation, and delivers it from bondage, that it may be the instrument of His purpose, a worshipping people who continually praise Him for the acts whereby He has delivered them, and whereby He has kept them in safety. He teaches this people, through painful struggles, to worship Him not self-interestedly as a means of securing their own prosperity, but for His own sake, for the praise of His glory, rehearsing His mighty works in creation, in nature, and in history. And Israel has a mission to the nations of the world, who are at last to be drawn into unity with her in the worship of the one God. Thus God purposes to unite mankind through a particular people, and to unite them, not in a programme of philanthropic and social progress, but in the worship of Himself. The end for which He has created men is that all their activities shall become an act of praise towards the perfect and eternal God. Meanwhile, the life and worship of Israel looks forward as well as backward; for the time shall come when God will intervene through His Messiah to vindicate His kingdom upon earth. As yet His people live by promise and in hope.

In the midst of the promise and of the hope Israel was beset by the agony of its Passion. God is just and all-ruling—and yet the innocent continually suffer. The more God discloses through His prophets the truths of His righteousness and His sovereignty, the more acute does this problem of suffering become. Again and again there confronts us in the Old Testament the figure of the man of God asking " why ? ". Habakkuk, upon his watch-tower, complains,

" Thou that art of purer eyes than to behold evil, and that canst not look on perverseness, wherefore lookest thou upon them that deal treacherously, and holdest thy peace when the wicked swalloweth up the man that is more righteous than he ? " (Hab. 1¹³.)

Jeremiah stands as it were by the death-bed of his nation, and cries

" The harvest is past, the summer is ended, and we are not saved. . . . Oh that my head were waters, and mine eyes a fountain of tears, that I might weep day and night for the slain of the daughter of my people." (Jer. 8²⁰, 9¹.)

Job, assured of his own integrity, is torn between faith in His Creator and rebellion against Him. In figures such as these the problem is seen in its intensity. But it was not only these outstanding men of God whose sensitive souls felt the Passion for, as the Psalms show again and again, it was deeply woven into the nation's thought and experience. The cry " how long ? " often sums up the burden of the Psalmist's plaint,

" Yea, for thy sake we are killed all the day long ;
    we are counted as sheep for the slaughter." (Ps. 44²².)

Again and again we find both the nation and the individual baffled by this problem, and by it driven first to despair and

then to faith, born of darkness, in the power of the inscrut-
able and all-wise God. The faith of Israel remains, while
the Passion of Israel is inescapable.

But during the exile in Babylon a prophet who taught of
God's sovereignty, righteousness and universal purpose as
" Saviour " of all men—

" Look unto me, and be ye saved, all the ends of the earth :
for I am God, and there is none else " (Isaiah 45²²)

—taught also that in this purpose a central place is being
taken or will be taken by a " Servant of the Lord " who
suffers. In the four passages, known as the " Servant
songs," the mission of the Servant and its climax in suffering are described. The first song describes the Servant's
mission to the nations, gentle, trustful, patient :—

" Behold my servant, whom I uphold ;
 My chosen, in whom my soul delighteth :
 I have put my spirit upon him ;
 He shall bring forth judgement to the Gentiles.
 He shall not cry, nor lift up,
 Nor cause his voice to be heard in the street.
 A bruised reed shall he not break,
 And the smoking flax shall he not quench :
 He shall bring forth judgement in truth.
 He shall not fail nor be discouraged,
 Till he have set judgement in the earth ;
 And the isles shall wait for his law." (Isaiah 42¹⁻⁴.)

The second song represents the Servant himself speaking of
his sense of weakness and failure, and of God's command
that he should minister to all the peoples of mankind :—

" Listen, O isles, unto me ;
 And hearken, ye peoples, from far :
 The Lord hath called me from the womb ;
 From the bowels of my mother hath he made mention of
  my name :
 And he hath made my mouth like a sharp sword,
 In the shadow of his hand hath he hid me ;
 And he hath made me a polished shaft,

In his quiver hath he kept me close ;
And he said unto me, Thou art my servant ;
Israel, in whom I will be glorified.
But I said, I have laboured in vain,
I have spent my strength for nought and vanity :
Yet surely my judgement is with the Lord
And my recompence with my God.
And now saith the Lord,
That formed me from the womb to be his servant,
To bring Jacob again to him,
And that Israel be gathered unto him :
(For I am honourable in the eyes of the Lord,
And my God is become my strength :)
It is too light a thing . . . to raise up the tribes of Jacob,
And to restore the preserved of Israel :
I will also give thee for a light to the Gentiles,
That my salvation may be unto the end of the earth."

—(Isaiah 49$^{1-6}$.)

Thus wide is the Servant's mission. And in the third song
the Servant himself speaks of the sufferings to which his
obedience leads :—

" The Lord God hath given me
  The tongue of them that are taught,
  That I should know how to speak a word in season
  To him that is weary :
  He wakeneth morning by morning,
  He wakeneth mine ear to hear as they that are taught.
  The Lord God hath opened mine ear,
  And I was not rebellious,
  Neither turned away backward.
  I gave my back to the smiters,
  And my cheeks to them that plucked off the hair :
  I hid not my face
  From shame and spitting.
  For the Lord God will help me ;
  Therefore have I not been confounded :
  Therefore have I set my face like a flint;
  And I know that I shall not be ashamed.
  He is near that justified me ;
  Who will contend with me ?

Let us stand up together :
Who is mine adversary ?
Let him come near to me.
Behold, the Lord God will help me ;
Who is he that shall condemn me ?
Behold they shall wax old as a garment ;
The moth shall eat them up." (Isaiah 50⁴⁻⁹.)

Finally, the fourth song describes the place of the sufferings in the purpose of God who saves :—

(*God speaks*) :

" Behold, my servant shall prosper,
He shall be exalted and lifted up,
And shall be very high.
Like as many were astonished at him
(His visage was so marred more than any man,
And his form more than the sons of men),
So shall he startle many nations ;
Kings shall shut their mouths at him,
For that which had not been told them shall they see ;
And that which they had not heard shall they understand."

(*The sinners speak*) :

" Who hath believed our report ?
And to whom hath the arm of the Lord been revealed ?
For he grew up before us as a tender plant,
And as a root out of a dry ground :
He hath no form nor comeliness ;
And when we see him
There is no beauty that we should desire him.
He was despised and rejected of men ;
A man of sorrows, and acquainted with grief :
And as one from whom men hide their face,
He was despised, and we esteemed him not.
—Surely he hath borne our griefs,
And carried our sorrows :
Yet we did esteem him stricken,
Smitten of God, and afflicted.
But he was wounded for our transgressions,
He was bruised for our iniquities :

The chastisement of our peace was upon him ;
And with his stripes we are healed.
All we like sheep have gone astray ;
We have turned every one to his own way ;
And the Lord hath laid on him
The iniquity of us all.
—He was oppressed, yet he humbled himself
And opened not his mouth ;
As a lamb that is led to the slaughter,
And as a sheep that before her shearers is dumb ;
Yea, he opened not his mouth.
(Excluded) from judgement was he taken away ;
And, as for his generation, who considered
That he was cut off out of the land of the living ?
For the transgression of the people was he stricken.
And they made his grave with the wicked,
And with the rich in his death ;
Although he had done no violence,
Neither was any deceit in his mouth.
—Yet it pleased the Lord to bruise him ;
He hath put him to grief :
When his soul shall make an offering for sin,
He shall see his seed, he shall prolong his days,
And the pleasure of the Lord shall prosper in his hand.
He shall see of the travail of his soul,
And shall be satisfied."

(*God speaks*) :

" My servant shall make many righteous ;
And he shall bear their iniquities.
Therefore will I divide him a portion with the great,
And he shall divide the spoil with the strong ;
Because he poured out his soul unto death,
And was numbered with the transgressors :
Yet he bare the sin of many,
And made intercession for the transgressors."

—(Isaiah 52¹³-53¹².)

Thus the Servant suffers unspeakable pains of body, and
men shrink from the horror of His appearance. But they
come to recognize that He was innocent and was suffering

for them. And God speaks to proclaim that the Servant's sacrifice enables men to have deliverance and peace.

Scholars have long debated the immediate reference of these passages. Some have urged that the Servant is the nation, either in its actual or in its " ideal " condition ; others that he is an individual. Some have thought that he last of the songs describes a past event, others that it is the prediction of one who shall arise and suffer in the future. Yet amid all these uncertainties, two facts stand out quite clearly, and both are facts of primary importance. *Firstly*, it is plain that the prophet in exile taught that God's purpose for mankind is somehow coupled with the sufferings of a Servant. *Secondly*, there is no instance in Hebrew literature, between the exile and our Lord's day, of any identification of the sufferer with the Messiah.[1] The Messiah was never pictured in such terms, and the prophecy stands in the book of Isaiah mysterious, baffling, uninterpreted by the race for whom it was written. Within the Old Testament there exists this proclamation of God's sovereign purpose wrought out in the life and death of a sufferer ; yet the Church of the Old Testament never made Messianic sense of this elusive poem.

But though Israel failed to perceive the truth, she was groping after it ; and some of the ideas of the Servant songs occur in some other O.T. passages. Thus, the writer of Zech. 9⁹ depicts a Messiah " just and having salvation ; lowly, and riding upon an ass, even upon a colt the foal of an ass." And the 22nd Psalm is still more akin to Isaiah 53. This Psalm opens with the cry of desolation from one who undergoes terrible persecution,

" My God, My God, why hast thou forsaken me ? "

The sufferer goes on to describe his intense pains amid the derision of a host of enemies. His prayer is answered, and

---

[1] In Jewish exegesis, represented by the Targums, the descriptions of the Servant's sufferings were applied to the nation, and only the descriptions of his success and glory to the Messiah.

the Psalm ends with a picture of men of every nation wor-shipping God, whose name has been vindicated and whose sufferer has been faithful.

" A seed shall serve him ;
It shall be told of the Lord unto the next generation.
They shall come and shall declare his righteousness
Unto a people that shall be born, that he hath done it."

Like the fourth servant-song, this Psalm depicts sufferings which issue in the praise of God by the nations, and like the song it was never drawn into the Jewish imagery of the Messiah who should come. The Passion of Israel meant more for Israel and for mankind than Israel ever knew.

For in the fulness of time Jesus Christ came, with the burden laid upon Him that He must fulfil the scriptures. He healed the sick, He cast out devils, He proclaimed the Kingdom of God and its righteousness ; but in the centre of His mission was the death which He died not only because the course of events led to it but because He chose to die " that the scriptures might be fulfilled." And the very parts of scripture, which the Jews had failed to inter-pret, Jesus the Messiah interpreted and executed, so that the theme of the suffering Servant was brought right into the centre of the themes, more familiar to his contem-poraries, of Son of David, Son of Man, Son of God. Hence the disciples after Pentecost found the death no longer a stumbling-block but the fulfilment of prophecy, and they preached Jesus as the Servant of God whom the 53rd chapter of Isaiah had foretold, and whose Passion the 22nd Psalm prefigured. (Acts 3[13, 26], 4[27-30], 8[32] ; I Peter 2[21-24]. Cf. Matt. 8[17], 12[18-20].) And it is hard to doubt that this identification, amounting to a recreation of Messianic ideas and of spiritual attitudes, goes back to the teaching of Jesus Himself, who found in the scriptures that He must die according to the will of God.

" The Son of Man goeth, even as it is written of him."
—(Mark 14[21].)

c

" For I say unto you, that which is written must be fulfilled
in me, And he was reckoned with the transgressors : for
that which concerneth me hath fulfilment." (Luke 22³⁷.)

" And Jesus cried with a loud voice . . . My God, My God,
why hast thou forsaken me." (Mark 15³⁴.)

In fulfilment not only of particular passages in the O.T.,
but of the whole Passion which the O.T. contains, Christ's
death was the act of divine power which broke the forces
of evil and set up God's Kingdom amongst men. While
the final interpretation is in S. John, where the Passion
is recorded as an act of victory and glory, the same fact
is implicit in the realistic record of S. Mark where the
humiliations of the Christ are the disclosure of the power
of God.

For, through the lonely death and the resurrection
which seals its triumph and the gift of the Spirit of Him
who died and rose, there is created a new Israel or Church
of God, in which the Gospel of God is proclaimed. It is
still God's purpose to unite mankind through a people ;
and this people does not mean a loose collection of believers
in Jesus, but a new nation to which the characteristic
descriptions of the old Israel—the Vine, the Temple, the
Bride—are transferred, and which has the same sense of
the solidarity of one race, brought to birth by a creative
act of God. Thus the Church is Israel still. But there
are two great differences: (1) The new race is drawn
from any and every earthly nation and from Jew or
Gentile, male or female, bond or free (Gal. 3²⁸), and (2)
the new race does not find death and suffering to be its
baffling problem. For by the Messiah's death it has been
created, and made a people unto God. The Church exists,
because He died. That which had been the cause of
despair and tension and offence throughout Israel's history
—the suffering of the righteous ones—has become the
centre of Israel's being. The Servant has become the
" light to lighten the Gentiles " because the Servant has
suffered and identified Himself with the death of all

mankind. (Heb. 2⁹, John 12³², Eph. 2¹³, ¹⁴.) In His death the Church rejoices and worships and shares. Of all the contrasts between the old Israel and the new Israel none is greater than this. For the one, death was the stumbling-block; for the other, a death is the centre of its existence, of its worship and of the way of unity which it offers to mankind.

II

The death and the Church—the one has sprung from the other. Yet the connexion is closer still. For it seems not only that Christ creates the Church by dying and rising again, but that within Him and especially within His death and resurrection the Church is actually present. We must search for the fact of the Church not beyond Calvary and Easter but within them.

It must first of all be remembered that some of the leading ideas and phrases in the Old Testament apply both to the individual Messiah and to the nation or a remnant within the nation. It is hard for the modern reader to realize to what lengths the personification of the nation is carried in the Old Testament; certainly it is carried further than is natural to our minds. Sometimes a description which seems to suit an individual figure applies to the nation as a whole :—

" Many a time have they afflicted me from my youth up,
    let Israel now say :
  Many a time have they afflicted me from my youth up,
    yet they have not prevailed against me.
  The plowers ploughed upon my back, and made long
    furrows." (Psalm 129¹⁻³.)

This is one of the many passages where the " I " of the psalmist refers not to a single person, but to the nation or to the righteous element within it; and many other instances could be given from psalmists and prophets. Now this " telescoping " of the individual and the nation occurs also in language about the nation's Messianic hope. The Son of God is the nation.

"When Israel was a child, then I loved him, and called my son out of Egypt." (Hosea 11¹.)

Yet the Son of God is also the Messiah who shall reign over the nation.

"Thou art my son; this day have I begotten thee . . . Kiss the son lest he be angry." (Psalm 2⁷, ¹².)

Of this latter passage Wellhausen wrote, " The Messiah is the Incarnation of Israel's universal rule, He and Israel are almost identical, and it matters little whether we say that Israel *has* or *is* the Messiah." [1] Again, the title " Son of Man " appears in the vision in Daniel 7 as a personification of " the people of the saints of the most high " to whom shall be given a dominion which shall not pass away. Again, the title " Christ " is used both of the anointed king and of the anointed people; and the title " Servant " in the book of Isaiah eludes modern attempts to define it, since it portrays at times an intensely individual figure and at times the people of God. In all these ways the Old Testament prepares us for the closest possible union between the Messiah and His people.

Now Jesus Christ assumed those titles and functions which in the scriptures are linked both with the Messiah and the nation—Χριστός, Son of God, Servant. About the title " Son of Man " it is hard to dogmatize. It has been urged that in the Gospels this title refers not to the Lord alone, but also to the remnant united with Him, so that the sufferings of the Son of Man mean the sufferings both of Christ and of His followers.[2] This interpretation of the actual title seems very doubtful, yet, even without it, the closeness between our Lord and Israel is unmistakable in His whole Messianic work. He is the Messiah, in a way which trans-

---

[1] Quoted by Sanday, art. " Son of God," *H.D.B.*, IV, 571.
[2] Cf. T. W. Manson, *The Teaching of Jesus*, pp. 211-234.

cends all human language and thought ; He is also *Israel*, the people of God. For when He comes to proclaim the Kingdom in Israel, to fulfil the law, to gather the lost sheep, to reign in Israel—His own reject Him. Israel rejects Israel, and in the isolation of Calvary Jesus alone is Israel, the Son, the Servant. The vineyard has been lost to its former husbandmen, and the *people of God* consists only of the *One* who, rejected by His own, is dying on the Cross, alone the Servant who obeys and alone the place where the name and the glory and the will and the promises of God are seen. Jesus Christ, in His solitary obedience, *is* the Church. Its existence does not begin with the addition of Jesus to men or of men to Jesus. The Israel of God is Jesus on the Cross ; and those who will be united with Him will enter an Israel which exists already.

It is indeed a paradox that the death of Jesus, an event of utter isolation from men, should be the means of fellow-ship between men and God, and between men and one another. The Marcan account of the Passion shows us a lonely Christ, bereft of contact with men and even for a time bereft of conscious contact with God. His mother and His friends have sought for Him, hearing it said that He is a madman ; the crowds cannot fathom His teaching ; the religious leaders of His people plot to destroy Him ; the disciples cannot understand the necessity of His death ; and He goes to die alone. As He hangs on the Cross, the people who pass by mock at Him, the chief priests deride Him, the thieves crucified together with Him revile Him, and His separation from men is complete. And finally He cries in the darkness, " My God, My God, why hast thou forsaken me ? " Yet in this lonely death there is present already the truth which underlies the words " church," " fellow-ship," and " unity."

(1) The death is—first of all—the deepest point of the Son of God's identification of Himself with men and of His entry into the stream of human life. If He is near to men in the joyful contact of His ministry in Galilee, teaching

and healing and blessing, He is nearer still as He goes to the Cross. Remote from all the superficialities of life and of society, the Christ enters by the way of the Cross into nearer and nearer contact with the grim human realities of sin and creatureliness and death. For death is not merely a physical fact, the cessation of the organic processes of life ; it has a moral meaning since it marks and declares the sinfulness and creatureliness and fragmentariness of mankind which is gripped by sin and falls short of the glory of God. Death in the New Testament, characterizes man in the essential contrast between man and God. It is due to sin (Rom. 5^{12}), it is universal, it enslaves men and dominates them like a king (Rom. $5^{14, \ 21}$), and " all flesh is as grass, and all the glory thereof as the flower of grass . . . ," and only " the word of the Lord abideth for ever." (I Peter 1^{24-25}.) The New Testament writers know man as, for all his achievements, a dying creature, confronted with the boundary and the fear of death, and death sums up the truth about man when he is seen in the light of the eternal God. Now into this death the Son of God came, tasting both of the fear of death and of the fact of death and of the moral meaning of death. Of the fear of death He tasted in Gethsemane,

" having offered up prayers and supplications with strong crying and tears unto him that was able to save him from death." (Heb. 5^7.)

Of the fact of death He tasted with the grim literalness expressed when S. Mark dares to call the dead Messiah " the corpse " (τὸ πτῶμα) :—

" Pilate . . . granted the corpse to Joseph." (Mark 15^{45}.)

And of the moral meaning of death He tasted by bearing it as the consequence of men's sin, identifying Himself with sinful men. The hard phrase of S. Paul, " Him who knew no sin he made to be sin on our behalf " (2 Cor. 5^{21}) finds its best commentary in the cry of dereliction from the Cross. For our Lord enters so deeply into the meaning and the pain and the darkness of a race cut off from God by sin that He seems momentarily to lose the vision of the Father, and He is never more man's brother and never more " totus in nostris " than in the cry of dereliction. In Galilee He was near to men, but the full meaning of sin before God was not disclosed ; on Calvary He is near to men in the death which sums up and reveals what man is, as creature and as sinner before God. Thus He came in order to die, so as to be man, in man, of man, going whither men must go. And His coming to die does not mean the negative act of a suicide seeking self-destruction, but the positive act of one whose love embraces man and all that is man's. " Whither thou goest, I will go."

Thus, the death on the Cross was prefigured throughout our Lord's ministry on earth. From the first, the will to die was a part of the Messiah's identification with men. By His baptism in Jordan He places Himself where the sinners had been bidden by John the Baptist to go, declaring thereby that He will cleanse sinners not as one who stands apart from them, but as one who shares utterly in the consequences of their sin. In His temptations in the wilderness He is again seen " in all things made like unto His brethren." And all His intercourse with men is a sharing of their lives which points to His death as its completion. The baptism in Jordan is linked with the baptism into the calamities of mankind (cf. Luke 12^{50}, Mark 10^{38}), as S. John tells us when he writes that Jesus " came by the water and the blood." (1 John 5^6.) In the manner of His coming there is disclosed already the meaning of " fellowship " between God and men.

(2) The death of the Lord means also the laying down of the self and the abandonment of all its claims. Throughout His life His will is wholly submitted to the Father's will, and He lives and dies not as pleasing Himself but as losing His will and His whole being in the Father and in mankind.

" Howbeit not what I will, but what thou wilt."
—(Mark 14^{36}. Cf. Rom. 15^3.)

His selfhood is so laid down, that His power and authority centre in His humiliation. Such is the impression of the earthly life of Jesus. But this self-abandonment does not belong to that earthly life alone, for it is the expression in history of the self-giving of the eternal God. S. Paul makes it clear that the first and great act of humiliation is the act whereby the Son of God is made man.

" Have this mind in you, which was also in Christ Jesus ; who, being in the form of God; counted it not a prize to be on an equality with God, but emptied Himself, taking the form of a servant, being made in the likeness of men ; and being found in fashion as a man, he humbled himself, becoming obedient unto death, yea, the death of the Cross." (Phil. 2$^{5-7}$.)

Thus, before the humiliations of the Messiah in His life and death upon earth, there is the divine self-emptying whereby He " came " and " was sent." For S. Paul the Incarnation is in itself an act of sacrifice than which none is greater ; Christmas is as costly in self-giving as is Good Friday. Only the Crucifixion is the deepest visible point of the divine self-giving which entered history at Bethlehem and which begins in heaven itself. " There was a Calvary above which was the mother of it all."

Now the Fourth Gospel unfolds this eternal love of God, uttered in the " sending " of the Son into the world and in the self-giving of the Son to the point of death ; and it shows how this truth is the basis of the Church. The narrative points us both to Christ in the flesh and to the eternal truth which His flesh reveals. Christ is depicted throughout His life upon earth as living and speaking and thinking in utter dependence on the Father.

" The Son can do nothing of himself, but what he seeth the Father doing ; for what things soever he doeth, these the Son also doeth in like manner." (John 5^{19}. Cf. 5$^{30-32}$, $^{42-44}$.)

" As the living Father sent me, and I live because of the Father ; so he that eateth me he also shall live because of me." (John 6^{57}.)

" I am not come of myself, but he that sent me is true, whom ye know not. I know him, because I am from him and he sent me." (John 7²⁸.)

" If I glorify myself, my glory is nothing ; it is my Father that glorifieth me." (John 8⁵⁴.)

This dependence of the Son means that the Son finds in the Father the centre of His own existence ; it implies a relationship of death to Himself *qua* Himself. The Son has nothing, wills nothing, is nothing of Himself alone. The self has its centre in/ Another. And this attitude and action of the Son in history reveals the character of the eternal God, the mutual love of Father and Son.

" Believe me that I am in the Father, and the Father in me." (John 14¹¹.)

" And now, O Father, glorify thou me with thine own self with the glory which I had with thee before the world was." (John 17⁵.)

And this eternal love and this " losing life to find it " in the very being of God is especially manifested when the Son of God moves towards His death.

" When ye have lifted up the Son of Man, then shall ye know that I am he, and that I do nothing of myself, but as the Father taught me, I speak these things. And he that sent me is with me ; he hath not left me alone ; for I do always the things that are pleasing to him." (S. John 8²⁸⁻²⁹.)

" Therefore doth the Father love me because I lay down my life, that I may take it again. . . . This commandment received I from the Father." (John 10¹⁷⁻¹⁸.)

And, thence, this divine love enters the disciples of Jesus so that they share in the self-negation and in the unity :

" that they may all be one ; even as thou, Father, art in me and I in Thee, that they also may be in us." (John 17²¹.)

Here then is a complete setting forth of the meaning of the Church ; the eternal love of Father and Son is uttered in the Christ's self-negation unto death, to the end that men may make it their own and be made one. The unity, in a word, means *death*. The death to the self *qua* self, first in Christ and thence in the disciples, is the ground and essence of the Church.

So in these two ways the death of Christ contains within itself the fact of the Church—by His baptism into our humanity, by His negation of the rights of self before God. But all this is true only because His death is followed by His resurrection. His entry into man's death is a mighty act of divine power, for God's power is manifested in self-emptying love, and to be made man, to die, to be buried is of the power of God no less than is the creation of the world. He died, and, being made nought with nothing of His own, He is in the Father's glory and in that glory He is raised from the dead.

" Christ was raised from the dead through the glory of the Father." (Rom. 6⁴.)

" It is Jesus Christ that died, yea rather that was raised from the dead." (Rom. 8³⁴.)

Thus in the nothingness of the death and the tomb there is a love so mighty that He lives and fills all things. S. John draws the death and the resurrection so closely together that the one is the inevitable divine sequence of the other ; the Cross is to him not a defeat needing the resurrection to reverse it, but rather a victory so decisive that the resurrection follows quickly to seal it ; the exalting on the Cross and the exalting to heaven hardly seem separate. And the New Testament, in its final impression, does not let us see Death, Resurrection, Ascension, Logos doctrine as a series of " stages," each of which adds something " more " of power and divinity. Rather do the power of God and the humiliation of the Christ appear coincident, so that in the death and the grave there is present the Word who was in the beginning with God. He that ascended . . . what is it but that he also descended ? He that humbled Himself, that was broken into the fragmentariness of man's death, what is it but that, risen, He fills all things and in Him all things consist ?

He died to self, morally by the will to die throughout His life, actually by the crucifixion. He died with men, as man, coming by the water and the blood. God raised Him, and in the death and resurrection the fact of the Church is present. For, as He is baptized into man's death, so men shall be baptized into His ; and, as He loses His life to find it in the Father, so men may by a veritable death find a life whose centre is in Christ and in the brethren. *One died for all, therefore all died*. To say this is to describe the Church of God.

CHAPTER III

THEREFORE ALL DIED

I

THE death and resurrection of the Lord happened once and can never be repeated. The deed was done in history, yet it is the entry into history of something beyond history which cannot be known in terms of history alone. " The time is fulfilled, and the Kingdom of God is at hand." But this event, born in eternity and uttering the voice of God from another world, pierces deeply into our order of time, so that the death and resurrection of the Christ were known not only as something " without " but also as something " within " the disciples who believed. That is the meaning of the Church.

This is no mere speculative paradox. It happened in human flesh and blood. At Cæsarea Philippi, Peter confesses that Jesus is the Messiah, and though this is a true confession, bewilderment follows since the Messiah at once predicts His death. The disciples cannot understand the Kingdom until they know the Messiah, and now having at last found Him, they see that they cannot know Him unless they face the necessity of His death. And the thought of the death baffles them. " They understood not the saying and were afraid to ask Him." (Mark 9[32].) In answer to their bewilderment the Lord teaches that they will never understand it except by sharing in it.

" If any man would come after me, let him deny himself and take up his cross and follow me." (Mark 8[34].)

" Are ye able to drink the cup that I drink ? or to be baptized with the baptism that I am baptized with ? "

—(Mark 10[38].)

" Take ye : this is my body. . . . This is my blood of the covenant, which is shed for many." (Mark 14[22-24].)

In each of these episodes the disciples are bidden to join the Lord in His act of dying ; and His words at the last supper about the body and the blood to be eaten and drunk form the climax to the teaching about the need for the disciples to identify themselves with His Passion. Their bewilderment may well be imagined ; they were told that *they* must die like the Christ and with Him. And whether this meant an outward physical death or an inner moral change it was remote from their belief and attitude. At the last supper, S. Luke tells us, " there arose also a contention amongst them, which of them is accounted to be greatest." (Luke 22[24].) The death is still an event *outside* them ; it is yet to become a happening *within* them.

Now we pass beyond the death and the resurrection to the story of the Church of Jerusalem as told in the first five chapters of the Acts. In place of the self-consciousness and love of contention ($\phi\iota\lambda o\nu\epsilon\iota\kappa\iota a$) of the former period there is now " fellowship " ($\kappa o\iota\nu\omega\nu\iota a$) between them. This " fellowship " is created by the Holy Spirit, and the " speaking with tongues " at Pentecost is probably an expression of the " fellowship " in a common ecstasy of praise.[1] But the " fellowship " is something deeper than ecstasy and emotion ; it penetrates into the whole lives

[1] It seems most likely that the " speaking with tongues " at Pentecost was not, as the writer of Acts interprets it, a " gift of divers languages," but ecstatic $\gamma\lambda\omega\sigma\sigma o\lambda a\lambda\iota a$ similar to that described in 1 Cor. 14 and elsewhere in the New Testament. The cries might be meaningless and might convey an impression of drunkenness (Acts 2[13]) to the onlookers, but they would be full of meaning to those who shared in the common ecstasy, and in the first expression of the $\kappa o\iota\nu\omega\nu\iota a$ or " fellowship " created by the Spirit of Jesus. Cf. Anderson Scott, " What Happened at Pentecost " in the volume *The Spirit*, ed. B. H. Streeter.

of the disciples, so that the word κοινωνία describes a oneness in thought, in mind, and in the sharing of goods, of sufferings, and of a life which is not their own but Another's.

The "fellowship" seems closely linked with the death of the Messiah. The Spirit who sustains it is the Spirit of Him who died and was raised up. "Being therefore by the right hand of God exalted and having received of the Father the promise of the Holy Ghost, he hath poured forth this, which ye see and hear." (Acts 2³³.) Behind the gift of the Spirit and the fellowship thereby created there is the divine plan of the death and resurrection of Jesus. While to the ordinary Jew the death is a scandal, the Christians dare to teach that it is a part of God's purpose for His "servant" and, applying the lesson to themselves, they are now glad to be "counted worthy to suffer dishonour for the Name." (Acts 5⁴¹.) From the point of view of the old religion two new facts emerge in the story of the Pentecostal church—the new "fellowship" with its width and depth, and the new attitude towards the death of a Messiah and the sufferings of a disciple. The "fellowship" and the death seem inseparable. "Fellowship" has been created since, starting with the death of Jesus, men have died to themselves as separate and sufficient "selfhoods" and have been found alive in one another and in the Spirit of the Lord Jesus. Underlying the fellowship of Pentecost and of the primitive Church there is the fact described some decades later when S. Paul says that the Christians were "baptized into his death" (Rom. 6³) and when S. Peter says that they are "elect . . . in sanctification of the Spirit, unto obedience and sprinkling of the blood of Jesus Christ." (I Peter I².) This latter passage illustrates the connexion, found elsewhere, between the crucifixion and the Spirit. Not only did the crucifixion make possible the giving of the Spirit, but the life bestowed by the Spirit is a life of which crucifixion is a quality, a life of living through dying.[1]

[1] John 7³⁹, I Cor. 2 (the whole chapter), Gal. 3¹, ², 5²²⁻²⁴, Rom. 8¹⁶⁻¹⁷.

The fellowship created at Pentecost grows far beyond the confines of Palestine and the Jewish race, and the Christians' understanding of its meaning and origin grows also. Wherever the fellowship spreads, those who share in it look back continually to the happenings in Jerusalem which have brought them into their new life, and remember that the Spirit who sustains the fellowship is the gift of the Messiah who died and rose. But this is not all. For in every place where Christians are found they dare to assert that the Christ is *in them*, and that their relation to Him is not only the memory of a past event but the fact of a present indwelling. The presence of the Spirit mediates the presence of the Christ Himself, so that to be " in the Spirit " is to be " in Christ." Nor is this the language of a few intense mystics only. S. Paul and S. John describe not isolated experiences of their own but the common life of the Christians, and the ordinary tempted and sinful converts are expected to understand the Apostles' language. If S. Paul says of himself " I have been crucified with Christ ; yet I live ; and yet no longer I, but Christ liveth in me " (Gal. 2[20]), he also says to Roman Christians whom he has not yet seen, " we were buried with him through baptism into death." (Rom. 6[4].) If S. John claims immediate union with Christ who is the life, he makes this claim as one of the many who have " fellowship with Christ and with the Father," and he believes that the life of the Christians means " I am the vine, ye are the branches . . . abide in me, and I in you . . . apart from me ye can do nothing." (John 15[4, 5].)

But how did this relationship come about ? and how was it sustained ? S. Paul answers these questions in passages which describe the beginnings of a Christian's life, and the struggles through which that life continues. That life begins with an act of faith and initiation which verily means " *death*." There comes first the response of faith in Christ crucified, when the believer recognizes his impotence and failure and lays hold upon God's act of love for him in the death of Christ. Faith means owning

that one is, of oneself and in oneself, nothing. The phrase
τὰ μὴ ὄντα, "things that are nought," explains faith as
S. Paul sees it; for the type of faith is Abraham who
"considered his own body now as good as dead," and who
trusted only in God "who quickeneth the dead, and calleth
the things that are not, as though they were." (Rom. 4¹⁷.)
And faith means also a deadness to the world's ideas of
worth and merit. "God chose the foolish things of the
world . . . the weak things . . . the base things . . .
things that are despised . . . yea, and things that are
not." (1 Cor. 1²⁷⁻²⁸.) [1] But the self which is lost in this
response is found again, and so S. Paul continues " but
of him are ye in Christ Jesus, who was made unto us
wisdom from God, and righteousness, and sanctification,
and redemption: that according as it is written, He that
glorieth, let him glory in the Lord." (1 Cor. 1³⁰⁻³¹.)

Nor is the Christian's death to self only a response to
the death of Christ as a past event; it is a present sharing
in His dying and rising again. In Baptism the death and
resurrection of Jesus become a present reality within the
converts:

" Or are ye ignorant that all we who were baptized into Christ
Jesus were baptized into his death ? We were buried therefore with him through baptism unto death; that like as
Christ was raised from the dead through the glory of the
Father, so we also might walk in newness of life. For if we
have become united with him by the likeness of his death,
we shall be also by the likeness of his resurrection; knowing
this, that our old man was crucified with him that the body of
sin might be done away, that so we should be no longer in
bondage to sin; for he that hath died is justified from sin.
But if we died with Christ, we believe that we shall also live
with him; knowing that Christ being raised from the dead
dieth no more; death no more hath dominion over him.
For the death that he died, he died unto sin once; but the
life that he liveth, he liveth unto God. Even so reckon ye also
yourselves to be dead unto sin, but alive unto God in Christ
Jesus." (Rom. 6⁸⁻¹¹.)

[1] Cf. Gal. 6¹⁴, Col. 2²⁰,

By the power of the Spirit who brings the self-giving of God into the convert's life the self-centred nexus of appetites and impulses is broken, and the life is brought into a new centre and a new environment, Christ and His Body. The response of faith has preceded the receiving of this divine action, the response of faith is continually needed in order to appropriate it; yet the Baptism is, like the Incarnation and the death of the Christ, a real action of God who recreates. Further analysis will add little to the interpretation of this passage; the best commentary is found in the saints whose hidden life has been the response to the fact of their Baptism.

Thus the Christians have looked back to the death and resurrection of Jesus on whom they first believed, they have received the Spirit of Him who died and rose again, they have known the dying and rising as a fact within themselves. Hence they are led to think both of the Christ and of themselves in a new way :

" For the love of Christ constraineth us ; because we thus judge, that one died for all, therefore all died ; and he died for all, that they which live should no longer live unto themselves, but unto him who for their sakes died and rose again. Wherefore we henceforth know no man after the flesh : even though we have known Christ after the flesh, yet now we know him so no more. Wherefore if any man is in Christ, he is a new creature : the old things are passed away ; behold, they are become new." (2 Cor. $5^{14\cdot17}$.)

A wealth of thought is compressed into this passage. Men are now found to be identified with Christ's death in such a way that they think of themselves no longer as separate and self-sufficient units, but as centred in Christ who died and rose again. They used to think of Christ as an isolated historical figure (" after the flesh ") ; now they think of Him as the inclusive head and centre of a new humanity, wherein a new creation of God is at work. The implication of this passage is far-reaching. Christ is here defined not as the isolated figure of Galilee and Judaea but as one whose people, dead and risen with Him,

D

are His own humanity. The fact of Christ includes the
fact of the Church. And this is not a novel speculation
added to the original Gospel; it springs from that Gospel.
The synoptic record is unintelligible apart from the
Messiah's death; the death is spiritually unintelligible
except the disciples share in it, and by sharing in it through
the baptism of the Spirit they and all the believers know
the death and resurrection as a present fact. Thus when
S. Paul describes the Church as the " Body " of Christ,
and the " fulness " of Christ, he is not indulging in mystical
adventures of his own; he is describing facts inherent in
the Messiah's work from its commencement. " One died
for all, therefore all died "; to know this is to know " the
Church which is His body, the fulness of him that filleth
all in all "

II

The Body of Christ is one of the central themes of the
Epistles of S. Paul's captivity. But this part of his teaching was foreshadowed in his earlier references to life " in
Christ," and in such passages as Gal. 3^{27-28} : " For as many
of you as were baptized into Christ did put on Christ . . .
ye are all one man ($\epsilon\hat{\iota}s$) in Christ Jesus." While in Romans
and in I Corinthians the relation of Christ to the Christians
had been likened to a human body in a metaphorical comparison (I Cor. 12^{12}, Rom. 12^4), in Ephesians and Colossians
the definite article is introduced and the Christians are
called " *the* body " of Christ. Caution is needed in the
interpretation of S. Paul's language, since the usage varies.
Sometimes Christ is likened to the whole body which is
Himself, sometimes He is the head and the Christians
are the body, and sometimes the imagery passes from
a body to a house or a temple. Nor is it certain whether
in speaking of the Church as the $\pi\lambda\dot{\eta}\rho\omega\mu\alpha$ or " fulness "
of Christ, S. Paul means " that which Christ fills " or
" that by which Christ is fulfilled or made complete." [1]

[1] Armitage Robinson argues for the latter view. Cf. his *Ephesians*,
pp. 42-44, 255-259.

But these uncertainties, inevitable in the description of a reality which transcends our thought, do not obscure the striking facts which S. Paul is asserting about the Christians and the Christ.

(1) The word σῶμα first points the reader towards Christ Himself rather than towards the Christians. For the word σῶμα in pre-Christian Greek, whether classical or biblical or hellenistic, did not mean a " body " of people or a society, in the manner of the English use of the word " body " or the Latin use of " corpus " as a social metaphor. Such a use is rarely found in Greek literature, or in the LXX or in the papyri. The word could mean a man (dead or alive), or a slave, or a mass or bulk of some substance, or a body of literature. It did not suggest a group of persons. Hence to call the Church τὸ σῶμα τοῦ Χριστοῦ was to draw attention to it not primarily as a collection of men, but primarily as Christ Himself in His own being and life. On the passage " as the body is one and hath many members . . . so also is Christ " (1 Cor. 12¹²) Calvin boldly comments, " He calls Christ the church." More cautious are Armitage Robinson's words: " He is no part, but rather the whole of which the various members are parts. . . . This is in exact correspondence with the image employed by our Lord Himself, ' I am the Vine, ye are the branches,' that is to say, not ' I am the trunk of the vine, and ye are the branches growing out of the trunk,' but rather ' I am the living whole, ye are the parts whose life is a life dependent on the whole.' " But neither Calvin's nor Armitage Robinson's words are startling if the sheer novelty of the Christian use of the word σῶμα is borne in mind. We do not know the whole fact of Christ Incarnate unless we know His Church and its life as a part of His own life. Yet the other language, in which Christ is called head over the body (Eph. 1²³, 4¹⁵) warns us against a mere immanentism and reminds us that to know the Church is not to know the inexhaustible truth of the Christ who has ever more to give to men. None the less the Body is the fulness of Christ, and the

history of the Church and the lives of the saints are the acts of the biography of the Messiah.[1]

(2) Christianity therefore is never solitary. It is never true to say that separate persons are united to Christ, and then combine to form the Church ; for to believe in Christ is to believe in One whose Body is a part of Himself and whose people are His own humanity, and to be joined to Christ is to be joined to Christ-in-His-Body ; for " so is Christ " and Christ is not otherwise. S. Paul shows us

---

[1] It is striking how unfamiliar to the Greek language is the use of " body " in the sense of a fellowship. In classical literature we find it meaning (a) a body, dead or alive ; (b) a person ; (c) a corporeal substance, e.g. λίθος ; (d) the whole of a thing, the sum of its parts, e.g. τοῦ κόσμου, Plato, Timaeus, 31 B. 32 C. τῆς πίστεως, Arist. Rhet. i. i. 3. In the papyri the same uses occur, with the addition of (e) a slave (as also in the LXX, cf. Gen. 36[6], 2 Macc. 8[11] and in Rev. 18[13]). In the N.T., besides familiar uses, σῶμα is used of

(1) Christ's physical body. Mk. 15[43], Heb. 10[10], Col. 1[22], 2[11].
(2) His body glorified. Phil. 3[21].
(3) The eucharistic body. Mk. 14[22], etc., I Cor. 10[16], 11[24-28].
(4) His Church. I Cor. 10[17], 12[12], Rom. 12[5], Eph. 1[23], 2[16], 4[4, 12, 16], 5[23, 30], Col. 1[18, 24].

The close connexion between the Body, the Church, and the eucharistic body is seen in I Cor. 10[16]. In some other passages the word σῶμα links the Christians very closely with the historical death and resurrection of Jesus ; e.g. in Col. I the use seems to slide easily between the fleshly body of Jesus and the no less actual body the Church.

" He is the head of the body, the Church." (Col. 1[18].)
" you . . . hath he reconciled in the body of his flesh through death." (Col. 1[21].)
" I fill up upon my part that which is lacking of the afflictions of Christ in my flesh, for his body's sake, which is the Church." (Col. 1[24].)

In one passage there may even be a hint that the Christians are the actual resurrection body of Christ,

" wherefore, my brethren, ye also were made dead to the law through the body of Christ ; that ye should be joined to another, even to him who was raised from the dead." (Rom. 7[4].)

For the connexion between these two uses of σῶμα see Schweitzer, Mysticism of Paul the Apostle, Ch. VI. For a full discussion, see Mersch, Le Corps Mystique du Christ, Vol. I, pp. 109-153.

that the Christian is confronted by the one Body at his conversion, in his experience of justification by faith, and at every stage in his growing knowledge of Christ. (a) Saul himself was converted by no solitary Jesus. The voice on the road to Damascus, " Saul, Saul, why persecutest thou *me* ? " declares that the disciples are His own risen humanity in whom He suffers.   The moment therefore that Saul turns to Christ he turns to the fact of the σῶμα Χριστοῦ.   (b) Similarly, justification by faith is never a solitary relationship with a solitary Christ. The man who is justified is an individual, but the Christ who justifies is one with His people as His Body ; and the act of faith, in releasing a man from self, brings him into dependence upon his neighbours in Christ.   Faith and justification are inseparable from initiation into the one Body.

" For ye are all sons of God, through faith, in Christ Jesus. For as many of you as were baptized into Christ did put on Christ . . . ye are all one man in Christ Jesus."   (Gal. 3²⁶⁻²⁸.)

" For in one Spirit we were all baptized into one body, whether Jews or Greeks, whether bond or free ; and were all made to drink of one Spirit."   (1 Cor. 12¹³.)

(c) Similarly also the Christian's growth in Christ is a part of the growth of the one Body and all its members. His knowledge of Christ grows, as the one Body grows by the due working of all its parts, and as Christ is made complete in all His saints.

" Till we all attain unto the unity of the faith, and of the knowledge of the Son of God, unto a full grown man, unto the measure of the stature of the fulness of Christ: that we may be no longer children, . . . but may grow up in all things into him, which is the head, even Christ ; from whom all the body fitly framed and knit together through that which every joint supplieth, according to the working in due measure of each several part, maketh the increase of the body unto the building up of itself in love."   (Eph. 4¹³⁻¹⁶.)

From the Church therefore the Christian never escapes; it is a part of his own existence since it is a part of the Christ Himself. And without the Church the Christian does not grow, since the Christ is fulfilled in the totality of all His members.

" Individualism " therefore has no place in Christianity, and Christianity verily means its extinction. Yet through the death of " individualism " the individual finds himself; and through membership in the Body the single Christian is discovered in new ways and becomes aware that God loves him, in all his singleness, as if God had no one else to love. He can speak of a conscious union between his single self and Christ: " He loved me, and gave Himself for me." Hence two kinds of language have always been legitimate for Christians, the one which dwells upon the Body of Christ wherein the individual is merged, the other which dwells upon the individual Christian in his conscious union with Christ. But both kinds of language describe what is really one fact. For the individual Christian exists only because the Body exists already. The self is known in its reality as a self when it ceases to be solitary and learns its utter dependence, and the " individuality " of Christians, with all its rich variety, springs from their death and resurrection in the Body which is one. In the Body the self is found, and within the " individual experience " the Body is present. Thus the losing and the finding are equally real. While the claim that individualism must die is unrelenting, and while Paul, Apollos and Cephas are " nothing," beyond Resurrection and in the one Body they are known once more and their singleness is seen. " Wherefore, let no one glory in men. For all things are yours; whether Paul, or Apollos, or Cephas, or the world, or life, or death, or things present, or things to come; all are yours; and ye are Christ's; and Christ is God's." (1 Cor. 3$^{21-24}$.)

III

That Christ died and rose, and that the Christians shared in His death and resurrection and became members of His Body, are historical events which the New Testament records. But history cannot exhaust the meaning of these events, since in them the powers of another world are at work and the beginnings of a new creation are present. God is in Christ reconciling the world to Himself : the powers of evil have been overcome, and a new order is entering the life of men and of nature. The Son of God is raised from the dead as the first-fruits of a race of men who shall be raised in Him, and of a world of nature which shall be freed from bondage into the glory of God. Now in this new order of creation and in this resurrection life the Church already shares. The world does not perceive this, but already the Christians have died and have been raised with Christ. " Ye died," says S. Paul, " and your life is hid with Christ in God." (Col. 3^3.) Thus, unknown to the world, the Church is drawn into a central place in the universe, sharing in the sovereignty of Christ, and S. Paul's description of the Church as the Body springs from his account of the exaltation of the Christ :

" he raised him from the dead, and made him to sit at his right hand in the heavenly places . . . and he put all things in subjection under his feet, and gave him to be head over all things to the church, which is his body, the fulness of him that filleth all in all." (Eph. 1^{20-23}.)

This heavenly status of the Church can hardly be exaggerated, but it is a sovereignty of dying and risen life, it is apprehended through faith in the Cross, its power is known in humiliation, and neither the resurrection of the Christ nor the place of the Church beside him can be perceived by the mind of the world.[1]

[1] (1) Christ's resurrection as a " first-fruits " of that of mankind. Col. 1^{18}, 1 Cor. 15^{23} ; cf. Rom. 7^4, 8^{34}.
(2) The Christians raised already with Christ. Eph. 2^{5-6}, 5^{14}, Col. 2^{12}, 3^1 ; cf. John 5^{21-24}, 10^{10}, 11^{25-26}, 1 John 3^{14}.

[Continued on following page.

But though the Church has died and is risen, the end is not yet ; and, by one of the many paradoxes of the New Testament, there is a dying and a rising still to be experienced, and the Church is the scene of dying and rising in every age of history. (i) There is, first of all, the struggle with sin within the Christian, the battle with the " ego " which still asserts itself. The struggle is a sharing in the Lord's Passion, and S. Paul yearns for his converts " till Christ be formed in you," and for his own part he goes on dying, " that I may gain Christ . . . that I may know him, and the power of his resurrection, and the fellowship of his sufferings, becoming conformed unto his death." (Phil. 3^{8-10}.) The death which the Christian died once is repeated in the conflict with the mind of the flesh and the old self-consciousness, until the mind of Christ fully possesses His people. (ii) There is also the existence of pain and tragedy in nature and in the world around the Christians, and here too they recognize the Passion of Christ. They do not fear the struggle ; S. Paul's physical afflictions are a source of strength and joy to him. For pain has been used by Christ, and has been given a new significance ; and taught by Him, the Christians can use it for love, for sympathy and for intercession. It enables them to enter more deeply into His Passion, it helps to wean them from any content with the present order and its false values, it makes them " members one of another " in a unity springing from the Cross, and pointing to a glory which is to be revealed. In the words of Dr. Karl Barth, " what seems at first sight to be human suffering becomes the action of God, the creator and redeemer. Demolition becomes edification. Disappointment and obstruction become energetic hastening and tarrying for the

(3) Christ's life-giving work in the Christians points to a future resurrection of their bodies. Rom. 8^{11}, Phil. 3^{21}, John 5^{25}, 6^{39-40}.

(4) Nature will share in the new creation. Rom. 8^{18-25}.

(5) But Christ's triumph is scandal and folly to the world. 1 Cor. 1^{23}, 2^{6-8}, 2 Cor. 2^{14-16}.

coming of the Lord. . . . Thus our tribulation, without
ceasing to be tribulation, is transformed. We must suffer,
as we suffered before, but our suffering is no longer a passive
perplexity . . . but is transformed into a pain which is
creative, fruitful, full of power and promise. . . . The
road which is impassable has been made known to us in
the crucified and risen Lord." [1]

Like the Christ, the Church is sent to execute a twofold
work in the face of the sufferings of men ; to seek to al-
leviate them, to heal them and to remove them, since they
are hateful to God—yet, when they are overwhelming
and there is no escape from them, to transfigure them and
use them as the raw material of love. So in every age
Christians have fought to remove sufferings, and have also
borne witness to the truth that they can be transfigured
and can become the place where the power of God is known.

So in these two ways—the inner conflict with sin and
the outer bearing of pain—the Church is a scene of
continual dying ; yet it is the place where the sovereignty
of God is known and uttered, and where God is reconciling the world to Himself. Here life is given in
abundance, and here the faithful discern the peace of
the resurrection. The passage which starts " one died
for all, therefore all died," ends " all things are of God,
who reconciled us to himself through Christ, and gave
unto us this ministry of reconciliation ; to wit, that God
was in Christ reconciling the world unto himself, not reckon-
ing unto them their trespasses, and having committed
unto us the word of reconciliation." (2 Cor. 5[18-19].) This
reconciling work of God is the history of the Christian
Church.

Behind this history lies the Redemption once wrought
by God, the breaking of the eternal into the order of time.
Before it there remains the " not yet," since dying and rising
are still to come. And this paradox of the " not yet"

[1] Barth on Romans 5[3-5].   Cf. Col. 1[24], 2 Cor. 6[9-10], 12[9-10], Phil.
1[20, 29], 2[17], etc.

runs through the New Testament. Christ is in us—yet the Parousia is in the future. The Church is here—yet the heavenly city is still to descend. The Christians have died and risen—yet still they must die and rise. But this puzzle of the " not yet " speaks of the inexhaustible and unimaginable character of God's purpose ; He has redeemed us, but it is not made manifest what we shall be. He has given Himself to us, but He has still more to give. And the " not yet " throws further light on the meaning of the Church. It exists in faith and hope, in a hidden life in Christ, by a power which can never be known in terms of the world's ideas of progress. It is the place where human personality is lost and yet found and enriched, and where all mankind shall be made one by the death and resurrection of the Christ. In terms of that death and resurrection the Church's history must be interpreted, and the doctrines concerning the Church must be studied and understood.

ADDITIONAL NOTE

For a fuller treatment of the concept of the Body in the New Testament, the reader is referred to J. A. T. Robinson, *The Body, a Study in Pauline Theology.*

CHAPTER IV

THE MEANING OF UNITY

I

IN showing us the Christ the New Testament has taken us beyond His historical life and death into a region as hard to define as it is real to Christian experience. This region is described when the writer of Hebrews says, " Jesus Christ is the same yesterday and to-day, yea and for ever " (Heb. 13⁸), and when S. Paul says, " Christ liveth in me " (Gal. 2²⁰). In this region of thought the word "mystical" at once suggests itself, and it is a word which has often been used to describe that union of the Christian with his Lord which is as real as was the union of the disciples in the days of His flesh. But in this region there lurks a subtle danger, since in it there is the temptation for a Christian to cling to the immediacy of his own experience of Christ, and so, in the very midst of the Body of Christ, to be ensnared into an individualism and self-satisfaction which belie the truth about the one Body. Against this danger the New Testament asserts two important safeguards : (1) the importance of the historical events of the life and death of Jesus in the flesh, and (2), the importance, to the individual member or group, of realizing that the one Body existed before his own conversion and has one continuous historic life in which he is called to share.

(i) United with Christ as they are, the Christians will not interpret aright their present union with Him unless they constantly look back to the events whence it has sprung, and remember that these events, wrought once for all, are the source of everything that the Christians

43

are and have and know. They are called upon not to advertise their own "experiences" but to praise God for, and to bear witness to, the historical events wherein the Name and the glory of God were uttered in human flesh. The faithful Christian will not draw attention to himself as an interesting specimen of life in Christ, but dying to all interest in himself and his "experiences" he will focus attention upon the redeeming acts of Christ in history, as the centre of man's prayers and praises for all time. In other words, the Church is Apostolic; it looks back to the deeds of Jesus in the flesh, and through these deeds it has been "sent" into the world.

(ii) From the deeds of Jesus in the flesh there springs a society which is one in its continuous life. Many kinds of fellowship in diverse places and manners are created by the Spirit of Jesus, but they all depend upon the one life. Thus each group of Christians will learn its utter dependence upon the whole Body. It will indeed be aware of its own immediate union with Christ, but it will see this experience as a part of the one life of the one family in every age and place. By its dependence upon the Church of history it will die to self-consciousness and self-satisfaction. And as with the group, so with the individual Christian; he will know his dependence upon the other members of the Body, wherein the relation of member to member and of function to function begets humility and love. The gifts that he possesses belong to the Body, and are useful only in the Body's common life. Thus through membership he dies to self-sufficing, and knows that his life in Christ exists only as a life in which all the members share.

In these two ways the Christians will forget themselves and bear witness to the redemption wrought once for all and to the society in which men die and rise.[1] In later

---

[1] These points are illustrated by S. Paul's life and writings. It is impossible to belittle his own special experiences and the independence which he claims in loyalty to them. (Gal. 1^1, 1^{16-17}, 2^{11}; I Cor. 9^{1-2}, etc.) Yet he knows that these things would betray him, were it not

language the Church is called "Apostolic" (sent by the
one redeemer in the flesh) and "Catholic" (living one
universal life); and both these notes of the Church are
essential to its existence as expressing the Lord's death
and resurrection, wherein its "Holiness" consists.   By
his place in the Body the Christian finds the Gospel of
death and resurrection active around and through him.
To "believe one Holy, Catholic and Apostolic Church"
is to die to self.

II

The relation therefore between the Christians and the
one Church is a part of their relation to Christ Himself.
Its oneness, in which they share, speaks of the truth about
Him.   Hence the student of the Gospel is at this point
compelled to study carefully the meaning of unity in the
New Testament, both in its inward essence and in its
outward structure.

Certainly the Epistles show us that there is a unity
between Christians everywhere.   We read of Christian
communities in Judaea, Samaria, Syria, Galatia, Asia,
Macedonia, Achaea, Rome and other parts of the world,
and each community is a fellowship in which every member
is called to live in lowliness and love towards his brethren.
Yet, when this has been said, the half has not been told
about the unity of Christian life, for, as we read the letters
of S. Paul and others to the local communities, we find
that these communities are not allowed to forget the
existence of the others and their close relation in life, work,
worship, wealth and poverty, pain and death.

The visits, the messages, the salutations, the hospitalities
at once express and foster an atmosphere of brotherhood
between the communities.   And how S. Paul cherishes
this brotherhood and how the communities responded to

for (a) his sense of debt to the older apostles as witnesses to the flesh
of Jesus (1 Cor. 15[1-8]); and (b) his sense of the Church's continuity
from them.   (1 Cor. 1[1-2], 14[36]; Eph. 2[20].)

him is seen vividly in the story of the " collection for the
saints " in Jerusalem, to which S. Paul devoted much
time and energy during his third missionary journey.
This " collection " was far more than an economic scheme
or an act of brotherly charity ; it was a test of essential
Christianity ; " for if the Gentiles have been made partakers of their spiritual things, they owe it to them also
to minister unto them in carnal things." (Rom. 15^{27}.)
And this collection issues in a worship which is one act
in which Gentile and Jewish communities share, " for the
ministration of this service not only filleth up the measure
of the wants of the saints, but worketh also through
many thanksgivings unto God." (2 Cor. 9^{12}.) Worship,
then, links the Christian communities. Pain also links
them :—

" ye, brethren, became imitators of the churches of God which
are in Judaea in Christ Jesus ; for ye also suffered the same
things " (1 Thess. 2^{14}),

" as ye are partakers of the sufferings, so also are ye of the
comfort." (2 Cor. 1^{7}).

This unity in pain is very significant ; it is not only a
unity by similarity and imitation, but the unity of one
single organism of joy and sorrow. Suffering in one
Christian may beget life and comfort in Christians elsewhere. " So then death worketh in us, but life in you."
(2 Cor. 4^{12}.) Thus the sorrows of a Christian in one place
may be all-powerful for Christians elsewhere. Such is
the range and depth of the unity of the Christians in the
scattered communities of the Mediterranean world.

But what is the nature and meaning of this unity ?
It is deeper than convenience, organisation, human
brotherhood. It is less formally expounded than tacitly
assumed. There is no Christian community mentioned in
the New Testament which has not behind it some authority
responsible to a larger whole, and there is no letter in the
New Testament (except the epistle to Philemon) which
does not show that the local society owes obedience to
someone who addresses it in the name of the larger whole.

Not of convenience alone, this unity is connected with the truth about Christ Himself. It is the unity of His own Body, springing from the unity of God, uttered in the Passion of Jesus, and expressed in an order and a structure. We must investigate the nature of this unity, and ask what is its relation to the Gospel.

(i) The meaning of unity is seen first of all in the word "ecclesia," which our English Bible translates "church." In the Greek Bible from the book of Deuteronomy onwards "ecclesia" is the normal rendering of the Hebrew "quahal," the congregation of Israel. Hence the use of the word by the Christian communities is striking; in many cities of the dispersion the Christians have been banished from the synagogues, and yet (no reader of the Septuagint could fail to see the audacious claim involved) they are themselves the ἐκκλησία of God. To them belong the promises and privileges of the Israel of God, and their unity is a unity of *race*. This race, drawn from Jews and Gentiles and yet one race in Christ, is formed in many local communities, and the important question arises: What is the relation between the local communities and the whole race? The word ἐκκλησία is used in the New Testament both for the local community and for the race as a whole, and, except in the Epistle to the Ephesians, the former use is far more frequent. Does it then follow that the local community is primary, and the important starting point? No, for the very word ἐκκλησία forbids us to think of any merely local community; the ἐκκλησία in a place is *the one race* as existing in that place, e.g. the "ecclesia" of Corinth is the one called-out-race of God which exists in Corinth, as in many other places. The one race exists first, precedes the local ecclesia and is represented by it. This fact was well put by P. T. Forsyth: "The total Church was not made up by adding the local churches together, but the local church was a church through representing then and there the total Church. . . . It was one Church in many manifestations; it was not many churches in one convention.

. . . The great Church is not the agglutination of local churches, but their prius ; . . . the local church was not *a* church, but *the* Church . . . the totality of all Christians flowing to a certain spot, and emerging there." [1] Thus the use of the word " ecclesia " in itself tells us an important truth about unity. The one universal Church is primary, the local society expresses the life and unity of the whole.

(ii) Behind this unity of the one race there stand the historic events which created it, and the unity is seen to be in a real sense a sharing in those events. The word translated " fellowship " is applied to a number of aspects of unity ; to the common life of the primitive Christians in Jerusalem (Acts 2^{42}), to the collection for the saints (2 Cor. 9^{13}), to the Eucharist (1 Cor. 10^{16}), to the sharing of the Christians in the Holy Spirit (2 Cor. 13^{14}, Phil. 2^{1}), to sharing in Christ's sufferings (Phil. 3^{10}), to union with the Father and the Son (1 John 1^{8}). But this wide and deep and many-sided unity is made possible only by a real contact with the historical events :

" that which we have seen and heard (i.e. the historical Incarnation) declare we unto you also, that ye also may have fellowship with us : yea, and our fellowship is with the Father, and with his Son Jesus Christ." (1 John 1^{8}.)

" Herein was the love of God manifested in us, that God hath sent his only begotten Son into the world (i.e. the historical event) that we might live through him. Herein is love, not that we loved God, but that he loved us, and sent his Son to be the propitiation for our sins." (1 John 4^{9-10}.)

Fellowship is essentially fellowship with the historical events. No book in the New Testament is more emphatic in its teaching about the fellowship and love of the brotherhood than the first Epistle of S. John ; and no book is more insistent that fellowship springs from and bears witness to the events of Jesus in the flesh. The events created the fellowship and the fellowship mysteriously shares in the events.

[1] Forsyth, *Lectures on the Church and Sacraments*, p. 40.

" Ye know the grace of our Lord Jesus Christ, that, though he was rich, yet for your sakes became poor, that ye through his poverty might become rich." (2 Cor. 8⁹.)

The unity is between men who, dying to themselves, give glory to the one historic redemption and are drawn into it in one Body. The Eucharist is a sharing in the body and the blood of Christ, and the means whereby the Christians are "one bread one body" (1 Cor. 10¹⁶⁻¹⁷), only because it brings them very near to His actual death in the flesh. (1 Cor. 11²⁶.)

(iii) Yet the New Testament leads us still more deeply into the meaning of unity. It takes us behind the one race and behind the historical events to the Divine unity from which they spring. "One Lord, one faith, one baptism, one God and Father of all." (Eph. 4⁵⁻⁶.) The unity which comes to men through the Cross is the eternal unity of God Himself, a unity of love which transcends human utterance and human understanding.

" Holy Father, keep them in thy name which thou hast given me, that they may be one, even as we are."
—(John 17¹¹.)

" Neither for these only do I pray, but for them also that believe on me through their word ; that they may all be one ; even as thou, Father, art in me, and I in thee, that they also may be in us : that the world may believe that thou didst send me. And the glory which thou hast given me I have given unto them ; that they may be one, even as we are one." (John 17²⁰⁻²².)

" That they may behold my glory, which thou hast given me ; for thou lovest me before the foundation of the world."
—(John 17²⁴.)

Before and behind the historical events there is the unity of the one God. This unity overcomes men and apprehends them through the Cross. "It does not mean that there is a calculable number of men who are at peace with themselves ; it means that the oneness of God triumphs over the whole questionableness of the Church's history."[1]

[1] Karl Barth, *Romans*, Eng. tr., p. 396.

Unity is God's alone, and in Him alone can anything on earth be said to be united.

In these ways the New Testament unfolds the secret of the Church's unity. (i) Christ's people are the *ecclesia*, the one race precedes its various parts. (ii) The people are united in the historical events of Jesus in the flesh. (iii) Behind the people and the events there is the eternal unity of God. Thus the inward and the outward are inseparable, and the Church's inward meaning is expressed in the Church's outward shape and structure as the *ecclesia* wherein the parts depend upon the whole.

III

The outward order of the Church therefore is no indifferent matter ; it is, on the contrary, of supreme importance since it is found to be related to the Church's inner meaning and to the Gospel of God itself. For the good news that God has visited and redeemed His people includes the redeemed man's knowledge of death and resurrection through his place in the one visible society and through the death to self which every member and group has died. And in telling of this one visible society the Church's outward order tells indeed of the Gospel. For every part of the Church's true order will bear witness to the one universal family of God and will point to the historic events of the Word-made-flesh. Thus Baptism is into the death and resurrection of Christ, and into the one Body (Rom. 6^3, 1 Cor. 12^{13}) ; the Eucharist is likewise a sharing in Christ's death and a merging of the individual into the one Body (1 Cor. 11^{26}, 1 Cor. 10^{17}) ; and the Apostles are both a link with the historical Jesus and also the officers of the one *ecclesia* whereon every local community depends. Hence the whole structure of the Church tells of the Gospel ; not only by its graces and its virtues, but also by its mere organic shape it proclaims the truth. A Baptism, a Eucharistic service, an Apostle, in themselves tell us of our death and resurrection and of the Body which is one.

The study of the Gospel and of inner unity has now forced us on to the study of the Church's outward order ; and the subsequent chapters of this book will deal with the growth of this order in history. Meanwhile its connexion with the Gospel is abundantly clear from the New Testament itself, and is illustrated in a striking way by the crisis in the Church at Corinth. The story of this crisis may well gather up the present discussion.

In Corinth the issues of the Gospel and the issues of Church order lie close together, not in any theories of S. Paul, but in a desperate conflict wherein the whole Christianity of the Corinthian converts is at stake. In the first Epistle to the Corinthians there is a great deal of teaching about the Gospel of the Cross.

" For the Word of the Cross is to them that are perishing foolishness, but unto us that are being saved it is the power of God." (1 Cor. 1[18].)

And there is also a great deal of teaching about order and the office of an Apostle. It is no accident that these two subjects figure side by side.

What is the trouble in Corinth ? It seems that the Corinthian Christians possess many spiritual and intellectual gifts, and have succumbed to the peril of thinking of these gifts as possessions of their own and interpreting them in terms of human wisdom, knowledge and individual ownership. The thoughts, " *we* have," " *we* know," " *we* are," take the place of the thoughts, " God has given," " God possesses us," " we are not, in ourselves and of ourselves ; but Christ in us is wisdom, righteousness and sanctification." In short, the Corinthians have taken the things of Christ in an individualistic way instead of merging themselves and their gifts in the one Body and so learning to die and live. Or, to put the same thing rather differently, they think of themselves as separate " selfhoods," —(I, mine, he, his)—instead of knowing themselves to be nothing. " Each one saith, I am of Paul, I of Apollos, I of Cephas, and I of Christ." In this verse three sins are described ; they dare to speak as an " each " instead of as a member (*each* one saith) ; then they dare to talk about themselves and their " positions " (I am) ; and finally they dare to speak about other Christians as if they were great individual personalities, a Paul, a Cephas, an Apollos. Those who say " I am of Christ " (the superior " non-party party " ?) are just as sinful, for their attitude is just as self-conscious. Thus an atmosphere of " great individuals and their great gifts " takes the place of the atmosphere of the Body and the Gospel. The sin is unspeakable, for it means a severing of Christ. " And is Christ divided ? "

Now, the sin of the Corinthians is both sin against the Gospel of the Cross and sin against the claims of the one Body of Christ. So S. Paul meets the situation by reasserting both the Gospel of the Cross and the truth about the structure of the Church. In 1 Cor. 1-4 the two themes are interwoven. First, he confronts their pride with the death of Christ, which is scandal and folly to the world, but the power and the wisdom of God ; it confounds the wisdom of the wise and brings to nought the things that are. Before the scandal of the Cross the Corinthians are nothing and know nothing, but Christ in them is " wisdom and righteousness and sanctification." They no longer belong to a world which thinks in terms of " I," " mine," " he," " his," for even Paul and Apollos and Cephas are nothing in themselves and of themselves. Thus thoroughly are the Corinthians faced with the Gospel of the Cross. But they are to learn this Gospel not only by looking back to a past event, but by finding its present expression in the one Body. By their place in the one Body they are to learn to be humble and dependent and to die to self. Let them consider the Body and exist only as members of the Body, and they will learn of Christ's Cross whereby men are lost as separate " selfhoods " and found as members of Christ and of one another.

In two ways specially S. Paul drives this truth home to the Corinthians. (i) He shows first of all that the Body to

which they belong is the universal historic family. " Paul
. . . unto the Church of God which is in Corinth . . . called
to be saints . . . with all that call upon the name of our
Lord Jesus Christ in every place, their Lord and ours."
(1 Cor. 1¹⁻².) The Corinthians are Christians only in dependence upon the one universal family, now represented
in Corinth. " What ? was it from you that the word of
God went forth ? or came it unto you alone ? " (1 Cor.
14³⁶.) By their place in the historic Church which exists
before them the Corinthians will die to pride. (ii) And
S. Paul shows further the hierarchical principle of mutual
dependence in the one Body. In Chapter 12, reverting to
the question of spiritual gifts which cause self-consciousness
and friction, he expounds this principle fully :—

" The eye cannot say to the hand, I have no need of thee :
or again the head to the feet, I have no need of you. Nay,
much rather, those members of the body which seem to be
more feeble are necessary. . . . Now ye are the body of
Christ, and severally members thereof. And God hath set
some in the Church, first apostles, secondly prophets, thirdly
teachers, then miracles, then gifts of healings, helps, govern-
ments, divers kinds of tongues. Are all apostles ? are all
prophets ? are all teachers ? are all workers of miracles ?
have all gifts of healing ? do all speak with tongues ? do all
interpret ? " (1 Cor. 12²¹⁻³⁰.)

To possess a gift is to feel no pride of possession, for only
in the life of the one Body is it of use or of significance ;
to lack a gift or function is not to feel hurt since the
member's selfhood dies in the one Body. Thus the hierarchical principle sets forth death and resurrection, and
the " still more excellent way " of divine love is uttered
in the Church's structure as in the Gospel of the Cross.

So Corinth learns the Gospel anew by learning the Church.
Both the individual Christian, and the exalted and spiritual
group of Christians, and the Church of Corinth as a whole
learn both of the Body and of the Cross. The structure,
historic and apostolic, does matter. Paul the Apostle
is a part of this structure ; not by his eloquence, or

distinction, or personal gifts, but by his *office* as Apostle he represents to the local communities the fact of the one ecclesia in which they die and live. " Paul called to be an apostle . . . unto the Church of God which is in Corinth." The structure of Catholicism is an utterance of the Gospel.

APPENDED NOTE

The use of the words εὐαγγέλιον, εὐαγγελίζεσθαι shows the connexion between the Gospel and the life of the Church.

In the LXX the verb is used of the bringing of the " good news " of the fulfilment of God's messianic promises. (Isaiah 40⁹, 52⁷, 61¹, etc.) Hence in the N.T. both verb and noun describe the actual fulfilment in the words and deeds of the Messiah. Thus (a) Jesus proclaims the " good news " of God, Mk. 1¹⁴, ¹⁵ ; of the Kingdom, Lk. 4⁴³, 8¹, 16¹⁶, etc. (b) The Apostles proclaim the " good news " about Jesus, or the " good news " which *is* Jesus Himself, Acts 5⁴², 8²⁵, 11²⁰ (cf. probably, Mk. 8³⁵, 10²⁹). (c) This " good news " of Jesus is seen as the " good news " of God, in the sense of God's whole saving work in His Son. Cf. Acts 20²⁴, Rom. 1¹ (of God), 1⁹ (of His Son), 2 Cor. 4⁴, 1 Thess. 2².

The Apostles and others proclaim this εὐαγγέλιον by word of mouth, and the κήρυγμα is in the forefront of their task. (Rom. 10¹⁴.) S. Paul was sent " not to baptize but to preach the Gospel " (1 Cor. 1¹⁷). But it cannot be inferred from this passage that preaching by word of mouth is the only way in which the Gospel is set forth, for many passages show that the whole life of the Church is to be a setting forth of the Gospel. Thus (a) the whole of an Apostle's ministry of conversion and of founding a Church is " in the gospel." (1 Cor. 4¹⁵.) (b) the life of the Christians is a sharing in it. (Phil. 1⁵, ²⁷.) (c) Unworthy conduct can hinder it. (1 Cor. 9¹².) (d) There was a brother whose " praise in it " was known. (2 Cor. 8¹⁸.) (e) The gospelling to the Gentiles of " peace " (Eph. 2¹⁷) and of the " unsearchable riches of Christ " (Eph. 3⁸) must include not only preaching, but their whole access to God in Christ.

In short, the whole work of an Apostle is a λατρεία ἐν τῷ εὐαγγελίῳ (cf. Rom. 1⁹), and the Gospel is οὐ λόγῳ μόνον (cf. 1 Thess. 1⁵). Every function of the Church proclaims it, and not least the Church's organic shape and structure.

CHAPTER V

THE GOSPEL AND CHURCH ORDER

I

UNITED by the death and resurrection of Christ, the Christians are conscious of what they are, " an elect race, a royal priesthood, a holy nation, a people for God's own possession." (1 Peter 2⁹.) They are neither Jews nor Gentiles, but (to use the phrase of Harnack) a *third race*, whose unity lies not in their opinions but in the redemptive act whereby they were begotten and born anew. " This conviction that they were a *people* . . . i.e. the transference of all the prerogatives and claims of the Jewish people to the new community as a new creation which exhibited and realized whatever was old and original in religion—this at once furnished adherents of the new faith with a political and historical self-consciousness. Nothing more complete or comprehensive or impressive than this consciousness can be conceived. Could there be any higher or more comprehensive conception than that of the complex of momenta afforded by the Christians' view of themselves as the true Israel, ' the new people,' ' the original people,' and the ' people of the future,' i.e. of eternity ? . . . Was the cry raised ' you are renegade Jews '—the answer came ' we are the community of the Messiah and therefore the true Israelites.' If people said ' you are simply Jews,' they reply ' we are a new creation and a new people.' If, again, they were taxed with their recent origin and told that they were but of yesterday, they retorted ' we only seem to be the younger people ; from the beginning we have been latent ; we have always existed, previous to any other people ; we are the original people of God.' If they were told ' you do not deserve to live,' the answer ran, ' we would die to live, for we are citizens of the world to come, and sure that we shall rise again.' "[1]

These are awful claims, yet the Christians could not shrink from making them, since the Christians were the Body and the fulness of the Christ in whom all things consist and in whom all things shall be summed up in the good purpose of God. But these claims involve corresponding perils. There is the peril of a self-consciousness which dwells upon " our privileges " rather than upon the glory of God in Christ ; of a partisanship which exaggerates particular experiences or aspects of truth ; of an intellectualism which misses the meaning of the redemptive act ; and (the most subtle because the most devout error) of a " spirituality " which rejoices in conscious union with Christ here and now and ignores the importance, for belief and conduct, of the historical coming of Jesus in the flesh and the historical society which links them to that coming. The peril, in short, is for the devout Churchman to turn his religion into a " glory to me," " glory to this movement," " glory to the Church " religion instead of a " glory to God " religion. These perils are already evident in the Apostolic age. We have seen the " spiritual group " in Corinth who need reminding of *historical* Christianity and of the one Body ; and very similar are the " spiritual " people in Ephesus to whom S. John in his First Epistle insists that Jesus came *in the flesh* and that love is based upon fellowship with this historical event. Passing into the second century we read of the " spiritual " people in Asia Minor to whom S. Ignatius urges the importance both of the *flesh* of Jesus and of the unity of the Church. And, above all, we find the Church in the second century beset by the struggle with Gnosticism,—the very popular tendency to ignore the historic basis of Christianity and to fit the Christ into a complex scheme of theosophical revelations.

[1] Harnack, *Mission and Expansion of Christianity*, pp. 240-241.

The struggle with Gnosticism, which threatened the very character and existence of Christianity, was the first of the battles between Christianity and its counterfeits. In this crisis, as in the others we have mentioned, the remedy lay in a twofold appeal—to the historical facts of Christianity and to the structure of the one Body which claims continuity with those facts. Thus the Church's reply to Gnosticism was to emphasize the Christian writings (which were gradually formed into the Canon of the New Testament) and the succession of Bishops as the organs of the Church's unity and continuity. In the greatest of the anti-gnostic theologians, S. Irenaeus, we find this twofold emphasis on Scripture and on the Apostolic succession. He is led to this twofold emphasis solely through his concern with the essential Christian revelation ; and S. Paul's dealings with Corinth have already shown that the structure of the Church expresses the truth about Christ and the Christians.

Now this structure grows, and it takes the form of an organism of Sacraments, Episcopacy, Scriptures and Creeds. This " order " has persisted ; it existed throughout all Christendom for fifteen centuries, and in a large part of Christendom it exists to-day. And the problem arises " Whence came it ? and what does it mean ? " Recent scholarship has shattered conclusively the theory that this development was influenced by the pagan mystery-religions [1] ; but, while this historical question has been settled, the theological question still remains—What is the place of this structure in essential Christianity ? Is it a spurious " institutionalism " which obscures the simple and primitive Gospel ? Or is it a convenient order which grew up as a result of its practical utility but which has no permanent necessity about it ? Or is it a development which grew in the Gospel and through the Gospel, and which expresses the Gospel and can be belittled only at the expense of the Gospel ? Here we face the central issue

[1] Cf. the essay by A. D. Nock in *Essays on the Trinity and the Incarnation*, edited by A. E. J. Rawlinson (1928).

of this book. In this present chapter the original relation of the growing structure to the Gospel will be described as a whole ; in the chapters which follow the meaning of particular parts of it will be tested ; and in the second part of the book both the structure and the Gospel will be seen in the light of later history.

II

In the Church of the New Testament we find Baptism, Eucharist, Apostles. In the subsequent centuries we find Baptism, Eucharist, the Bishops, the Bible, the Creeds. In what sense do these marks of the Church declare or obscure the Gospel of God ?

(1) *Baptism.* From the very earliest times this appears as an act of Christ whereby the baptized person is brought into a new relation to Christ and His Body. The response of continual faith is needed for this new relation to grow. None the less Baptism is the Divine act creating the new relationship :—

" but ye were washed, but ye were sanctified, but ye were justified in the name of our Lord Jesus Christ, and in the Spirit of our God " (1 Cor. 6¹¹).

" As many of you as were baptized into Christ did put on Christ " (Gal. 3²⁷).

" Are ye ignorant that all we who were baptized into Christ Jesus were baptized into his death ? " (Rom. 6³),

" one Lord, one faith, one baptism " (Eph. 4⁵),

" according to his mercy he saved us, through the washing of regeneration and renewing of the Holy Ghost " (Titus 3⁵),

" not laying again a foundation of repentance from dead works, of faith toward God, of the teaching of baptisms, of laying on of hands, and of the resurrection of the dead, and of eternal judgement " (Heb. 6¹⁻²),

" which also after a true likeness doth now save you, even baptism " (1 Pet. 3²¹),

" except a man be born of water and the Spirit, he cannot enter into the kingdom of God " (John 3⁵),

" repent ye, and be baptized every one of you in the name of Jesus Christ unto the remission of your sins " (Acts 2[38]).

The inevitable meaning of these passages, singly or as a whole, is that Baptism is a divine act which has in itself a real effect ; it is joined to resurrection and judgement in a catalogue of awful verities in Hebrews 6[2].   It is interesting to recall the examination of New Testament evidence made by the late Dr. H. T. Andrews, the Congregationalist scholar, in a chapter included in Dr. P. T. Forsyth's *Lectures on the Church and Sacraments*.   After examining 1 Cor. 6[11], 1 Cor. 15[29], Eph. 4[5], 5[26], Titus 3[5], Dr. Andrews concludes : " In the light of these statements it is difficult to believe that the more neutral phrases, e.g. ' baptized into Christ,' ' baptized into one body,' imply a merely symbolical interpretation of baptism.   With this evidence before us it seems very hard to resist the conclusion (however little we may like it) that if the Epistles do not enunciate the ecclesiastical doctrine of baptismal regeneration, they at any rate approximate very closely to it."   On Eph. 4[5] Dr. Andrews comments, " why is baptism assigned a place in this great hierarchy of spiritual realities ? . . . if baptism is merely a symbol and nothing more, it is difficult to find the reason which led S. Paul to set it on so high a pinnacle."   " It cleanses from the defilement of sin. (1 Cor. 6[11], Eph. 5[26].)   It creates the mystical union between the believer and Christ (Rom. 6[3], Gal. 3[26]), and it is the means whereby he is incorporated into the Church the Body of Christ." [1]

Baptism, therefore (with the laying-on-of-hands as its normal completion [2]) is the first significant fact about a Christian.   It declares that the beginning of a man's Christianity is not what he feels and experiences but what God in Christ has done for him.   And his feelings and experiences and virtues have meaning not in themselves in isolation but as bearing witness to the one Body in which

---

[1] *Lectures on the Church and Sacraments*, pp. 145-150.

[2] Cf. Acts 8[14-17], 19[1-7], Heb. 6[2], Titus 3[5], and probably 2 Tim. 1[6].

alone the individual can grow to full manhood. The life of a Christian is a continual response to the fact of his Baptism; he continually learns that he *has* died and risen with Christ, and that his life is a part of the life of the one family.

(2) *The Eucharist* likewise sets forth Christ crucified and the one Body, and shows the constant relation between these truths,

" as often as ye eat this bread, and drink the cup, ye proclaim the Lord's death " (1 Cor. 11²⁶),

" we, who are many, are one bread, one body : for we all partake of the one bread " (1 Cor. 10¹⁷).

A subsequent chapter will discuss the development of Eucharistic life and doctrine. Meanwhile the close connexion between the showing forth of the Lord's death, and the unity of the Body suggests inevitably that the minister in the Eucharist will be, not only the representative of a local group, but the organ of the one universal and historic society, so that the rite proclaims the dependence of the local community upon the one family of God.

(3) *Apostles and prophets* also bear witness to the Gospel and to the Body. The prophets teach, predict, expound ; but their work finds its true meaning and power only in the context of the Body and of the historical facts of the Christ. It is the essential function of the Apostles to represent these facts, and their significance is twofold ; they are " sent " to bear witness to the historical events, and they are officers of the one people of God, which is behind and before all local communities. As time goes on the form of the ministry develops ; while in the apostolic age there was a local ministry of presbyter-bishops and deacons and a " general " ministry of Apostles, a change takes place, and in the second century there appears the ministry of Bishops with a growing emphasis upon their necessity as links with the Apostles. A subsequent chapter will deal more fully with the growth of the ministry. And

if the Apostles, by their place in the structure, set forth
the Gospel, then there will be needed in subsequent ages
a similar ministry (distinct from presbyters and from
prophets) with a similar relation to the Gospel and the
Body. The Apostle, and the Bishop after him, is the
link with the historic events and the organ of the one Body
into which Corinth must die in humble dependence.

(4) *The Canon of Scripture* likewise sets forth the historical redemption and the one Body. The scriptures of
the old Israel of God are still the books of God's people,
and they become the Bible of the new Israel, which knows
itself to be the Messianic people, the inheritor of the promises.
The new Israel uses this Bible as Christ has taught, and
finds in the scriptures the age-long plan of God that the
Messiah should die, and redeem His people. " The Son of
man goeth, even as it is written of him." (Mark 14[21], cf.
Luke 22[37], 1 Peter 1[11].) Thus taught, the Apostles in the
earliest days of the new Church expound from the scriptures
how that Isaiah spake of the death, and David of the resurrection (Acts 2[25-28], 8[32-33], cf. 1 Peter 2[21-24].) From this
redemption there springs " an elect race, a royal priesthood,
a holy nation, a people for God's own possession " (1 Peter
2[9]). Thus the Christians find the scriptures made intelligible by the two themes (*a*) the redemptive death and rising ;
(*b*) the redeemed race. And when to the books of the old
covenant the Church gradually added the books of the
new covenant the same themes were still dominant in
the new Canon, namely the redemptive acts of Jesus and
the redeemed people of God. To understand the Bible, it
is necessary to share in Christ's death and resurrection,
and to be a member of His people.

(5) Similarly, the *Apostles' Creed* and the *Nicene Creed*
emerge in the life of the Church as sign-posts to the historic
events and to the general experience of Christians as
against speculative tendencies which would ignore both.
The Apostles' Creed gathers up the facts of the historical
redemption into which the Christians are baptized, and the
future hopes of resurrection and eternal life to which the

redemption points.[1] The Nicene Creed has a similarly
" evangelical " origin and meaning. To allege that it
represents a philosophizing of the Christian faith is to miss
the point altogether ; the fact is that the Church adopted
it as a defence against the philosophical speculations of
Arianism and as a safeguard of the Church's common
experience of redemption through Christ. It will be shown
in a later chapter that this Creed uses only one unbiblical
and metaphysical term, not to wed the Church to a particular philosophy, but to assert that the one Christ the
Mediator is as divine as God the Father, and to direct the
minds of the Christians to the historical redemption which
stands before and behind any scholasticisms or philosophies
which may seek to express it. In F. D. Maurice's words,
the Creeds are " a defence of the scriptures and of the poor
man against the attempts of doctors to confuse the one
and to rob the other." [2]

Such are the outward marks of the Church. The Gospel
has created them, and in the Gospel their meaning is to be
found. But their testimony is one and united, and to treat
them in isolation from one another is to miss their meaning.
Both in the earliest stage of the Church's life, and in the
fully developed structure this interdependence of the
various elements is plain.

(1) At the last supper both the Eucharist and the Old
Testament scriptures and the Apostolate seem inseparably
linked as expressions of the Gospel. The Lord is about to
die ; He interprets His death by the *scriptures* (" the Son of
man goeth as it is written of him "), and equally by the
eucharistic act (" take eat, this is my body ") and the death
creates a new people of God of whose unity the *Apostles* are
the organs. It is indeed hard to say that any one of these

---

[1] Writing of the teaching of the Acts of the Apostles, Dr. Foakes-
Jackson and Dr. Kirsopp-Lake say, " The most striking comparison
with Acts is not offered by any book in the New Testament, but
rather by the Apostles' Creed," *Beginnings of Christianity*, Vol. II,
p. 199.

[2] *Kingdom of Christ*, Vol. II, p. vii. (*Everyman* edition.)

is before or after the other in importance, for Bible, Eucharist, and Apostolate are intertwined in the Lord's own utterance of the Gospel on the eve of His death.

(2) In the fuller structure also the various elements seem inseparable. Faced by the spiritual perils, which Gnosticism typifies but which recur again and again, the Church appeals to the scriptures, which are slowly being formed into the Canon, and to the historic Episcopate which has taken the place of the Apostolate; and these are both facts which point the Christians away from what is partial or subjective, to Jesus in the flesh, and to the one universal Church. Both the Canon of Scripture and the Episcopate are " developments," and it would seem highly arbitrary to select one of these and to call it essential, while rejecting or ignoring the other. It would be more reasonable to seek in both of them, through their close inner connexion and their place in the life of the one Body, the utterance of the Gospel of God.

Misunderstanding and misuse arise if the marks of the Church are used or treated separately, or if any one of them is appealed to in isolation as the basis of Christianity. Thus the Gospel may be seriously obscured by a piety which emphasises Christ's presence in the Eucharist and dwells too little upon His presence in the baptized; or by a use of the Creeds as scholastic definitions, which ignores their close relation to the Eucharist and to the scriptures; or by a reverence for Scripture, which ignores the ministry and the Creeds as organs of the society wherein Scripture grew. But in each of these cases (and they are typical of many other perversions) deliverance comes not by discarding the gift of God which has been misused but by recovering its true relation to the other gifts. The remedy for a misuse of Creeds is to see that Creeds are a sign-post to Scripture and accordingly to turn to Scripture; but Scripture will be misused unless the Episcopate points us to the continuous life of the one Body in which Scripture emerged. And the Episcopate will be perverted unless it knows itself as nothing in isolation and as significant only as an organ of the

one Body, which, by the healthy relation of all its parts,
sets forth the Gospel. Thus all these marks of the Church,
by their interdependent working, point the Christian to
the historic redemption and to the one divine society,
and show him the meaning of his life in Christ. " He
gave some to be apostles, some prophets, and some
evangelists, and some pastors and teachers." Divine
action does not cease ; if He gave the Canon of Scripture,
He gave also the sacraments, the ministry, the Creeds.
But all these avail for His purpose only when, " fitly
framed and knit together through that which every joint
supplieth," they are used unto the building up of the
Body of Christ.

III

Developments thus took place, but they were all tested.
The tests of a true development are whether it bears witness to the Gospel, whether it expresses the general consciousness of the Christians, and whether it serves the
organic unity of the Body in all its parts. These tests
are summed up in the scriptures, wherein the historical
Gospel and the experience of the redeemed and the nature
of the one Body are described. Hence, while the Canon
of Scripture is in itself a development, it has a special
authority to control and to check the whole field of
development in life and doctrine. Judged by these tests
and by Scripture which sums them up, the marks of the
Church which we have just described are abundantly
vindicated, since they were the means whereby the Gospel
of God prevailed over one-sided theories and perversions
of Christian life. The theologians of the second century
who dwell most upon Church order—S. Ignatius and
S. Irenaeus—are precisely those whose whole theology is
most controlled and pervaded by Scripture.

The question at once arises whether the Papacy is an
equally legitimate development, growing out of a primacy
given by our Lord to S. Peter and symbolizing the unity of

the Church.   The answer must be found in these same tests.
A Papacy, which expresses the general mind of the Church
in doctrine, and which focuses the organic unity of all
the Bishops and of the whole Church, might well claim to
be a legitimate development in and through the Gospel.
But a Papacy, which claims to be a source of truth over
and above the general mind of the Church and which
wields an authority such as depresses the due working
of the other functions of the one Body, fails to fulfil the
main tests.   That is where the issue lies ; and the fuller
discussion of the ministry, of the sacraments, and of
authority must precede a fuller answer to the question of
the Papacy in history.   But meanwhile it must be insisted
that neither the apostolic nor the sub-apostolic ages nor
the period in which Creed, Canon and Episcopate emerged
knew the See of Rome as having any monarchical place
in the one structure.   The structure itself is the Catholic
fact.   How far the Papacy expresses this main fact or
distorts it is a subsequent historical question.[1]

The study of the historical death and resurrection of
Jesus has led us to the study of the Apostolic Church, and
thence, in one organic movement, to the study of
" Catholicism."   The impact of the Gospel has led on to
the structure of the Church.   What, then, is the relation
between the Gospel and " Catholicism ? "   It seems
impossible to understand them separately.   For we cannot
appeal back to the authority of Jesus Christ without
being led to face the Church and its outward marks.   To
know Jesus we must pass beyond His life and example
to His death and resurrection, and these events were
intelligible only through the scriptures which foretold
them and through the Apostles who shared in them when
they died with Christ and were raised together with Him.
This dying and rising means the one Body ; we know
Christ through dying in its one life, and the marks of
the Church help us to die by pointing us to the universal
family whose membership is death and life in Christ.

[1] Cf. Ch. XI, and the Appendix.

F

In short, the only appeal back to Jesus which is logically and spiritually coherent is an appeal to the Gospel of God uttered in the one Body by its whole structure. However much it may have suffered perversion in history, this structure proclaims the Gospel by pointing men beyond this or that experience, this or that achievement, this or that movement or revival, to the universal society in which all these are made full. If we would draw near to the naked facts of Calvary and Easter, we can do so only in the one fellowship whose very meaning is death to self.

The Catholicism, therefore, which sprang from the Gospel of God is a faith wherein the visible and ordered Church fills an important place. But this Church is understood less as an *institution* founded upon the rules laid down by Christ and the Apostles than as an *organism* which grew inevitably through Christ's death and resurrection. The Church, therefore, is defined not in terms of itself, but in terms of Christ, whose Gospel created it and whose life is its indwelling life.

But the Church's order does not imply that those who possess it are always more godly than those who are without it. For it does not bear witness to the perfection of those who share in it, but to the Gospel of God by which alone, in one universal family, mankind can be made perfect. It is not something Roman or Greek or Anglican ; rather does it declare to men their utter dependence upon Christ by setting forth the universal Church in which all that is Anglican or Roman or Greek or partial or local in any way must share by an agonizing death to its pride. Many fruits of the Spirit will be found apart from the full Church order ; yet those fruits and all others will grow to perfection only through the growth of the one Body in which Christ is all in all fulfilled, and it is the Church order that in every age bears witness to this one Body of which every movement, experience, " ism," achievement, must know itself to be a fragmentary part.

To assert that Church order is thus related to the Gospel is unpopular in many modern theological circles. It is widely assumed that a deeper understanding of that Gospel brings an indifference to Church order. But Baptism and Episcopacy are part of the utterance of God's redemptive love, and they proclaim that men's love is made perfect only by the building up of the one Body in which alone, by the due working of all its parts, the truth that is in Jesus is fully learnt. And no man, whether " churchman " or " Quaker," can love his fellow-men so well that he can cease to learn, from Baptism and the order of the Church, of the loving act of God in Christ and of the society in whose universal life that act will be realised by mankind.

.   .   .   .

The structure of the Church has now been described in general terms. But certain parts of it demand fuller discussion, and the chapters which follow will deal with the Church's ministry, the Church's worship, and the Church's authority in doctrine, and with their relation to the Gospel of God.

CHAPTER VI

The Gospel and Episcopacy

I

Discussions of the primitive Christian ministry have filled a large place in modern theological literature. The adherents of almost every post-reformation Church-system have sought to prove that their own form of ministry has the sanction of the New Testament, and the debates have often been tedious. Hence many welcomed with relief the conclusions reached by Dr. Streeter in his book, *The Primitive Church*—that there was a great variety of forms of ministry in the Apostolic age, that there was no single type of Church order, and that in the words of *Alice in Wonderland*, " Everybody has won, and all shall have prizes."

It seems, however, that both Dr. Streeter and many of those whose conclusions he criticizes have omitted some important questions. For when the historian has ascertained that there was a great variety of ministries, and that a development took place, the question remains : What does this development mean ? is it an indifferent thing ? or does it rather express some truth about the Body and the Gospel of God ? With this question the present discussion will be chiefly concerned. Previous controversies have dwelt upon Episcopacy mainly as a form of government, and there is greater need to consider its relation to the Gospel.

The historical problem is well known. Whereas in the Apostolic age we find " local " ministries of presbyter-bishops and deacons, and a " general " ministry of Apostles and prophets, there appears from early in the second century a threefold ministry of Bishops, presbyters and deacons, an order which soon becomes universal, with great importance attached to the succession (in more than one sense of the word) of the Bishops from the Apostles. What, now, is the important question to ask about this development ?   Not, surely, whether our Lord and the Apostles laid down by definite commands that such and such order was to be followed, but whether the development speaks of the Gospel and the one Body, so that the Bishop by his place in the one Body bears that essential relation to the Gospel which the Apostle bore before him.   To burrow in the New Testament for forms of ministry and imitate them is archæological religion :   to seek that form of ministry which the whole New Testament creates is the more evangelical way.   And our view of the ministry had better be evangelical than archæological.

II

The story falls into four main stages :   (a) our Lord and the Apostles as described in the Synoptic Gospels and the Acts ;   (b) the Apostolate as seen in the Epistles in relation to other ministries ;   (c) a transitional stage, about which we have little information, but which seems to be reflected in the Pastoral Epistles ;   (d) the final development, of which S. Ignatius' letters give an important theological exposition.   At each stage we must consider especially the function of the ministry in relation to the Gospel and to the one Body.

(a) The first impression of the Gospels is that the training and institution of the twelve Apostles was one of the main tasks of our Lord.   So unclerically minded a thinker as F. D. Maurice wrote, " If we called the four gospels ' the institution of a Christian ministry ' we might not go very far wrong." [1]   Yet critical study bids us question this impression.   For if we take S. Mark's Gospel alone we find that the word ἀπόστολος is used only in 3^{14} (where

[1] *The Kingdom of Christ*, Vol. II, p. 90.

the text is doubtful) and in 6³⁰; and Hort maintained
that the word here referred to one special mission in
Galilee and implied no permanent office.¹ Apart from the
title ἀπόστολος the Twelve are indeed often mentioned
in Mark ; to them is given " the mystery of the kingdom "
(Mark 4¹¹), and to them the meaning of the Lord's death
is unfolded at the last supper (Mark 14¹⁷⁻²⁵), and a large
part of the Lord's ministry is devoted to training them.
But, again, Hort raised the critical question (which every
candid historian must face), whether this ministry was
a special office or merely a type of general Christian discipleship, whether the Twelve were a definite order or
merely, as disciples, the nucleus of the Church in general ?
On this question, S. Mark's Gospel alone gives no certain
answer. But a saying of Jesus common to Matthew and
Luke may throw some light on the problem.

" Ye shall sit on twelve thrones, judging the twelve tribes
of Israel." (Matt. 19²⁸, Luke 22³⁰.)

The saying is mysterious, and we cannot be certain as
to its context ; but it suggests that the Apostles, being
twelve in number, are to have special leadership in a new
Israel which shall replace the twelve tribes.

Now while the evidence of S. Mark alone is inconclusive
as regards a definite Apostolic order, and the evidence of
a single " Q " passage strongly suggests such an order,
the evidence of S. Luke makes this interpretation quite
explicit. If we may not stress the fact that as gospel-
editor he uses the word ἀπόστολος as a very distinctive
title (cf. Luke 17⁵, 22¹⁴, 24¹⁰), there remains the evidence
of Acts, not only in single passages but in the whole drift
of the narrative. There he describes the Twelve as appointed by Christ to teach and to rule and to dispense
the gifts of the Spirit. (Cf. Acts 1²⁻²⁶, 2³⁷⁻⁴², 5¹², 6¹⁻⁶,
8¹⁴⁻²⁴.) So definite is their number and their order, that
the vacant place of Judas has to be filled by the appoint-

¹ *The Christian Ecclesia*, pp. 23-26 (1914 edn.)

ment of Matthias. The Apostles actively direct the Church life and expansion ; their teaching is a mark of Church fellowship, they ordain the Seven, and they send two of their own number to lay hands on the Samaritans that they may receive the Holy Spirit. Thus S. Luke makes it clear that the training and sending of the Twelve by Christ was not for a temporary mission, nor yet for a general discipleship, but for a unique office, to order and unite the Christians in one fellowship, in union with the historic events of which the Apostles are witnesses. If S. Luke's picture of the Apostles is a fictitious one, then we must cease to treat his writings as a serious historical document ; and there is no reason to doubt that he rightly interprets the very important place ascribed to the Twelve by S. Mark and by the mysterious " Q " saying which we have quoted.

The Apostolic office is shared equally by all the Apostles. The commission given to S. Peter (Matt. 16[18-19]) and the leadership ascribed to S. Peter in the Acts can involve no more than a primacy which focuses and expresses the one authority of the Apostles as a whole. For in Matt. 18[18] the commission to bind and loose is given to them all ; in Eph. 2[20] the Apostles, and not Peter alone, are the " foundation " ; and there is no evidence in the New Testament that they recognized a supremacy in Peter. All share in one Apostleship whose duties are to represent the historical Christ and to unite and feed the Christian flock.[1]

(b) Turning to the story of the expanding Church, we are faced by a wide and confusing use of the word " apostle." It is applied to a company far wider than the Twelve ; to S. Paul and S. Barnabas (Acts 14[14]), to S. James (Gal. 1[19]), to Epaphroditus (Phil. 2[25]), to Andronicus and Junias (Rom. 16[7]), apparently to Silas (1 Thess. 2[6]), but not to Timothy or to Apollos. In

[1] For the position of Peter, cf. the paper by Armitage Robinson, *The Malines Conversations*, pp. 89-102 ; C. H. Turner, *Catholic and Apostolic*, pp. 181-205.

1 Cor. 15[7] apostles are mentioned as witness of the Resurrection in addition to the Twelve ; 2 Cor. 8[23] speaks of "apostles of Churches," meaning presumably missionaries sent by local churches, and S. Paul complains of false apostles, 2 Cor. 11[13]. So there is a use of the word wider than the Twelve or even the Twelve together with outstanding Christians like S. James or S. Paul, a use suggesting "missionary" or "delegate" in a very extended sense. What then is the relation between "apostles" in the restricted and in the wider sense ? It might be argued that the wider sense was original, and that S. Luke shows us a tendency to restrict the word, a tendency which grew and in the end predominated. It seems that light may be thrown upon this problem by the facts about S. Paul's apostleship, since S. Paul claims to be a great deal more than a "missionary" in the wide and vague sense of the word.

What, then, is the character of S. Paul's apostleship ? Is he an Apostle in a special sense, sharing with the Twelve, and perhaps with one or two others also, a unique rank and authority ? Or is he an apostle only in the wider and vaguer sense ? Certainly, in 1 Cor. 15[9] he is "least of the apostles," where "apostles" are distinct from the Twelve, and in 2 Cor. 11[5], 12[11], he says that his claim to apostleship is at least as good as that of his opponents. Such references can indeed be explained if "Apostle" vaguely means "missionary." But elsewhere S. Paul shows that his apostleship is something far more definite, (i) it is related to a general mission to evangelize the Gentiles, and to build them up into unity with the one ecclesia (Rom. 11[13], Eph. 3[1-13]) ; (ii) it is a position of tremendous authority (1 Cor. 4[14-21] and cf. 1 Cor. and 2 Cor. *passim*) ; (iii) it is not an authority limited to a single Church, but an authority which represents to the local churches their dependence upon and submission to the universal Church behind them,

"even as I teach everywhere in every church " (1 Cor. 4[17]),

" if any man seem to be contentious we have no such custom, neither the churches of God " (1 Cor. 11¹⁶),

" The rest will I set in order whensoever I come " (1 Cor. 11³⁴).

" What ? Was it from you that the word of God went forth ? Or came it unto you alone ? " (1 Cor. 14³⁶).

Thus S. Paul has an office of ruling and integrating. It is not too much to say that " Paul the apostle to the saints in Corinth " may, in the light of the Epistle as a whole, be paraphrased, " Paul whose ministry and rule represents to the saints in Corinth their membership in and their dependence upon the one Body of Christ."

Can we now draw any general conclusion ? About the title ἀπόστολος we cannot always dogmatize. Its use no doubt has varied, and may possibly have been at first vague and wide, and later restricted, S. Luke showing this tendency to restriction. Yet apart from names and terms, we can be certain of this ; there was a ministry, restricted in numbers and of definite authority, not attached to local churches but controlling local churches on behalf of the general Church. This ministry included at least the Twelve with S. James, S. Paul, and S. Barnabas in addition, and its functions were (i) to link the Christians with the historical events of Jesus from whom this Apostolate has received a solemn and special commission ; (ii) to represent the one society, for only in the context of the one society can a local church grow into the fulness of Christ. Amid all the uncertainties of the Apostolic age, it is clear that there is no Church mentioned in the New Testament which does not own the authority of an Apostle or apostolic man who represents the wider general Church.

But what is the spiritual meaning of this Apostolic order ? The Church, says S. Paul, is " built upon the foundation of apostles and prophets." (Eph. 2²⁰.) Here are two elements in the setting-forth of the Gospel. *Prophets* pray, interpret, exhort, console. Sometimes the functions overlap ; thus S. Paul the Apostle was a prophet also, and so, later on, were the Bishops Ignatius and

Polycarp. Through them God speaks His word in this or
that situation or crisis. Their work is free, inspired, spontaneous. But prophets are members of an Apostolic
Church, and their work and witness will lack its full meaning
unless attention is also given to the Body's continuous life
and universal character. So prophecy finds its full meaning
and power only in the context of that other " foundation,"
the *Apostles*. Prophets speak ; Apostles, not by speech
alone but by their organic place in the Body, declare the
facts of Jesus crucified and risen, facts before which all speaking is nothing, and all prophets and Apostles are as dead
men. For Apostles represent unity and continuity, being
sent by our Lord who Himself was sent by the Father, and
declaring in effect, " He came, He died, He rose, we are sent
and the Body is One." The Lord's Commission, recorded
in S. John 20[21], " as the Father hath sent me, even so send
I you " no doubt refers to the mission of His whole Church.
All Christian life has this character of apostolicity or
" sentness," but the order of Apostles especially represents
it and its place in the one family.

Two episodes specially illustrate this deep relevance of
the Apostles' office to the Gospel and to the Body.

The first is the episode in Samaria, described in Acts
8[14-17]. " Now when the apostles which were at Jerusalem
heard that Samaria had received the word of God, they
sent unto them Peter and John : who, when they were
come down, prayed for them, that they might receive the
Holy Ghost : for as yet he was fallen upon none of them :
only they had been baptized into the name of the Lord Jesus.
Then laid they their hands on them, and they received
the Holy Ghost." Now this event in Samaria is significant
in the light of the whole teaching of the New Testament
about the one ecclesia. When the Samaritans become
Christians they are not to think of themselves as initiated
into a Samaritan fellowship with its own isolated experience
and spiritual life. They are to know that to be Christ's is to
be included in the one life of the one people of God which
sprang from the historical events in Jerusalem ; the Holy

Spirit who shall descend upon them is the Spirit who bears witness to the historical events, and who is known in the growth of the one universal fellowship. And these truths are vividly declared by the sending of S. Peter and S. John to lay hands on the Samaritans ; and this function is restricted to them not because some special grace passes through them as an isolated channel, but because God, by using certain organs for certain functions, proclaims the fact of the one Body in which alone men can grow into the fulness of Christ. The Apostles, as organs of the universal Church, lay hands upon the Samaritans.

The second instance is the crisis in Corinth, of which we have already seen the issue. The Corinthians learn of the Gospel of the Cross by learning their utter dependence in membership of the one Body ; they are Christians only through being of the one ecclesia. Such is the truth about the Gospel and the Body ; and of this truth S. Paul's apostleship is the expression. " Paul an apostle to the saints in Corinth " fulfils the same essential rôle as Peter and John in relation to the Samaritans.

In these two episodes the Apostolic *office* is seen to set forth the Gospel. So far as we can see, the elimination of the Apostles would mean that a vital truth about the Body and the Gospel would lack organic expression. No doubt there was variety of practice ; but an important principle with regard to the nature of the Apostolate is apparent, and, if this principle becomes more prominent, it would seem that its growing prominence was not an addition to the Gospel but a fuller expression of the Gospel. Towards the close of the Apostolic age it becomes increasingly important to stress unity and continuity with Jesus in the flesh. The First Epistle of S. John shows the dangers of a sporadic spirituality and prophecy which are unrelated to the coming of Jesus in the flesh and to the one fellowship, and the need for continuous emphasis upon the historical events and upon the one fellowship. What if this emphasis is not left for letters and sermons only, but is embedded in the very structure of the Church ?

(c) We reach the stage when the first Apostles have almost finished their work on earth. Their place in the Body has been a parable of unity and hence of death and resurrection. They have appointed elders in every Church and ordained them by the laying on of hands. And with the passing of the Apostles the need for similar functions will not be less and may be even greater. Hence, the principle embodied in the Apostles is extended to others. The *Pastoral Epistles* (whether they be Pauline or partly Pauline or not Pauline at all) give us a picture of Timothy and Titus as Apostolic men, appointed by an Apostle for work in Ephesus and in Crete respectively ; they are to appoint and ordain elders (which presumably means the giving of a χάρισμα similar to that which they themselves received by laying on of hands) to rule, to remove false doctrine, to maintain continuity of teaching, and in short to *integrate*, so that the Christians in Ephesus and in Crete shall share more securely in the life and faith of the one Body. Even if the ministry of Timothy and Titus was not a permanent order, we see in its functions the same integrating principle. And here is no " officialism " alien to the Gospel, but simply a growth, believed to be under the direction of an Apostle, of those organs of the Body which (as in Samaria and in Corinth) have been expressions of the Gospel. The *Pastoral Epistles* have much to say about the central facts of the Christian revelation ; what they say about Church order is not alien from this, but springs essentially from the same religion.

(d) A transition ensues, roughly in the generation after the deaths of the first Apostles. The literary records are so scanty that we cannot trace its movement, but we can see its results. From early in the second century there appears a separation between the Bishops and the presbyters in the local churches, and a threefold ministry of Bishops, priests and deacons. How the new distinction between Bishop and presbyter came about, the evidence does not allow us to affirm. Perhaps " Apostolic men " (like Timothy and Titus) became localized and

stabilized into Bishops (as Bishop Gore thought), or perhaps certain presbyters were elevated so as to become
presiding-bishops (as Bishop Lightfoot thought), or perhaps there was a variety of causes.[1] The central feature of
this developed structure consists of the Bishops—an order
distinct from the presbyterate—who rule in each Church,
celebrate the Eucharist, are consecrated by the laying
on of hands, and are regarded as the successors of the
Apostles in office and as the organs of the Church's unity.
This full structure appeared gradually ; thus in Clement
of Rome (chapters 42 and 44) succession is emphasized
without any reference to a distinct order of Bishops, whereas
in Ignatius of Antioch (*passim*) the Bishop is the organ of
unity without any mention of succession. But in all the
extant literature of the sub-apostolic age one or other or
both of these principles—unity and continuity—is apparent,
and we know that the episcopal structure which combines
them both became universal by the second half of the
second century. (Irenaeus, *Adv. Haer.* III,iii.1; Tertullian,
de Praeser. Haer. 32.) There is no trace of opposition to this
growth, and there was even a belief that the Apostles had
ordered it.[2]

III

The crucial question, however, for theology is this. Does
this developed structure of Episcopacy fulfil the same place
in the Church and express the same truth as did the
Apostles' office in Samaria and in Corinth and throughout
the Apostolic Church ? If " Paul the Apostle " represents an important truth by his place and function in the
one Body, does the Bishop represent the same truth ?

In answering this question we turn to the letters of
S. Ignatius of Antioch, an ardent advocate of the necessity

[1] Cf. a number of suggestions by W. K. Lowther-Clarke, *Episcopacy*, p. 39.

[2] Cf. 1 Clement 42, 44 (of leading men over and above the presbyters) ; Ignatius, *ad Trall.* 7 (meaning rather doubtful) ; Clement,
Quis Dives 42, and Tertullian, *ad. Marc.* iv. 5 (of Episcopacy set up
by S. John in Asia).

of Bishops. S. Ignatius was sent to Rome to be martyred in or about the year 116 A.D., and during his journey as a prisoner he wrote letters to various churches in Asia Minor and to the Church in Rome. These letters show an intense sense of the unity of the whole Church, in prayer and in suffering and in outward structure, and the writer's intense belief in Episcopacy as a necessity of the Church's life and worship. Now why does he take so great an interest in the status of the Bishops ? Is he developing an " institutionalism," rigid and alien to the Gospel, or is he, as Dr. Streeter has urged, a morbid character with a psycho-neurotic obsession about the importance of a Bishop ? [1] An examination of S. Ignatius' whole teaching suggests neither view, but rather that his interest in Bishops springs directly from his sense of the Christian Gospel.

S. Ignatius' Christianity has about it a Pauline ring. He has died already, and he is on his way to Rome to die once more. The Christians are " united and elect by a true passion " (Eph. 1) ; they are " branches of the Cross, and their fruit imperishable—the Cross whereby He through His passion inviteth us, being His members" (Trall. 11). " Permit me to be an imitator of the Passion of my God," cries S. Ignatius (Rom. 6), and repentance means to " return to the Passion, which is our resurrection " (Smyrn. 5). Now as with S. Paul, so with Ignatius, the Gospel is expressed in the fact of the Church, which is the very act and life of Christ Himself.

" Ye are stones of a temple, which were prepared before-hand for a building of God the Father, being hoisted up to the heights through the engine of Jesus Christ, which is the Cross, and using for a rope the Holy Spirit." (Eph. 9.)

The ministry is important as linking the Christians with the historic events of Jesus Christ, since Christian experience is

[1] For the considerable discrepancy between Dr. Streeter's exposi-tion of S. Ignatius and the actual contents of the Epistles of S. Ignatius, see an article by Dr. G. A. Michell in the *Church Quarterly Review*, July, 1931.

not a spirituality unrelated to history, but bears witness to its derivation from Jesus in the *flesh*. In several striking passages S. Ignatius joins together the ministry and the *flesh* of Jesus.

" But your prayer will make me perfect, that I may attain into the inheritance, wherein I have found mercy, taking refuge in the Gospel as the flesh of Jesus and in the Apostles as the presbytery of the Church." (*Philad.* 5.)

" I salute your godly Bishop and your venerable fellow-presbytery and my fellow-servants the deacons, and all of you severally and in a body, in the name of Jesus Christ, and in His flesh and blood, in His passion and resurrection, which was both carnal and spiritual, in the unity of God and of yourselves." (*Smyrn.* 12.)

Thus the Church is one Body ; its members glorify not themselves and their experiences, but the one historic Christ. And its worship is one ; the Eucharist is not the act of any local group, but of the one Body, represented by its organ of unity in any place. Hence the Eucharist is to be celebrated only by the Bishop.

" Since love doth not suffer me to be silent concerning you therefore was I forward to exhort you, that ye run in harmony with the mind of God : for Jesus Christ also, our inseparable life, is the mind of the Father, even as the Bishops that are settled in the furthest parts of the earth are in the mind of Jesus Christ. So then it becometh you to run in harmony with the mind of the Bishop ; which thing also ye do. For your honourable presbytery, which is worthy of God is attuned to the Bishop, even as its strings to a lyre. Therefore in your concord and harmonious love Jesus Christ is sung . . . it it therefore profitable for you to be in blameless unity, that ye may be partakers of God always." (*Eph.* 3, 4.)

" Be careful to observe one Eucharist (for there is one flesh of our Lord Jesus Christ and one cup unto union in his blood ; there is one altar, as there is one Bishop, together with his presbytery and the deacons my fellow-servants), that what-soever ye do, ye may do it after God." (*Philad.* 4.)

"Let no man do aught of things pertaining to the Church apart from the Bishop. Let that be held a valid Eucharist which is under the Bishop or to whom he shall have committed it. Wheresoever the Bishop shall appear, there let the people be; even as where Jesus may be, there is the universal Church." (*Smyrn*. 8.)

"Do nothing without the Bishop!" Is this the remark of an institutionalist who has lost the simplicity and spirituality of the early Gospel? Certainly there is no false pride of office on S. Ignatius' part; he calls himself a fellow-servant with the deacons (*Smyrn*. 12), and says that the Bishop should be silent. "In proportion as a man seeth that his bishop is silent let him fear him the more." (*Ephes*. 6.) "Let not office puff up any man, for faith and love are everything, and there is nothing better than these." (*Smyrn*. 6.) For the Bishop does not have a greatness of his own, he is the organ of the one Body who represents to the Christians their dependence within the Body, and to the local Church its dependence within the historic family, whose worship is one act. Just as the Apostles had represented these truths, so now do S. Ignatius and the other Bishops. The structure is now more definite, it is specially related to the Eucharist; and whereas the Apostle had charge of a wide range of communities, the Bishop is "localized" in one. But the structure still expresses the Gospel.

Thus the same truth lies behind the Lord's commission to the Twelve, the episode of Peter and John laying hands on the Samaritans, the dealings of Paul the Apostle with the Corinthians, and the Episcopate which prevailed from the second century. At every stage we have taken the evidence at its lowest; and, even so, the presence at every stage of a principle about the ministry and the Body has been plain. The principle prevails; for the impact of the Gospel moulds the form of the Church, and its order itself proclaims that the Christ has come in the flesh and that His people are one family.

IV

" Everybody has won, and all shall have prizes,"—in the sense that the primitive Church undoubtedly contained not only Bishops but presbyters, deacons, prophets, and congregations as well. But the " prizes " correspond to distinct functions in the Body, for as time passed each type of ministry found its right relation to the whole, and the backbone of the whole was and is the Episcopate, succeeding the Apostolate.

" Apostolic succession " is a phrase with several meanings. (1) First of all, the succession of Bishop to Bishop in office secured a continuity of Christian teaching and tradition in every See. Each followed the teachings of his predecessor, and so the succession of Bishops was a guarantee that everywhere the Christians were taught the true Gospel of Jesus Christ in the flesh. Having no such succession, the Gnostics had no claim to be the authorized teachers of the faith.

" Anyone, whose eyes are open to the facts, can see this tradition from the Apostles in manifest form in every Christian community throughout the world. We can give the names of the Bishops whom the Apostles appointed in the several churches, with the list of their successors from that day to this ; and no one of them thought or taught anything like the phantasies of the Gnostics." (Irenaeus, *Adv. Haer*. III, iii. 6.)

After describing the succession of Bishops in Rome and Syria and Ephesus, S. Irenaeus concludes :—

" Seeing that we have so many lines of proof, there is no need to seek elsewhere for the truth which we can get thus easily from the Church ; for into it, as into a treasury, the Apostles poured prodigally all that there is of truth, in order that he who will may draw from it the water of life. This is the entrance to life, all else are thieves and robbers." (Op. cit., III, iv. 1.)

Thus the succession of Bishops is a safeguard of continuous teaching. This last passage shows that while the Church as a whole is the vessel into which truth is poured, the Bishops are an important organ in its discharging of this task.

(2) The Bishops also succeeded the Apostles in the sense that they performed those *functions*, of preaching and ruling and ordaining, which the Apostles had performed. It is in this sense that the actual word " successors " διαδόχοι was first applied to the Bishops ;[1] and we have seen that they plainly succeed the Apostles in relation to the Gospel and the Body. The Bishops' place as celebrant in the Eucharist, interceding for his flock and family, sums up this whole relationship.

(3) The phrase " Apostolic succession " is also used to signify that grace is handed down from the Apostles through each generation of Bishops by the laying on of hands. Concerning this third meaning of succession there has been a classical controversy. Bishop Headlam has urged that Apostolic succession *in this sense* did not become a doctrine until S. Augustine's time, and that there is no evidence for belief in it in the Fathers of the previous centuries. As against this view other scholars, notably Bishop Gore and Dr. Cuthbert Turner, have urged that Apostolic succession in this sense was implicit, if not explicitly referred to, in the Church of the second and third centuries also.[2]

If, however, Episcopacy is seen primarily as an organ closely related to the Gospel, and to the one Body, then Bishop Headlam's contention seems to be irrelevant. Grace is bestowed always by our Lord Himself and through the action of His whole Church. Every act of grace is His act and the act of the one Body which is His. And the succession of Bishops is not an isolated channel of grace, since from the first Christ bestows grace through

---

[1] Hippolytus, *Refutatio*, Procem.

[2] Cf. A. C. Headlam, *The Doctrine of the Church and Christian Reunion*, pp. 124-133, and a criticism by N. P. Williams, *Lausanne, Lambeth and South India*, pp. 74-90. In these two passages the issue is stated in the shortest and clearest way.

every sacramental act of His Body. But certain actions in this work of grace are confined to the Bishops; and thereby the truth is taught that every local group or Church depends upon the one life of the one Body, and that the Church of any generation shares in the one historic society which is not past and dead but alive in the present. Thus the Church's full and continuous life in grace does depend upon the succession of Bishops, whose work, however, is not isolated but bound up with the whole Body.

In these ways—as the guardian of teaching, as the performers of the Apostles' own functions, as an organ in the one Body's continuous life in grace,—the Bishop sets forth the Gospel of God.

The meaning of the Episcopate is vividly seen in the rites of Consecration and Ordination, of which the earliest descriptions are found in the " Apostolic Tradition " of Hippolytus (c. 225 A.D.). Both rites are performed in the midst of the Eucharist, that is, in the context of the death and resurrection of Jesus Christ. (a) The Bishop-elect is chosen by the presbyters and people, and three Bishops lay hands upon him, so that his consecration is the outward act of our Lord in His whole Church, and so that " in its Bishop every single church transcends its own limits and comes into contact with and merges into other churches, not in the order of brotherly love and remembrance alone, but in the unity of mysterious and gracious life." [1] (b) The priest-to-be is ordained by the laying on of the hands of the Bishop and the presbyters, and he receives grace from our Lord by an inward and an outward act of our Lord, through His death and resurrection, and through the one Body both in its world-wide existence and in its historic past which is really present in the Communion of saints. Here is not only a single congregation ratifying the call to an individual and adopting him as its minister; here is an act of the Lord, expressed plainly and outwardly through His whole Church whereof

[1] G. Florovsky, *Sobornost*, March, 1934.

the parts derive their power from the whole. For " so also is Christ " (I Cor. 12^{12}), and the rite sets forth the Gospel. Every act of grace is the act of the whole Church ; and Bishop, presbyters and people exercise their share in the one priesthood of Christ. But each order by its own function represents a part of the truth and, by learning its dependence, glorifies not itself but Christ whose Body is one.

" Built upon the foundation of apostles and prophets," the Church finds both to be essential to its existence as the one Body in whose completeness the Gospel is proclaimed. Both were in the New Testament " foundation," and both fulfil their function for the whole of time. In every age prophetic movements bear witness to Christ, and Christian fellowship is manifested in new and diverse ways ; and in every age the Episcopate represents that general church life of which the prophets must know themselves to be a part, and that universal family in which all fellowships are made full. But the meaning of the Episcopate is seen, not in isolation, but in close connexion with the whole Body of Christ and its presbyteral and congregational elements. To sever this connexion is to corrupt the meaning of Episcopacy. Such corruptions have been many ; the centralization of the Papacy, the turning of Bishops into " prelates," the obscuring of their meaning by the outward divisions of Christendom have all tended to conceal the true place of the Bishop in the Church and in the Gospel, and his true character as a Father-in-Christ. Stripped of alien excrescences the episcopate will stand out, not as something " Anglican " or " Roman " or " Greek," but as the organ of the one people of God before and behind all that is local or sectional.

We are led, therefore, to affirm that the Episcopate is of the *esse* of the universal Church ; but we must beware of mis-stating the issue. All who are baptized into Christ are members of His Church, and Baptism is the first mark of churchmanship. Yet the growth of all Christians into the measure of the stature of the fulness of Christ means their growth with all the saints in the unity of the one Body, and of this unity the Episcopate is the expression. It speaks of the incompleteness of every section of a divided Church, whether of those who possess the Episcopate or of those who do not. And those who possess it will tremble and never boast, for none can say that it is " theirs." It proclaims that there is one family of God before and behind them all, and that all die daily in the Body of Him who died and rose.

CHAPTER VII

Worship

THE Christians are bidden to pray and to worship. In order to learn what this means they turn first of all to the pattern prayer, given by our Lord to His disciples in Galilee. In the Lord's Prayer the whole meaning of prayer is summed up.

But the Lord's Prayer cannot be understood apart from the whole ministry and teaching of Jesus. Its significance is unfolded as Jesus moves forward in His work for men ; for in this work, and above all in His death and resurrection, there is revealed the meaning of the words around which the Lord's Prayer centres—the Father, the Name, the Kingdom, the will. God's Fatherhood is shown forth in many acts and words of Jesus which culminate in the " Abba Father " of Gethsemane, and in the " Father, forgive them " and the " Father, into Thy hands " of Calvary. The Father's Name is " glorified " in the Passion (John 13[31]), the Father's will is wrought out by the sacrifice of the will of Jesus. (Heb. 10[5-10].) Thus the key-words of the Lord's Prayer —" Father," " Name," and " will "—set before us a picture of the whole work of Jesus Christ, and to pray the Lord's Prayer in His Name we must leave Galilee and go up to Jerusalem, where we see the Father's Name and Kingdom and will expressed in the Passion. In short the basis of Christian prayer is not the Lord's Prayer alone, but the Lord's Prayer and the Lord. Prayer in His Name means prayer through all that He is and all that He has done.

Hence, if we would pray the Lord's Prayer aright, we must
use it in the light of its interpretation in the whole of the
New Testament. In two parts of scripture especially do
we find the Lord's Prayer thus interpreted—in the teaching
about prayer in the last Discourse and Prayer in S. John's
Gospel (chs. 13-17), and, in the prayers contained in
S. Paul's Epistles. And, since the significance of S. Paul's
prayers is not always remembered, it may be useful to dwell
upon them and to ask what light they throw upon the
meaning of Christian worship.

S. Paul's Epistles frequently refer to his practice of
prayer. He brings before God both the needs of his converts and his own plans and anxieties. And his Epistles
reveal something of his method and conception of prayer.
He does not plunge at once into petitions ; he starts his
prayers by giving thanks, and a long thanksgiving often
precedes the offering of petitions. The thanksgivings in
his letters cover a wide range of subjects ; he thanks
God for the historical events whereby He has redeemed the
Christians, for the divine plan which lies behind these
events, and for the fellowship of the Christians which springs
from them ; and often his mind passes from God as redeemer to God as creator, as he thanks Him for His grace
in creating and sustaining all things. This wealth of
thanksgiving comes first ; and only when the whole action
of God has been thus thankfully commemorated does
S. Paul use petition, so as to bring into the action the
matters for which he would intercede. The Epistle to the
Ephesians shows clearly the various elements in an act of
Christian worship as S. Paul conceives it.

1³⁻¹⁴ *Blessed be the God and Father of our Lord Jesus Christ*
     in placing us in the heavenlies in Christ,
     in predestinating us to sonship,
     in the death of Christ on the Cross,
     in His age-long plan of summing-up all things in Christ,
     " to the end that we should be unto the praise of his
        glory."

1[15-23] *Wherefore I also . . . cease not to give thanks for you,
praying*
    for your wisdom and enlightenment,
    for your realization of the wonder of His redemption,
    and of His glory in the saints,
    and of Christ risen, Ascended and sovereign,
    and of the meaning of the church which is His Body.

3[14-21] *For this cause I bow my knees to the Father, praying*
    that the Spirit and the Christ may dwell in you ;
    that, in union with all the saints, you may know Christ's
      love ;
    that you may be filled with all the fulness of God ;
    that to Him whose power in us is greater than we know
      there may be uttered praise in the Church and in
      Christ for ever.

We may compare the acts of thanksgiving and prayer in
the Epistle to the Colossians :—

1[3-6] *We give thanks to God the Father of our Lord Jesus Christ*
    for the Christians' faith and life in Christ ;
    for their loving union with all the saints ;
    for their hope for the days to come ;
    for the Gospel, fruitful in all the world.

1[9-11] *For this cause also we do not cease to pray*
    that you may have a full knowledge of His will ;
    that you may be strengthened to endure.

1[12-18] *Giving thanks unto the Father*
    for setting us amongst the saints ;
    for redeeming us in His Son,
    who is the creator and the goal of all things,
    and who is head over the Body the Church.

In the case of the Colossians S. Paul has, as so often,
a deep anxiety, for the perverse tendencies at Colossae
threaten the whole character of Christianity there. But in
all his prayers S. Paul does not think first of the anxiety or
of the topical needs of the moment. He begins by giving
thanks, and dwelling upon certain great themes. (i) God

has redeemed us through the death of Christ. (ii) The Christ is the creator and sustainer of all things. (iii) The Church is one fellowship in union with which all prayer and thanksgiving are offered. Thus the Christian who prays in S. Paul's manner first recollects certain great truths, summarized in historical pictures—the picture of our Lord in His life and death, the picture of our Lord's creative care in the world around us, the picture of our Lord's present life in His whole Church. He who prays looks first at this divine action ; for it is *there* that prayer starts, and not with human needs and human feelings, and into this divine action the whole of life must, by thanksgiving, be brought. The Christians are to be thankful (εὐχαριστεῖν) at all times and for all things (Eph. 5²⁰, Col. 3¹⁵, Phil. 4⁶, 1 Thess. 5¹⁷, 2 Thess. 2¹³). Thanksgiving is the one alternative to " filthiness, foolish talk and jesting " (Eph. 5⁴), it is the Christians' response to God's redemptive will (1 Thess. 5¹⁸), it is linked with all eating and drinking (Rom. 14⁶, 1 Cor. 10³¹), it is the end of the collection for saints (2 Cor. 9¹²), and the essence of true religion is the praise of God just as the essence of paganism is the neglect of it (Rom. 1²¹, Rev. 11¹³, 14⁷, 16⁹, Acts 12²³). All life, therefore, is, for a Christian, eucharistic ; and the worship does not start with common needs, but with the divine action of the redeemer, and into this action it brings all common life.

Thus S. Paul's prayers are not primarily petitions, nor primarily mystical acts of contemplation ; they are primarily LITURGICAL, not in the sense that he reads them out of a book, but (in the more fundamental sense of the word " Liturgy ") that his method is first to recall the action of God, in Christ's redemption and in the one Body, and only then to utter his petitions by bringing into this action the topical needs with which he is concerned. He " *gives thanks, praying* . . . " ; and such is prayer " through Jesus Christ our Lord," through all that He is and all that He has done, and through His Body wherein He is made complete.

Similarly, the great doxologies in the New Testament draw out these different elements in worship :—

God the creator.   " For of him, and through him, and unto him, are all things.   To him be the glory for ever.   Amen."
—(Romans 11³⁶.)

God the redeemer.   " Unto him that loveth us, and loosed us from our sins by his own blood ; and he made us to be a kingdom, to be priests unto his God and Father ; to him be the glory and the dominion for ever and ever. Amen."   (Rev. 1⁵⁻⁶.)

The Church.   " Now unto him that is able to do exceeding abundantly above all that we ask or think, according to the power that worketh in us, unto him be the glory in the church and in Christ Jesus unto all generations for ever and ever.   Amen."   (Eph. 3²⁰⁻²¹.)

God.   " Now unto the King eternal, incorruptible, invisible, the only God, be honour and glory for ever and ever. Amen."   (1 Tim. 1¹⁷.)

This last element springs from the first three ; from the wonder of creation, of redemption, and of the Church, the mind of the worshipper passes to the thought of God who is beyond imagination, perfect, eternal, awful, unknown. God has drawn near through the tenderness of the Incarnation and the Cross, yet this very nearness brings the sense of awe before One whose love and wrath are past all comprehension.

Now both S. Paul's prayers and the doxologies of the New Testament do but express what is already present in the Lord's Prayer, if it be prayed " through Jesus Christ." The Father in heaven, His Name, His Kingdom and His will are uttered in the whole redemptive action of the Christ. Recollecting this action the Christian knows the Father to whom He prays, and He humbly asks for his daily bread, for the forgiveness of his sins, and for deliverance from the evil one, and as he prays he is drawn away from self into the loving purpose of God.

.   .   .   .

Yet when all this has been said, the half has not been told about Christian worship. For as the death and resurrection of the Lord are both unique events in history and also happenings within the Christians, so in like manner the divine action which is the centre of worship is not only one upon which the Christians gaze, but one which lives and moves *within* them. If this fact is contained within the truth of " the Body of Christ," it becomes clearer still when we think of two of the special words concerning worship, δόξα the Glory of God, and ὄνομα the Name of God. Both these words describe first an action which the Christians commemorate, and then an action which passes within them.

The *Name* of God in the Old Testament is the sum of His attributes (cf. Exodus 3[15]), and His character in redemption (cf. Isaiah 52[6], 63[14]. Psalms 20[5], 54[1], 124[8]). His Name is outwardly manifested as His " glory," and it rests upon Israel (cf. Deut. 12[11], Numbers 6[27], Jeremiah 23[6]). Now in the fulness of time the Father, who had bestowed His Name upon Israel, gives His Name to Jesus in an intimacy far transcending the old Messianic ideas. He gives His Name to the Son and glorifies His own Name in the Son by the death and resurrection.

" Wherefore also God highly exalted him, and gave unto him the name which is above every name ; that in the name of Jesus every knee should bow, of things in heaven and things on earth, and things under the earth, and that every tongue should confess that Jesus Christ is Lord, to the glory of God the Father." (Phil. 2[9-10].)

" Now is my soul troubled ; and what shall I say ? Father, save me from this hour. But for this cause came I unto this hour. Father, glorify thy name. There came therefore a voice from heaven, saying, I have both glorified it, and will glorify it again." (John 12[28].)

" I manifested thy name unto the men whom thou gavest me out of the world. . . . Holy Father, keep them in thy

name which thou hast given me, that they may be one, even
as we are." (John 17⁶, ¹¹.)

Thus the Name is disclosed by the Son's life and death ; and,
thence, from being an event outside the disciples, it passes
to become a happening within them. They are brought
" within " the Name, it becomes the sphere of their existence.
They are baptized into it, they confess it, praise it, love it,
proclaim it, bear it, and in it they pray, give thanks, heal,
suffer, die. The Name is thus not only the background of
all Christian life and worship, but also mysteriously present
within the Christians. With a depth and reality of which
Jeremiah can hardly have dreamed, the Christians can pray,
" Thou, Lord, art in the midst of us, and we are called by
thy name ; leave us not, O Lord our God."

The *Glory* of God is His self-manifestation. It is seen
in the heavens which " declare the glory of God," and in
Israel in whom His glory rests. The glory, both of the
heavens and of Israel, is shown forth in Jesus Christ, " and
we beheld his glory, glory as of the only begotten from the
Father, full of grace of truth." (John 1¹⁴.) Now there
is a striking contrast between the normal use of δόξα in
classical literature, and the distinctively Christian use of
δόξα in the New Testament. In classical literature the
word is used of the honour and distinction which a man
possesses for himself, and also of a man's opinion. But
in the New Testament the word is used mainly of the
Glory of God, which is seen specially in His *self-giving*.
The Father's glory is seen in His love for the Son, and the
Son's glory in His love for the Father. Christ's glory is
not His own (John 8⁵⁰), and yet it is His own through His
selfless union with the Father (John 17⁵). This eternal
Glory is manifested in the death on the Cross whereby
the Father glorifies the Son, and the Son the Father. And,
as with the Name, so with the Glory, it is to be found *within*
the Christians.

" All things that are mine are thine, and thine are mine :
and I am glorified *in them.*" (John 17¹⁰.)

Through this glory the Christians are redeemed (Rom. 6⁴),
and into it they are drawn (Rom. 8²¹, ³⁰), (1 Peter 4¹⁴) ;
they hope for it as a future inheritance not yet fully theirs
(Col. 3⁴), and meanwhile " with unveiled face, reflecting
as a mirror the glory of the Lord," they are " transformed
into the same image from glory to glory." (2 Cor. 3¹⁸.)

Thus, like the word " body," the words " Name " and
" Glory " speak both of a redemptive action and of an
indwelling power. The implication of this, for the meaning of worship, is far reaching. It is not merely the
act of Christians who gaze upon an action of God ; it is
rather the act of Christ Himself in them. Christ in His
Body glorifies the Father, and His members share in what
He does. The Holy Spirit prays within the Christians.
It is as though a stream of love flows forth from God
to mankind and returns to God through Christ ; the
Christians cast themselves into the stream, and while their
own efforts are called forth in full measure, the stream,
which is the essence of worship and prayer, is that of
God Himself. When S. Paul writes, " Unto him be the
glory in the Church and in Christ Jesus " (Eph. 3²¹),
he seems to say in effect, " May God be praised in the
Church,—yes, that means in Christ Jesus who is the life
of the Church ; it is His own act." And all seems to be
summed up in one sentence when he says,

" For how many soever be the promises of God, in him is
the yea: wherefore also through him is the Amen, unto the
glory of God through us." (2 Cor. 1²⁰.)

Christ, S. Paul here tells us, is the fulfilment of God's
promises ; He is also as Man the perfect response to those
promises, a response made to God's glory in and through
His people. Worship is the act of Jesus Christ, God and
man, and the whole of the New Testament sets forth this
act in heaven and upon earth.

.   .   .   .

It is now possible to sum up the character of Christian prayer, having seen how the New Testament as a whole interprets it. It fits into neither of the two great classes into which Dr. Heiler divides prayer in his monumental work *Das Gebet*,—the prophetic and the mystical. Heiler presses the antithesis between these two types of prayer very far. He sees the prophetic tradition as that which emphasizes petition and the soul's spontaneous cry to God about the needs of men, a tradition which he connects with the Hebrew prophets, with Jesus Christ and with the Reformers. He sees the mystical tradition as that which emphasizes meditation and contemplation and the desire for union with God, a tradition found often in Catholicism and, according to Heiler, less genuinely Christian in its essence. But Heiler's whole thesis seems to suffer from the fact that he never discusses the connexion between Christian prayer and Christ's redemption, and that he treats our Lord solely as a man of prayer and as a teacher about prayer without reference to His place as the redeemer, who sums up the prayers of those who came before Him and who is the centre and focus of the prayers of those who now approach God through Him. Heiler places Jesus in the long line of " great men of prayer," and the unique meaning of prayer " through Jesus Christ our Lord " is therefore missed. If, however, the Lord's prayer and the phrase " through Jesus Christ " be interpreted in the whole light of the New Testament, then clearly Christian prayer is primarily neither mystical nor prophetic in its essence, but *liturgical*. It is the sharing by men in the one action of Christ, through their dying to their own egotisms as they are joined in one Body with His death and resurrection. And if prayer be primarily liturgical, then (of Heiler's two types) meditation will precede petition. The Christian sets before his mind the Father's name and Kingdom and will, with reflection and thanksgiving, and only after this does he pass on to petition.

Taught, therefore, by the New Testament, the Christian

will expect two truths to be present always in Christian worship. (i) Firstly, the centre of worship, in practice, will not be the needs and feelings of men but the redeeming acts of God and the eternal truths which these acts reveal. The language and the structure of worship will point away from the changing and the topical to the divine action in the death and resurrection of Jesus, and to the same action now present in heaven and in the whole Church. Hence the regular and ordered movement of Liturgy is not a cumbrous addition to Christian prayer; rather does it express the New Testament fact of worship as the divine action into which all spontaneous and congregational prayer is ever merged. Such spontaneous prayer is needed, but it is never the centre. The centre is the High Priestly act of Jesus Christ in heaven and in history. (ii) Secondly, it follows that all worship is the act of the one Body of Christ. The voice of the single Christian is drawn into the voice of the Body and represents the Body. The two or three gathered together in Christ's name represent the Body in that particular place.[1] The most seemingly private and spontaneous prayers are a part of the one act of Christ in His Body and of the prayer of the one Spirit who cries in us "Abba Father." Hence a Christian congregation assembles not to offer "its own worship" to God, but to join as one small fragment in the one act of Christ in His whole Church in heaven and on earth. "At that season Jesus answered, and said, I thank thee, O Father, Lord of heaven and earth." (Matt. 11[25].) In the thanksgiving of Jesus His people now share, and in them the Spirit cries "Abba Father", and joins them both with His prayer in Gethsemane and with the final "Father into thine hands" on Calvary.

This interpretation of worship in the New Testament has sought, like the interpretation of the ministry in the previous chapter, to be evangelical rather than archæological. Our method must not be to burrow within the

---

[1] Cf. S. Cyprian, *de Unitate Ecclesiae*, Ch. XII.

New Testament for descriptions of worship in order to imitate these models ; we must turn rather to the New Testament as a whole, since it is in itself an act of worship, the Yea of God's self-utterance through Christ towards men, and the Amen of Christ's response uttered through men to the glory of God. Gospels, Acts, Epistles, Apocalypse together set forth this one act of worship ; and whenever Christians meet to pray there are present these truths of God creator and redeemer, of the Body of Christ, and of the Name and the Glory of God. But these truths also demand their due outward expression in the Church's acts of common worship, by an outward structure which points beyond men's needs and feelings to the divine sacrifice on the Cross and in heaven, and beyond the individual and the local fellowship to the continuous life of the universal Church.

" The Lord Jesus in the night in which he was betrayed took bread." The outward act is not lacking. In this act He summed up the meaning of His death upon the Cross, and in this act, therefore, there is present the whole truth of the Name and the Glory of God and of the one Body. Whenever the Lord breaks bread in His Church there will be present these same truths, and they will demand expression. Hence the true background to the Church's Eucharist is not the description of services contained in the New Testament, but the New Testament as a whole. That there should have been a development in the Eucharistic rite seems inevitable. Just as there was a growth in the understanding of the Christ from the primitive belief in his Messiahship to the deep and final beliefs of S. Paul and S. John, so also there was a growth in the understanding of that rite wherein the unspeakable death of the Lord is uttered. And the test of true development will *not* be, whether the Catholic Eucharist corresponds literally to what was done in the Upper room, or in Corinth (1 Cor. 11) or at Troas (Acts 20), *but* whether the Catholic Eucharist expresses the act of Jesus, creator and redeemer, as interpreted by the whole New Testament meaning of worship THROUGH JESUS CHRIST OUR LORD. If the Eucharist sets forth the Lord's death and resurrection, and the eternal truths which this action reveals, and the presence of this action within the Christians as one Body, then it will indeed sum up all that the New Testament teaches about worship. "Do all in the Name of the Lord."

H

CHAPTER VIII

LITURGY

I

IF the meaning of Christian prayer is, as we have seen, to be found not in the Lord's Prayer alone, but in that Prayer as interpreted in the light of the whole of the New Testament, so also the meaning of the Christian Eucharist is to be found not in the last supper alone but in the last supper as interpreted by the whole of the " Yea " and " Amen " of worship in the New Testament.

And if this be the right way in which to interpret the Eucharist, it follows that the problems concerning the precise manner of the institution of the rite, important as they are, are less important than the debates of modern scholars have suggested. It has been urged that the rite owes its existence or its main interpretation to S. Paul or to the Christians of Antioch in Syria. But it seems impossible to believe that the Jewish Christians would have tolerated such an innovation in Christian practice in the Gentile Churches without intense controversy, and of such controversy there is no trace. It is therefore hard to doubt that S. Paul " received " the main essentials of the rite from the Church's existing practice.[1] The difficulty, however, remains that the evidence that our Lord *commanded* the disciples to repeat His actions of the last supper is very slight, the only certain reference to

[1] Cf. A. E. Morris, *Jesus and the Eucharist* (*Theology*, Reprints No. 13), at once the fullest and the most conclusive discussion of this point.

a command being in S. Paul's account in 1 Cor. 11²³⁻²⁶.
But the dominical origin of the rite does not stand or fall
with the authenticity of the command to " do this."   The
Lord gave much of His most important teaching not by
verbal orders but by His actions and their creative effect
within His Church.

The meaning of His actions is determined by the whole
meaning of His life and work ; and it is here that the crucial
point with regard to the institution of the Eucharist lies.
Its interpretation depends upon the whole interpretation
of His ministry.   If Jesus is merely a prophet and a teacher,
then His solemn actions on the night before He died might
have a meaning limited to that time and place ; but if
He is the Messiah proclaiming the Kingdom of God, then
His action in setting up a new covenant in His blood has
a significance reaching far beyond His own life and death.

Our study of the meaning of the rite must therefore
take into account all the references to it in the New
Testament.   But the narratives of the last supper come
first :—

Mark 14²²⁻²⁵.   " And as they were eating, he took bread,
and when he had blessed, he brake it, and gave to them, and
said, Take ye ; this is my body.   And he took a cup, and when
he had given thanks, he gave to them ; and they all drank of
it.   And he said unto them, This is my blood of the covenant,
which is shed for many.   Verily I say unto you, I will no more
drink of the fruit of the vine, until that day when I drink it
new in the kingdom of God."

Luke 22¹⁵⁻²⁰.   " And he said unto them, With desire I have
desired to eat this passover with you before I suffer : for I
say unto you, I will not eat it, until it be fulfilled in the
kingdom of God.   And he received a cup, and when he had
given thanks, he said, Take this, and divide it among yourselves : for I say unto you, I will not drink from henceforth
of the fruit of the vine, until the kingdom of God shall come.
And he took bread, and when he had given thanks, he brake
it, and gave to them, saying, this is my body [which is given
for you : this do in remembrance of me.   And the cup in

like manner after supper, saying, This cup is the new covenant in my blood, even that which is poured out for you. "]

1 *Corinthians* 11[23-25]. " For I received of the Lord that which also I delivered unto you, how that the Lord Jesus in the night in which he was betrayed took bread ; and when he had given thanks, he break it, and said, This is my body, which is for you : this do in remembrance of me. In like manner also the cup, after supper, saying, This cup is the new covenant in my blood : this do, as oft as ye drink it, in remembrance of me."

The bracketed verses in the Lucan narrative very likely do not form part of the true text. They are omitted in the Codex Bezae, and the weight of scholarly opinion favours the view that they are not genuine and are an interpolation from 1 Cor. 11.[1] Other problems and difficulties, some of them insoluble, arise out of these narratives, but it would seem less profitable to dwell upon them than to collect the facts which stand out quite plainly about our Lord's actions at the supper.

(1) It is clear at the outset that the accounts in S. Mark and in 1 Cor. 11, in contrast with that in the Bezan or shorter text in S. Luke, are in striking agreement. In both of them our Lord declared that His death was an act of sacrifice ("shed for many," Mark ; "which is for you," 1 Cor.), and in both He declared also that the death created a new covenant between God and men ("blood of the covenant," Mark ; "new covenant in my blood," 1 Cor.). The rite therefore sets forth the new covenant in the death of the Messiah (cf. Exodus 24[8], Jer. 31[31]). This is plain from these two narratives, which are independent and confirm one another and are the earliest of our group of sources. Against their combined testimony

---

[1] Cf. Hort, *Introduction*, pp. 63-65. H. N. Bate has suggested that the original text of Luke 22 ended with v. 18 and that it thus contained no reference to the institution of the Eucharist (*J.Th.S.*, July, 1927, p. 362). Bishop Gore favoured this view, *A New Commentary*, ad loc.

any inferences that may be derived from the Bezan text of S. Luke are dubious indeed.[1]

(2) The giving of a covenant implies at once the creation of a people, a new nation which looks back to the Lord's death, as its origin and its bond of unity, just as the old Israel looks back to the deliverance from Egypt. (3) But the disciples will not only form a nation created by the death; by eating the bread and drinking the cup they will be brought within the death. In an unutterable way they partake of it; it is no longer only an event outside them, it becomes something within them to feed and to nourish them. And (4) the Lord's action looks forward to the Messianic banquet in the Kingdom of God; His present eating and drinking with His disciples pre-figures an eating and drinking which are to come (Mark 14[25]).

Thus did the Lord speak and act. His words and actions were His final unfolding of the meaning of His death, and in them the whole meaning and power of the death were present. The disciples were brought into the death; His dying is become their food. The rite is

[1] In the Bezan text of S. Luke, in contrast with S. Mark and S. Paul, there is no connexion expressed between our Lord's actions and His death or a covenant. Thus the Lucan account has been used as the basis of a view of the rite which severs it from redemptive and sacrificial ideas. The covenant theme, is, however, shortly afterwards mentioned in the verse " I appoint, διατίθεμαι, unto you a kingdom " (22[29]). Otto maintains that in Luke's special source verse 29 followed verse 19a, so that the narrative ran, " This is my body, and I appoint you unto a kingdom ! " (*Reich Gottes und Menschensohn*, pp. 223-234.)

Dr. J. W. Hunkin (late Bishop of Truro), in the *Evangelical Doctrine of the Holy Communion*, essay i, prefers the evidence of the Bezan text of Luke to the evidence of Mark and 1 Cor. in reconstructing the last supper. The primitive Eucharist was thus a fellowship meal unconnected with Christ's death or with the last supper, and the phrase " This is my blood " and the sacrificial character of the rite originated with the prophets of the Church in Antioch in Syria. Dr. Hunkin's arguments are answered point by point in A. E. Morris (op. cit.), whose conclusions it is hard to resist. " Why prefer unsupported Luke above Mark supported (quite independently, as Hunkin admits) by 1 Corinthians ? " (p. 12).

therefore the first effective and creative link between the
death and the disciples ; the death outside them is declared
to be a death within them, and the whole truth of the
σῶμα Χριστοῦ is here set forth.   Yet even this is not all.
For to the meaning of redemption the rite adds also the
meaning of creation. Jesus " gave thanks " and " took
bread."   Thanksgiving uttered over bread was of enormous
significance to a Jew ; it meant the conscious offering to
God of God's own created gifts to be blessed and so released
for use by men. And if, as seems most likely, the last
supper was not the Passover meal but the meal on the eve
of the Passover known as the Kiddush,[1] then the Lord's
action is still more explicitly linked with the thought of
creation.   For we know the customary form of the Passover
Kiddush, which Jesus in " giving thanks " would have
recited.

" Blessed art thou, O Lord our God, King Eternal, who
createst the fruit of the vine.

" Blessed art thou, O Lord our God, King Eternal, who has
chosen us from all peoples, and hast exalted us above all
tongues, and hast sanctified us by thy commandments. And
thou hast given us in love, O Lord our God, Sabbaths for rest,
and appointed times for gladness, festivals, and seasons of
joy ; this Sabbath day, and this feast of unleavened bread,
the season of our freedom.

" Blessed art thou, O Lord our God, King Eternal, who hast
kept us alive and preserved us, and enabled us to reach this
present season. Blessed art thou, O Lord our God, King
Eternal, who bringest forth bread from the earth."

[1] The problem is whether the last supper was the Passover meal,
as S. Mark assumes (Mark 14[14]), or whether the Passover day began
on the afternoon of the Crucifixion, as S. John assumes (John 18[28],
19[14]). There are strong reasons for preferring the Johannine
chronology ; for a lucid discussion the reader is referred to Balm-
forth, S. Luke (Clarendon Bible), pp. 261-265. For the resulting
interpretation of the Eucharist, as instituted not at the Passover
meal but at the Passover Kiddush, see Hicks, *Fulness of Sacrifice*,
pp. 215-222.   The fullest treatment is in Oesterley, *Jewish Background of the Christian Liturgy*.

Thus we may, from our knowledge of contemporary Jewish custom, picture our Lord, while feasting with His disciples on the night before His death which was also the night before the Passover, joining in the regular act of thanksgiving to God for creation, for the preservation of His chosen people, for the Sabbath, for the coming festival of His people's deliverance in which He would not be able to share ; and then, knowing of the death by which He shall be cut off from Israel but by which the new Israel shall be made, He adds to this thanksgiving His own rite which sets forth His death. For the climax of God's mercies in history (creation, preservation, Sabbaths, Passover, people of God) is the death of the Christ, in which God's whole work in the world and in Israel is summed up. This climax is set forth in the " newer rite." By sharing in the broken body and in the blood outpoured, the disciples will find interpreted both the crucifixion and the whole divine creation whose secrets the crucifixion unlocks.

No less momentous than all this is the rite performed by Jesus at the last supper. By it He invests His death with its meaning for mankind, and by it He declares the power of this death in redemption and its place in God's creation. Standing at a central point in the Gospel the rite is interpreted in the light of the whole of that Gospel, for in it the whole truth of the phrase " through Jesus Christ " is focused.

The whole of the New Testament, therefore, is the source wherein the meaning of the Eucharist is to be found. And we must pass on from the narrative of the supper to the other passages in the New Testament which refer to the Eucharist, though these can barely express the depth of meaning in the taking and the breaking of the bread by Jesus.

In *Acts* we find references to " the breaking of the bread " as a rite held regularly by the Christians. (Acts $2^{42, 46}$, 20^7.) We are told nothing as to the character and significance of this rite, but a definite service on the Lord's day is implied in Acts 20^7, where at Troas S. Paul discoursed to an assembly gathered to break bread on the first day of the week. It is hardly possible that this rite at Troas differed greatly, in intention and meaning, from the rite which S. Paul, at a date not far distant and during the same journey, describes in writing to the Corinthians. The awfulness and objective character which S. Paul connects with the rite at Corinth (however little the Corinthians may perceive it) would surely apply also to the rite at Troas.

S. Paul's only surviving teaching about the Eucharist is found in I Cor. 10^{16-22} and 11^{17-36}. (1) In the first passage he is warning his converts against compromise with idolatry, and he mentions the Eucharist incidentally for the purpose of contrasting it with idol-feasts.

> " Wherefore, my beloved, flee from idolatry. I speak as to wise men; judge ye what I say. The cup of blessing which we bless, is it not a communion of the blood of Christ? The bread which we break, is it not a communion of the body of Christ? seeing that we, who are many, are one bread, one body: for we all partake of the one bread. Behold Israel after the flesh: have not they which eat the sacrifices communion with the altar? . . . Ye cannot drink the cup of the Lord, and the cup of devils: ye cannot partake of the table of the Lord and the table of devils."

Here S. Paul is protesting against the sharing by Christians in sacrificial feasts in heathen temples. Why? Because the alleged meaning of those feasts is a partaking in the life of the deities in whose honour they are held; and in such rites the Christians can have no part, since in the Eucharist they partake of the life of Jesus Christ. The analogy presupposes that a real conveying of the life of Jesus is made in the Eucharist, and it is special pleading to interpret S. Paul's meaning otherwise. And there is present also the further and inseparable thought, that to partake of Christ is to partake of the very life of the Body or fellowship, " we who are many . . . are one bread, one body." The one loaf symbolizes the unity of all the Christians.

(2) In the second passage, S. Paul is dealing directly with abuses at the Eucharist in Corinth. He records solemnly the institution of the rite by Jesus, and then continues,

" For as often as ye eat this bread, and drink this cup, ye proclaim the Lord's death till he come. Wherefore whosoever shall eat the bread or drink the cup of the Lord unworthily, shall be guilty of the body and the blood of the Lord. But let a man prove himself, and so let him eat of the bread, and drink of the cup. For he that eateth and drinketh, eateth and drinketh judgement unto himself, if he discern not the body. For this cause many among you are weak and sickly, and not a few sleep."

Here S. Paul reiterates in awful language that the reality of the Lord's body is *there;* it must be discerned, failure to discern it by faithful partaking brings judgement of a terrible kind, because the gift is *there*.[1] There is no suggestion that faith or any human attitude creates the gift for the individual. The reality of the gift is as emphatic as are the other truths which these two Pauline passages set forth. (i) The rite proclaims the Lord's death ; (ii) the rite is a sharing in the life of Christ and therefore a sharing in the one Body which is His people. As in all Christian thinking about τὸ σῶμα, the Eucharist and the Church are inseparable. In these ways S. Paul discerns the meaning of the rite as declaring the meaning of the Gospel and of the Church as the Body of Christ.

S. John marks a further stage in the interpretation. If the Synoptists and S. Paul show how the rite declares the death of the Lord, S. John shows how it expresses not

[1] We may refer once more to Dr. Andrews'chapter on the " Sacraments in the New Testament " included in Dr. Forsyth's *Lectures on Church and Sacraments*. " To S. Paul, therefore, the Bread and the Wine of the Eucharist are not merely emblems of the sacrifice that was once offered for the sins of the world ; they are the vehicle by means of which the virtue of that sacrifice is appropriated by the participant," p. 151. The whole chapter is an important examination of the N.T. evidence.

the death only but the whole life, death and exaltation of the Word-made-flesh. He does not record the institution of the rite, but he unfolds its meaning in the discourses upon the Bread of Life in chapter 6. It has sometimes been urged that this teaching refers not to the Eucharist but to the whole work of Christ whose Incarnation feeds the souls of men. If, however, this is so, the chapter shows the place of the Eucharist in Christianity just as strongly as if its reference were more directly eucharistic. For the language of " bread " and " eating " and of " blood " and " drinking " is the Christians' eucharistic language, and to express the Incarnation in the language of the Eucharist betokens the importance of the rite just as emphatically as to express the Eucharist in terms of the Incarnation. And, throughout the account of the feeding of the five thousand and the discourses which follow, the reader's mind is often led directly to the Eucharist. The Passover is nigh (6⁴), Jesus gives thanks before distributing the loaves (6¹¹), and the thanksgiving is as prominent in the writer's mind as is the feeding, for he refers a little later to " the place where they ate the bread after the Lord had given thanks " (6²³).

The main teaching of this chapter is clear. The feeding of the multitude is a symbol of a heavenly feeding which Jesus has in store for men (vv. 26-27). Jesus Himself is the heavenly food, the bread from heaven, and His feeding of men is a part of His work of raising the dead to life (vv. 35-40). And the bread is his " flesh which is for the life of the world," that is the death which He shall die (v. 51). Thus far the discourse has said more vividly what S. Paul had already taught, of the real feeding and of the feeding through the power of a death. But the discourse has added a further fact : the power to feed and to give life is derived from the Father, and hence the Incarnation and the Eucharist reveal the truth about the Father and the Son. Behind the life, the death, the feeding, there is the eternal relation of Father and Son which the life, the death, and the feeding reveal. Hence the scandalous character of the rite is apparent. It is visible, tangible, earthy; and the common, vulgar word for eating (τρώγειν) tells of its earthiness. Yet in this earthy action the truth of the eternal God is learnt and is active to save the souls and bodies of men.

The Jews "strove with one another saying, How can this man give us his flesh to eat?" The idea is an impossible one for them. Can the carpenter's son from Nazareth be the giver of food and of life to all mankind? Jesus does not answer their difficulty. He only reasserts the scandalous truth once again and insists on its necessity for salvation. For the Jews the Eucharist, like the death of the Messiah in the flesh, is a scandal (vv. 52-59). To the disciples, however, He throws some light upon this now intolerable paradox:—

"Doth this cause you to stumble? What then if you should behold the Son of Man ascending where he was before? It is the spirit that quickeneth; the flesh profiteth nothing: the words that I have spoken unto you are spirit and are life" (vv. 61-63).

The eating of the flesh is a hard thought: harder still is the thought of the Son of Man ascending into heaven, yet this will make all plain. In the power of the ascended life and of the Holy Spirit the Christ will feed them with Himself; His words and works and sacraments are to be understood in the light of His completed work and His ascended life. All these stupendous truths, and nothing less, lie behind the Eucharist—the flesh of Jesus, the death, the ascension, the Father and the Son, the Spirit. The *flesh* must be eaten . . . here is history, concrete fact, Χριστὸς ἐν σαρκί. Yet history and fact have their significance in what lies beyond them. Like the Incarnation itself, the Eucharist is the breaking into history of something eternal, beyond history, inapprehensible in terms of history alone. And no man cometh, except it be given him of the Father.

Thus do S. Paul and S. John interpret the Eucharist.

They make explicit what is there from the beginning ; for if the power of the Christ's death creates the rite and is present in it, then there is in it also the whole New Testament revelation of Father, Son, and Spirit and of the Church which is His Body, and of the creation made by Him. Custom, interpretation, language varies. Sometimes the emphasis is upon the Eucharist and the Cross, sometimes upon the Eucharist and the Incarnation or the heavenly Priesthood ; variety of language about the rite is no stranger than variety of language about the Christ Himself. But underlying the language there is something greater than the language can express, and something which is creating language and thought and worship. For the fact behind and within the Eucharist is not the last supper alone, nor yet the last supper as interpreted by S. Paul and S. John, but the whole Gospel of the Name and the Glory of God in Christ. The rite has within itself something which disturbs and causes change. Perhaps one of the signs of this disturbance is the separation of the Eucharist from the " agape " or " love-feast " with which it was at first associated. Just as our Lord, in the awe and isolation of the Passion was set apart from mankind so as to be the nearer to them by death, so also the Eucharist had to be set apart from common meals in an awe and mystery whereby its nearness to common life was to be realized more deeply. The Gospel which moulded the structure of the Church moulded also the form of the Church's worship. This worship was and is the *Liturgy*, the divine action whereby the people of God share in the self oblation of the Christ.

II

The Liturgy declares the Gospel of God. λειτουργία means service offered to God, and Christ as Man is the λειτουργὸς. And the inner λειτουργία of the Church's self-offering is expressed in fixed forms so that it may represent not the topical needs and moods and feelings of men, but the changeless and enduring facts about Christ's work for men,—in history, in heaven and in His one Church. Now while the study of liturgies is complex, there being many types (Antiochene, Egyptian, Gallican, Roman), they all have certain general features, since all are expressions in language and action of the one λειτουργία of Christ. All early liturgies include the reading of scripture, the singing of Psalms, a prayer of intercession, an offering to God of the bread and wine as His created gifts, and a central Eucharistic prayer, which sets forth the successive stages of God's revelation and which culminates in the consecration of the bread to be His body and the wine to be His blood, after receiving which the Church offers itself in union with Christ to the Father. The following is the Eucharistic prayer from the Apostolic tradition of Hippolytus, and is the earliest such prayer that is now extant (c. 225 A.D.). It gives what is (with certain variations, which we shall note presently) the main structure of the Church's Eucharistic prayers:—

> Bishop : The Lord be with you.
> Congregation : And with thy spirit.
> Bishop : Lift up your hearts.
> Congregation : We lift them up unto the Lord.
> Bishop : Let us give thanks unto the Lord.
> Congregation : It is meet and right.

(i) We give thanks unto Thee, O God, through Thy beloved Son Jesus Christ, whom in the last times Thou didst send unto us to be Saviour, Redeemer, and messenger of Thy will ; who is Thine inseparable Word through whom Thou hast made all things, and who was well-pleasing unto Thee. Him Thou didst send from heaven into the womb of the Virgin, and being born in her womb was incarnate and shown to be Thy son, born of the Holy Spirit and the Virgin. He, in fulfilment of Thy will and preparing for Thee an holy people, stretched forth his hands when He was suffering that He might deliver from suffering those who believed in Thee.

(ii) Who when He was being given over to His willing suffering that He might dissolve death, break the chains of the devil, tread hell underfoot, illuminate the righteous, set a bound (to death) and manifest forth the Resurrection, having taken bread, gave thanks unto Thee and said : Take eat : this is my body which is broken for you. Likewise also the cup, saying : This is my blood which is poured out for you. When ye do this, ye make my memorial.

(iii) Being mindful then of His death and resurrection we offer to Thee the bread and the cup, giving thanks unto Thee as thou has deemed us worthy to stand before Thee and act as priest unto Thee.

(iv) And we beseech Thee to send Thy Holy Spirit upon the sacrifice of Thy (Holy) Church.

(v) Which do Thou in uniting it give to all the saints who partake for fulfilment of the Holy Spirit unto the strengthening of faith in truth, that we may praise and glorify Thee.

(vi) Through Thy son Jesus Christ, through whom unto Thee be glory and honour—to the Father and the Son with the Holy Spirit in Thy Holy Church, now and for evermore. Amen.

Variations, of course, exist in the great liturgies. The Roman rite dwells specially upon the commemoration of the *death* of Christ ; the Byzantine liturgies commemorate God's work in creation, leading up to His redemptive acts in a summary of all history, and thence passing to the whole story of Christ's birth, ministry, death, resurrection and ascension. Other differences concern the idea of consecration ; some rites presuppose that consecration is God's action in response to the whole prayer ; some (as the Latin rite) connect consecration with the recital of the words " This is my body," " This is my blood " ; and others (as the Eastern rites) connect it with the invocation of the Holy Spirit upon the bread and wine. Yet for all these differences it is as possible to speak of " the Liturgy " underlying its many presentations as it is to speak of " the Gospel " underlying the four gospels. All have certain common elements. In all there is *thanksgiving ;* in all there is *commemoration ;* in all there is the note of *mystery* since Christ is present to feed His people ;

in all there is the *fellowship* of those who are united with one
another and with the whole Church, and in all Christ gives
Himself in *sacrifice*. In the Liturgy, therefore, there is
wrought out the action of God which S. Paul describes in
his prayers in Ephesians and Colossians. To read these
Epistles is to contemplate the action; to share in the
Liturgy is to be drawn into its heart and centre.

Of these elements in the Christian Eucharist it is probable
that those of *thanksgiving* and *commemoration* have aroused
the least controversy and misunderstanding, while the
meaning of *mystery* and *fellowship* and *sacrifice* has been
the subject of many disputes in the history of the Church.
It is in the light of the Gospel and of the doctrine of
the Church as σῶμα Χριστοῦ that the meaning of these
elements is plain.

Mystery means that Christ by His body and His blood
feeds His people with Himself, and that the presence
of His body and His blood is not the result of the individual's faith, but, like the Incarnation itself, a presence
of Jesus which faith may receive and which unfaith may
reject. The gift is *there*, by the act of the Lord in His
Church, just as Christ Incarnate was *there* in Galilee for
men to receive or to reject. Such is the way of the Gospel
of God. But of the mystery there were, in the Church
of the first five centuries, several explanations all held
within the Church's tolerant embrace. Thus some patristic
writers simply assert that Christ feeds the souls of men,
without explaining how; [1] some use language of " type "
and " symbol " and " representation " [2]; some emphasize

[1] E.g. S. Ignatius, *Eph.* 5. 20; Tertullian, *De Carn. Res.* 37;
Clement, *Paed.* I, 6. 38; Origen, *In Lev. Hom.* VII, 5; Athanasius,
Ap. C. Ar. 5. 11; Cyril of Jerusalem, *Catech.* xiii. 19, xxii. 3.

[2] Tertullian, *Adv. Marcionen* i. 14, iii. 19, iv. 40; Theodoret, *Dial.*
i, ii; *Prayers* of Serapion 1; Augustine, *In Psalm,* III. In dealing
with this kind of teaching it is important to remember the truth
which Harnack well expressed in these words: " What we nowadays
understand by ' symbol ' is a thing which *is not* what it represents;
at that time ' symbol ' denoted a thing which in some kind of way
really *is* what it signifies," *History of Dogma,* II, 144.

a change wrought in the elements by consecration so that they are the body and blood of Jesus while still remaining also bread and wine.[1] The Church was content that these theories should be held side by side. But whatever theory is adopted the mystery calls forth awe and worship from those who share in the Liturgy. " Holy things for holy people " cries the deacon in the Syrian rite, "One is holy, one Lord Jesus Christ " reply the people. And, by the nearness of Jesus who feeds and the awfulness of Jesus who has redeemed men by His death, the liturgy sets forth the Gospel. Alike in the New Testament and in the Liturgy the Christians' ever-deepening union with Jesus increases their awe and wonder and sense of a great unknown which lies before them. Alike in the New Testament and in the Liturgy the prayer to God as Father is set in the context of Calvary, as is seen in some of the rites where the moment of commemorating the Passion is the moment where men " are bold to say, Our Father." And the presence of Jesus here and now is but the fore-taste of the union which is to come. The feasting is " until His coming again " ; and " it doth not yet appear what we shall be."

But the mystery of the body and the blood is mis-understood without the " one bread, one body " of *Fellow-ship*. S. Paul's teaching is driven home in S. Augustine's words :—

" If you wish to understand the Body of Christ, hear the apostle speaking to the faithful ' now ye are the Body and members of Christ.' If you then are the Body and members of Christ, the mystery of yourselves is laid upon the table of the Lord, the mystery of yourselves ye receive. To that which you are, answer ' Amen,' and in answering you assent. Be a member of the Body of Christ, that the Amen may be true." (*Sermons* 272.)

" The mystery of yourselves ye receive ! " The fellowship between Christians is not only a very close corollary of

[1] E.g. Cyril of Jerusalem, *Catech.* xix. 7, xxi. 3, xxii. 1, etc. ; Gregory of Nyssa, *Catech. Lect.* 37 ; Ambrose, *De Mysteriis*, 43-54.

their acts of receiving the Lord's Body—it is included within every act of communion, for the eucharistic Body and the Body the Church are utterly one. In a sermon to the newly-baptized S. Augustine says :—

> " I promised you, who have been baptized, a sermon in which I would explain the Sacrament of the Lord's table. . . . You ought to know what you have received, what you are about to receive, what you ought to receive daily. That bread, which you see on the altar, . . . is the body of Christ. That cup . . . is the blood of Christ. In this way the Lord willed to impart His body and His blood, which He shed for us for the remission of sins. If you have received well, you are what you have received." (*Sermons* 227.) [1]

Nor is the Body, thus received, a merely local fellowship of Christians ; it is the one universal Church. For the Eucharist is never merely the act of a local community, but always the act of the great Church, wherein the local community is merged. This is expressed in the restriction of leadership in the rite to the ministry of Bishops and presbyters, a restriction which does not lower the place of the laity in the rite but reminds them that their place is one with the whole Church of God in history and in heaven.

Sacrifice is a figure of speech which the early Christians, from their knowledge of the typical Jewish sacrifices, could use as one amongst many images to describe the work of Christ. The essence of the old sacrifices was the offering of an animal's blood which represented its life. The death was necessary to release the blood, but the essence of sacrifice was the offering of the life. Now Jesus Christ was a priest and offered sacrifice in a sense far transcending the ancient imagery ; and the Epistle

---

[1] This sermon is printed in full in Hebert, *Liturgy and Society*, pp. 85-86. Cf. *Sermon* 229, and Chrysostom, *In* 1 *Cor.* xxiv, 2. Similar teaching had been given by S. Cyprian, who likens the mixing of water and wine in the chalice to the uniting of the people with Christ's offering. Cf. Bayard, S. Cyprian, *Correspondance*, Vol. II, *Ep.* 63.

to the Hebrews bids us think of His priesthood in two ways. *Firstly*, it is an eternal fact about His heavenly life. " A priest for ever after the order of Melchizedek," the Son of God for ever possesses the character of one who gives His life utterly in love. His eternal priesthood and sacrifice are the eternal element of self-giving love in the Godhead, the element which S. John describes as the eternal love of the Son for the Father and of the Father for the Son. *Secondly*, this eternal self-giving or priesthood is uttered in time and history in the life and death of the Incarnate Son, and when wrought out in a world of sin and pain the life of sacrifice involves death and destruction. None the less the essence of the sacrifice is the giving of life, though the death is the mark and the significant fact about the life, making it for ever " the life whereof the abiding characteristic is to have died." Thus, priest eternally and priest on earth, our Lord is priest *now* in His relation to the Father, forever giving to the Father as Son of Man a life of which the death once died in history is the revealing mark and character. And the Christians' present access to the Father has been created by the Lord's sacrifice ; it is only through facing the Cross and its disclosure of the awful realities of sin and of God's forgiving love that men have free access to God in sonship, and it is only by looking constantly to Christ's sacrifice that they approach God aright and in His name. Hence the divine action to which the Christians look and which they commemorate as a finished event in history and as an eternal fact in heaven, is an action whereof priesthood and sacrifice are a scriptural description. The Christians look back to the sacrifice of Calvary and they look up to the eternal sacrifice which it reveals.

Nor is this all. As the Glory and the Name are realities *outside* the Christians, and also facts *within* them, so likewise is priesthood. The Body of Christ shares in His priesthood, for in His Body He lives His life of utter self-giving in the midst of pain and sin. Hence S. Peter describes the Christians,

" ye are·an elect race, a royal priesthood, a holy nation, a people for God's own possession." (1 Peter 2⁹),

and hence the New Testament uses priestly language in describing the Christian life as a whole (Rom. 12¹, 15¹⁶ ; Phil. 2¹⁷, 4¹⁸ ; Heb. 13¹⁵⁻¹⁶). To a biblically-minded Christian the words " priest " and " sacrifice " signify, first, the fact of Christ, and, next, the whole Body of Christ with its single life and ministry of self-oblation and intercession in the midst of a world of sin. So different is this priesthood from all Jewish and pagan priesthood that there is an inevitable tendency to avoid the application of priestly language to the Christian ministry or to the Christian rites lest the associations of Judaism or paganism might be present. Yet since Christ is Priest, in His eternal nature and in His actions in history, and since His Body shares in His priesthood, it follows that the special ministries (which represent the Church universal) are priestly ; and it follows also that the Eucharist, wherein the whole truth of Christ and His Church is focused, is an act of sacrifice.

It was by a gradual process that the language of sacrifice became applied to each of the main aspects of the Eucharist. That the process was due to no alien influences is shown by the frequent protests that Jewish and pagan rites are carnal and that only spiritual sacrifices are acceptable to God.[1] It is in this spiritual context that the sacrificial idea of the Eucharist grows. Sometimes, as in the Didache and in S. Ignatius, the language of sacrifice is used with no clear definition of what is meant.[2] Sometimes, as in Irenaeus, it is used of the bread and wine which are offered as the first-fruits of creation.[3] Sometimes, as in Justin, it is used of the praises and thanksgivings of the Christians.[4] But all this does not exhaust the sacrificial meaning of the rite. Hints of something deeper appear. For

[1] Cf. *Barnabas* II, 4-10 ; *ad Diognetum* III, 4, 5 ; Justin, *Dial.* 22 ; Irenaeus, *Adv. Haer.* IV, xvii. etc.

[2] *Did.* 14, Ignatius, *Eph.* 5, *Magn.* 6, *Trall.* 7, *Philad.* 4.

[3] *Adv. Haer.* IV, xvii. 5, IV, xviii. 1.   [4] *Dial.* 117.

(i) the rite commemorates the Passion (Justin, *Trypho.* 41), and not only the Passion but also the resurrection (Ignatius, *Smyrn.* 6) and the whole Incarnate life (Justin. *Dial.* 70). And (ii) the offerings in the rite are joined to Christ who is the Priest in heaven (Iren., *Adv. Haer.* IV, xvii. 6). Thus it looks back to the death-once-died, it looks up to the Priest in the heavenly places. But it is not until S. Cyprian that we find a writer who says that the sacrifice in the rite is the Body and Blood of Christ. "The Passion of the Lord," he says, "is the sacrifice which we offer." (*Epistles*, 63. 17.)

Now is there, as has often been urged, a real change of doctrine to be found in S. Cyprian's teaching? Is the idea of offering Christ in the Eucharist novel and inconsistent with the more primitive teaching? The answer will surely be found, not by considering the sacrificial terminology of the Eucharist in isolation, but by recalling the place of sacrifice in the whole fact of Christ and in the Church's whole life as His Body. Christ is eternally Priest. His life is ever one of self-oblation which "shows" to the Father and to men the sacrifice wrought once for all in history. His presence in heaven is as a sacrifice, and in the Eucharist His presence cannot be otherwise. He is there, as One who gave Himself on the Cross and who there and then unites His people to His self-giving to the Father in heaven. Hence when S. Cyprian speaks of the Body and the Blood as a sacrifice, he is only making articulate what is inherent in the Eucharist just because it is inherent in Christ Himself. And the sacrificial language, applied first to the bread and wine and to the prayers and praises of the Christians, is applied finally to the Body and Blood of Christ. Behind the language there is the Gospel of God, since Christ's unique act in history is the source of what the Christians do (Cyprian, *Epistles* 63. 14). Around the language there is the doctrine of the Church as Body (cf. *Epistles*, *passim*, and *De Unitate Ecclesiae*). And within this twofold context sacrifice and priesthood have their meaning.

It is only when this twofold context is forgotten that abuses can arise. Thus (1) sacrifice has sometimes been identified exclusively with death or destruction or with this act in its ritual embodiment without real emphasis upon the resurrection and ascension and heavenly priesthood. It was through this distortion that there arose the mediæval views that each Mass is a repetition of the sacrifice of Calvary, and thence the Reformers' reaction against the whole idea of the rite as a sacrifice. Again (2) sacrifice has sometimes been regarded as if Christ's action were quite separate from the Father's and as if He were, on Calvary and in the Eucharist, propitiating an estranged Father on man's behalf. Now certainly the New Testament teaches that Christ is a propitiation for sin (Rom. 3$^{21-26}$, 1 John 2^1), but both S. Paul and S. John make it clear that the initiative in the act of propitiation belongs to God Himself. The awful death is needed to disclose the horror of sin as well as the forgiving love of God ; but the whole action is that of God Himself. " God loved us, and sent His Son to be a propitiation." (1 John 4^{10}.) " God commendeth His own love towards us, in that, while we were yet sinners, Christ died for us." (Rom. 5^8.) Hence while both Calvary and the Eucharist are a " sacrifice for sin," both are the utterance of God's own self-giving towards men. God in Christ offers ; the Church His Body beholds the offering in all its costliness, and is drawn into it. The sacrifice is the action of God in Christ and in His Body. (3) Abuses have also come through a false separation between the ministerial priesthood and the one Body, as if the priest, as an individual and in virtue of rights inherent in himself, were offering in each Mass a separate sacrifice to God. But ministerial priesthood—an indelible order as it is—is the priesthood of the one Body focused in certain organs which act for the Lord and for the Body. And against individualistic views of priesthood Catholicism itself protests in the teaching of S. Paul and S. Augustine :—

" The whole redeemed city itself, that is the congregation
and society of the saints, is offered as a universal sacrifice to
God through the High Priest, who offered Himself in suffering
for us in the form of a servant, that we might be the body of
so great a Head. . . . This is the sacrifice of Christians, ' the
many one body in Christ,' which also the Church celebrates
in the sacrament of the altar, familiar to the faithful, where
it is shown to her that in this thing which she offers she herself
is offered." (*De Civitate Dei*, X. 6.)

III

The Christian who seeks to remember the Gospel of God
and to realize all that it implies finds in the Liturgy the
reminder which he seeks. For there he looks upon Him
whom he has pierced, and, as he sees the drama of what
God has done in Christ, he shares in the death once died
and finds his life no longer his own but united with Christ
and with the people of God. And if the ritual of the
later Eastern or Western Church, with its pattern of
music and form and colour, seems far away from the
rite in the Upper Room, he remembers that the background
to the Upper Room is the whole truth of Christ in His
birth and life and death and resurrection and ascension
and in His universal Church and in all creation, whose
beauty and variety are summed up in His liturgical act.
He will test the evangelical character of a rite not by its
precise resemblance to the rites within the New Testament
but by its setting-forth of the whole action of worship
which is the New Testament itself, and the whole Gospel
of creation and redemption.

It is still the Messiah who gives thanks and breaks
bread ; and herein is still summed up the life of the
Church, the Gospel of God, and the meaning of the whole
life of man.

The Church's life is gathered around the Liturgy since it
it is not only the most important of a series of rites, but
the divine act into which all prayers and praises are drawn.
The divine office and all other Christian services are links

between one Eucharist and the next, and the private prayers of all Christians are (however unconsciously) a part of the Body's one offering of which the Eucharist is the centre. Here also Holy Matrimony and Ordination find their true context and climax ; and here also every worshipful thought and deed and word of men is gathered up and explained, since here the Christians, with all that they have and do and desire, are offered in union with the death and resurrection of Jesus and the one family of God.

The Gospel of God is here set forth, since the bread and wine proclaim that God is creator, and the blessing and breaking declare that He has redeemed the world and that all things find their meaning and their unity only in the death and resurrection of the Christ who made them. Here therefore Christian doctrine, with the scriptures and the creeds, finds its true context. *Lex orandi, lex credendi.*

And the meaning of all life is here set forth, since men exist to worship God for God's own sake. The Christian does not share in the Liturgy in order to live aright ; he lives aright in order to share in the Liturgy. For the Liturgy is not an exercise of piety divorced from common life, it is rather the bringing of all common life into the sacrifice of Christ. The bread and the wine placed upon the altar are the gifts of the people betokening the food and work and toil and livelihood of men, brought to Christ to bless and to break to the end that all creation may be summed up in His death and resurrection, to the glory of God, the Father. Here is seen, in the words of the Creed, " the Communion of Saints," the fellowship both of holy things and of holy people, united in the Christ by whom all things were made. ἄγια ἀγίοις.

ADDITIONAL NOTE

Important new work on the origins of the Eucharist will be found in J. Jeremias *The Eucharistic Words of Jesus* and in Gregory Dix *The Shape of the Liturgy.* While the questions of the Lucan text and the relation of the Supper to the Passover cannot be regarded as closed, I find nothing to disturb the view expressed in this chapter as to the new and creative elements in our Lord's actions.

CHAPTER IX

The Truth of God

I

Jesus Christ is not only the Way and the Life. He is also the Truth ; and the Church, which is His Body, is commissioned to teach the Truth. How shall the Church know where to find what is true, and, how, after finding it, shall the Church assimilate it so as to proclaim it with authority to men ?

The answer to these questions has, in Christian history, been sought specially in two phrases, " the authority of the Bible " and " the authority of the Church." Some have turned to the Bible as a whole or to the New Testament, and have said in effect, " Propositions about God which we find here are true ; those which we do not find here are unwarranted or false." Others have turned to the Church as a divine institution and have said in effect, " This institution is divinely inspired. What it teaches (semper et ubique et ab omnibus) is true." We are not to say that either of these methods is wrong ; but neither of them goes deep enough. The deeper questions are these. What does the Bible mean by " Truth " ? What did our Lord mean when He said " I am the Truth " ? and what does the word " truth " mean on the lips of the Church's teachers ? It is not enough, and it may be even misleading to assert that Truth is found in the Bible and in the Church. We must ask, " What is this Truth which has created both the Church and the Bible ? "

In our quest of the meaning of " Truth " we shall start by examining the two words ἀλήθεια (truth) and σοφία (wisdom) as used in the New Testament ; and this examination will provide a basis for our consideration of the nature of Christian doctrine and the authority of the Christian Church.

(1) ἀλήθεια is used in the Old Testament of *God's steadfastness* in providence and in redemption.   The Truth is a quality of the living God in action.

> Psalm 100[5], " his truth endureth to all generations."
>
> Psalm 31[5], " thou hast redeemed me, O Lord, thou God of truth."
>
> Psalm 85[10], " mercy and truth are met together."
>
> Micah 7[20], " thou wilt perform the truth to Jacob."

Thus the Truth is God's saving plan as He rules in history with righteous purpose.   Karl Barth well reproduces the Old Testament meaning of " Truth " when he writes, " Truth is not what we think and say, but what God has done, will do, and is doing." [1]   Such is the background to the word ἀλήθεια in the New Testament, and the same *redemptive* note is present in S. Paul's and in S. John's use of the word.

> Gal. 2[5, 14], " the truth of the gospel."   Cf. Col. 1[5].
>
> Rom. 15[8], " Christ hath been made a minister of the circumcision for the truth of God, that he might confirm the promises made unto the fathers.
>
> Eph. 1[13], " Ye also, having heard the word of the truth, the gospel of your salvation."
>
> 1 Tim. 2[3], " God our Saviour, who willeth that all men should be saved ; and come to the knowledge of the truth."
>
> 2 Tim. 2[25], " repentance unto knowledge of the truth."

Thus Truth is uttered in God's redemption through Christ, and men learn the Truth through repentance as well as through intellectual processes, and apprehend the Truth in their life as well as in their thinking,

---

[1] *Epistle to Romans*, Eng. tr., p. 301.

" the new man, which after God hath been created in righteousness and holiness of truth " (Eph. 4²⁴),

" having girded your loins with truth " (Eph. 6¹⁴),

" God chose you . . . unto salvation in sanctification of the
Spirit and belief of the truth " (2 Thess. 2¹³).

Nor is the teaching of S. John essentially different ; the
emphasis is upon the Incarnation rather than upon the
Cross, but the redemptive note is present. " The word was
made flesh and dwelt among us, and we beheld his glory,
. . . full of grace and truth " reminds the reader at once of
Psalm 85, " His salvation is nigh them that fear him, that
glory may dwell in the land. Mercy and truth are met
together, righteousness and peace have kissed each other."
In some passages possibly the word ἀλήθεια has a Greek
tone to its meaning ; but, if this is so, the Greek idea
is thoroughly baptized into the redemptive Gospel. For
God's Truth is not an abstract value to be contemplated ;
it is active to save in Christ. Christ is the Truth (John 14⁶),
God's word is Truth (17¹⁷) and the disciple is he that *does* the
Truth,

" If ye abide in my word, then are ye truly my disciples ; and
ye shall know the truth, and the truth shall make you free."
                                        —(John 8³².)

More, still, S. John links truth with the Passion of our Lord,

" Sanctify them in the truth : thy word is truth. As thou
didst send me into the world, even so sent I them into the
world. And for their sakes I sanctify myself, that they themselves also may be sanctified in truth." (John 17¹⁷⁻¹⁹.)

Crucifixion—Truth—the life of holiness, all these are
linked ; and very similar is the teaching of the First
Epistle of S. John that " truth " and " love " are closely
related. (1 John 1⁶, 2 John ³, 3 John ¹.) In short, the
Christian use of the word ἀλήθεια in the New Testament
suggests that Truth centres in the redemptive death of

Christ, and that it is learnt in the common life of the society created by that death.[1]

(2) The use of the word σοφία, Wisdom, in the New Testament, is equally striking. Wisdom is an attribute of God Himself. (Rom 11³³, Eph. 3¹⁰, James 3¹⁷.) It is manifested in Christ " in whom are all the treasures of wisdom and knowledge hidden." (Col. 2³.) Nay more, Christ is Himself the Wisdom of God, for to Him are ascribed those functions of creating, sustaining the universe, ruling over history and disclosing God's purpose to men, functions which belong to the Wisdom of God in the wisdom literature. (1 Cor. 8⁶, 10⁴; Col. 1¹⁶⁻¹⁷; cf. Prov. 8²²⁻³⁶, Wisdom 7²² ff.) And Wisdom is set forth in the death of Christ, in direct contrast to human wisdom and as `the negation of the wisest ideas of the world.

" For the word of the Cross is to them that are perishing foolishness; but unto us which are being saved it is the power of God . . . we preach Christ crucified, unto Jews a stumbling-block and unto Gentiles foolishness, but unto them that are called, both Jews and Greeks, Christ the power of God, and the wisdom of God." (1 Cor. 1¹⁸⁻²³.)

It is shortly after this account of Wisdom disclosed by the Cross that S. Paul passes on to describe the Wisdom which dwells in the Christians to whom the Spirit gives a knowledge of the things of God.

" Howbeit we speak wisdom among the perfect; yet a wisdom not of this world, nor of the rulers of this world, which are coming to nought: but we speak God's wisdom in a mystery, even the wisdom that hath been hidden, which God foreordained before the worlds unto our glory: which none of

---

[1] C. H. Dodd, in *The Bible and the Greeks*, pp. 70-75, suggests that, in some instances both in LXX and in N.T. " in the passage from the Hebrew אֱמֶת to the Greek ἀλήθεια there is a certain inevitable shift of meaning," resulting in a certain " Hellenizing " of the thought. This does not, however, affect the supremacy of the *redemptive* idea in connexion with Truth, both in S. Paul and in S. John.

the rulers of this world knoweth. . . . But unto us God revealed them through the Spirit: for the Spirit searcheth all
things, yea, the deep things of God." (1 Cor. 2⁶⁻¹⁰.)

Thus the Christians, brought into the Wisdom of the
crucified, are led on to the life of Wisdom in the Spirit.
S. Paul prays that the readers of " Ephesians " may be
given " a spirit of σοφία and ἀποκάλυψις in the γνῶσις of
God " (Eph. 1¹⁷), and that in the Colossians " the word
of Christ may dwell richly in all wisdom." (Col. 3¹⁶ ;
cf. 1²⁸.) The range of this Wisdom is as wide as the whole
world, for the whole world, created by God, becomes intelligible in the light of the crucifixion wherein the character and method of divine government are disclosed.
He who redeemed men is also He who created the world
and in whom all things shall be summed up, and the fellowship which shares in His death and resurrection shall be
led by the Holy Spirit to interpret all life and all history.
This work of interpretation involves all the activities of
the human intellect and every part of science and art and
research ; yet the process of knowledge is not by these
activities alone. For there are secrets of the meaning of
the world which are unlocked through a knowledge which
is linked with the life and love of the society which shares
in the Cross ; a knowledge which grows through the building
up of the one Body in love,

" that your *love* may abound more and more in knowledge
and all discernment " (Phil. 1⁹),

" until we all attain unto the unity of the faith, and of the
knowledge of the Son of God, unto a fully-grown man, unto the
measure of the stature of the fulness of Christ " (Eph. 4¹³).

Christian knowledge (γνῶσις) and Christian love (ἀγάπη)
lie close together, and Christian theology is not only a
detached exercise of the Christian intellect ; it is the life
of the one Body in which Truth is both thought out and
lived out.

In the light of the meaning of the words " Truth " and " Wisdom " in the New Testament the nature of the Church's doctrine and authority becomes plain. These facts emerge inescapably from our biblical study.

(1) The Wisdom of God is working through all created life, and far and wide is the sustainer and the inspirer of the thought and the endeavour of men. The Church will therefore reverence every honest activity of the minds of men ; it will perceive that therein the Spirit of God is moving, and it will tremble lest by denying this, in word or in action, it blaspheme the Spirit of God. But Wisdom cannot be thus learnt in all its fulness. The mind and the eye of man are distorted by sin and self-worship ; and the Wisdom which the Spirit of God unfolds throughout the world can lead to blindness and to deceit unless men face the fact of sin and the need for redemption.

Hence, (2) the Church proclaims the Wisdom of God, set forth in its very essence in the crucifixion of Jesus Christ, a Wisdom learnt when men are brought to the crisis of repentance and to the resulting knowledge of self and of God. The Wisdom of the Cross seems at first to deny the wisdom of the Spirit of God in the created world ; it scandalizes men's sense of the good and the beautiful. But the Christians, who have first faced the scandal, discover in the Cross a key to the meaning of all creation. The Cross unlocks its secrets and its sorrows, and interprets them in terms of the power of God.

Thus (3), the Wisdom uttered in the Cross has created the Church and is expressed through the Church's whole life as the Body of Christ crucified and risen. The Church's work in thinking and interpreting and teaching is insepar-able from the Church's life in Christ. Its authority is Christ Himself, known in the building up of the one Body in Truth and in Love. Hence " orthodoxy " means not only " right opinion," but also " right worship " or " true glory," after the Biblical meaning of the word δόξα ; for life and thought and worship are inseparable activities in the Body of Christ. καὶ ἐθεασάμεθα τὴν δόξαν αὐτοῦ.

In these three ways the Church will be faithful to the Biblical meaning of Truth, by reverencing the works of God everywhere and the Spirit of God manifested in the endeavours of men's minds ; by keeping before itself and before men the scandal of the Cross ; and by remembering that orthodoxy means not only correct propositions about God, but the life of the One Body of Christ in the due working of all its members.

II

It follows that the Church can never be said to have apprehended the truth. Rather is the Truth the divine action which apprehends the Church. Dimly it understands what it teaches. For the more the Church learns of God, the more it is aware of the incomprehensible mystery of His being, in creation and in transcendence and on the Cross. Christ has made God known as Father, Creator, Saviour, and has made possible a new access for men in sonship to God ; yet the more God is known as Father, Creator, Saviour, the more " other " is He found to be from all that men can express or imagine of a Father, a Creator, a Saviour. " If any man thinketh that he knoweth anything, he knoweth not yet as he ought to know ; but if any man loveth God, the same is known of him." (I Cor. 8^{2-3}.) The more the Church knows, the more is it aware that a great unknown lies ahead. " For now we see in a mirror, darkly ; but then face to face : now I know in part ; but then shall I know even as also I am known." (I Cor. 13^{12}.) " . . . it doth not yet appear what we shall be." (I John 3^{2}.) The Church's perilous office of teaching is inseparable from the Church's worship of the mystery whereby it exists.

Ineffable, therefore, is the revelation of God, which creates and which uses the teaching Church. Human language can never express it. Yet the Church, like its Lord, must partly commit it to human speech and thought, and is indeed commissioned to do this in every age and civilization. Hence have appeared the Canon of Scripture and the Creeds ; both express and both control the Church's teaching. But, since Truth and life and worship are inseparable, the scriptures and the Creeds are not given for use in isolation. They form, with the ministry and the sacraments, one close-knit structure which points the Christians to the historical facts wherein God is revealed, and to the life and experience of the universal society. The Creeds, therefore, have authority not as scholastic definitions of Christianity, but as a part of the structure which points behind scholasticism and philosophy to the Messianic work of Jesus. They point away from speculative theories which would swamp the Gospel, and from partial or ephemeral definitions which would distort its proportions. But the Creeds are not in themselves the Christian Faith ; Christians do not " believe in the Creeds," but, with the Creeds to help them, they believe in God.

Creeds are dangerous documents. That they are so is no modern discovery, but a fact fully realized in the ancient Church. S. Hilary, one of S. Athanasius' staunchest supporters in the Nicene struggle, wrote, " We are compelled to attempt what is unattainable, to climb where we cannot reach, to speak what we cannot utter. Instead of the bare adoration of faith, we are compelled to entrust the deep things of religion to the perils of human expression." (*de Trin.* II, 2. 4.) But, for all the dangers which accompany them when they are used apart from the scriptures and the Church's whole evangelical structure, the Creeds none the less proclaim the Gospel. They point to the redemption once wrought and, in the phrases with which they close, to the Christian hopes which spring from that redemption. Into the name of God, Father, Son and Spirit, the convert or the child of a convert is baptized ; and the Apostles' Creed describes the reality present in the act of Baptism and the destiny towards which the act is pointing.

I BELIEVE in God the Father Almighty, Maker of heaven and earth :

And in Jesus Christ his only Son our Lord, Who was conceived by the Holy Ghost, Born of the Virgin Mary, Suffered under Pontius Pilate, Was crucified, dead, and buried, He descended into hell ; The third day he rose again from the dead, He ascended into heaven, And sitteth on the right hand of God the Father Almighty ; From thence he shall come to judge the quick and the dead.

I believe in the Holy Ghost; The holy Catholic Church; The Communion of Saints ; The Forgiveness of sins ; The Resurrection of the body, And the life everlasting.   Amen.[1]

Into the same threefold name the Church's Eucharistic praises are drawn, as the Christians sing in the Liturgy the Creed which emerged from the close of the Arian conflict :—

WE BELIEVE in one God, the Father Almighty, Maker of heaven and earth, And of all things visible and invisible :

And in one Lord Jesus Christ, the only-begotten Son of God, Begotten of His Father before all worlds, God of God, Light of Light, Very God of very God, Begotten, not made, Being of one substance with the Father, By Whom all things were made : Who for us men, and for our salvation came down from heaven, And was incarnate by the Holy Ghost of the Virgin Mary, And was made man, And was crucified also for us under Pontius Pilate.   He suffered and was buried, And the third day He rose again according to the Scriptures, And ascended into Heaven, And sitteth on the right hand of the Father.   And He shall come again with glory to judge both the quick and the dead : Whose kingdom shall have no end.

And we believe in the Holy Ghost, The Lord and giver of

---

[1] Until recently the view was widely accepted that the " Apostles' Creed " is based upon the Old Roman Creed which dates from very early in the second century.   Dr. F. J. Badcock, in *The History of the Creeds*, has challenged this view with evidence upon which a number of scholars are at present suspending judgement.   But the question of the precise origin of this Creed does not affect its place in the Church's life as the widely accepted specimen of the many Baptismal Creeds (very similar in structure and contents) used throughout East and West.   The existence of varieties of " the Baptismal Creed " is analogous to varieties of liturgies all expressing " the Liturgy."

life, Who proceedeth from the Father and the Son, Who with the Father and the Son together is worshipped and glorified, Who spake by the Prophets. And we believe one Holy Catholic and Apostolic Church. We acknowledge one Baptism for the remission of sins. And we look for the resurrection of the dead, and the life of the world to come.[1]

If these two Creeds—known as the Apostles' and the Nicene—be examined as to their place in comparative religious ideas and literature, it will be at once apparent that the faith which they proclaim is not Greek, speculative, philosophical, but historical, Biblical, semitic, eschatological, a faith which does not make general propositions about the nature of God, but which looks back to certain events in history wherein God has acted and which looks forward to God's own consummation of these acts " for us men and for our salvation." In the light of early Christian history the character of the Creeds is indeed very striking. Christianity has entered the Hellenic atmosphere, it has used the Greek tongue, its theologians have largely been Greeks—and yet its Creeds show that it has baptized its Greek adherents into a Messianic faith in a God who reveals Himself through acts in history. The Biblical Gospel has overcome the speculative mind. And the simple, pictorial language of " he came down," " he ascended," is not the language of a time or of a school of thought, but the inescapable language of the human race and of common life. Language less " mythological " in form is less permanent. A Creed which substituted for these pictorial phrases the language of " modern thought " or of any scheme of thought would be the Creed of an ephemeral scholasticism,

[1] This Creed was adopted by the Council of Chalcedon in 451, that is to say, it represents not the Council of Nicaea of 325 (which adopted a shorter creed) but the mind of the Church *at the close* of the struggle which followed Nicaea. Whether it was originally a Creed of Jerusalem (as Hort urged) or a local Creed of Constantinople (as Dr. Badcock urges), does not affect its authority as expressing the Church's faith ratified at the close of the Arian controversy (381) and reaffirmed at the close of the other Christological controversies (451).

K.

and not the Creed of a Gospel before which all scholasticisms must bow.

Nor does the one term, ὁμοούσιος (" of one substance "), which the Creed borrows from philosophy, commit the Church to any philosophy of οὐσια or substance. This one term asserts that Christ is as Divine as the Father; and that all that constitutes Deity and all, whereby God is God, belongs to Jesus Christ. Nor does the Chalcedonian language of the " Two Natures " commit the Church to any particular philosophy. It rather calls a halt to the speculations of the fifth century, and asserts that their possibilities have become exhausted. Christ is as Divine as the Father; the truth for which Alexandria has contended is right. He is also as human as ourselves; the truth for which Antioch has contended is right. Yet He is not Divine *because* He is perfectly human; God and Man, even God and perfect Man, are not synonyms, nor differently graded instances of the same species. Thus the doctrine of " Two Natures " merely asserts the scriptural revelation, and, by its exclusion of pseudo-pantheism, protects the " *Truth*," which, since it is ἡ ἀλήθεια of the scriptures, centres in the work of a Mediator.

Yet the Creeds can be abused, as the scriptures can be abused. Emil Brunner has well described the right and the wrong use of the Creeds :—

" Danger lurks wherever the confession of faith in Jesus Christ is formulated into a Creed and elaborated by a scientific theology. It is not that in themselves either dogma or theology imply or involve an intellectualism of this kind. On the contrary ! if we examine the impelling motives in the history of dogma we shall see that the opposite is true : Christian dogma has acted as a kind of breakwater, erected by the Christian church as a defence against the seething ocean of intellectualism by which it was surrounded." (*The Mediator*, p. 594.)

Thus the Creeds are misused when they are interpreted apart from the Gospel which is behind them and the whole organism of worship of which they form a part. When thus divorced from their true context—baptismal and eucharistic—in the Church's life, the Creeds can obtain a scholastic use which is alien from the true mind of the Church. Brunner has thus pictured the misuse of dogma :—

"Dogma and theology exist for the sake of the Christian message and not vice versa. When this relationship has been reversed, and when dogma is confused with the actual message, the danger which threatened the Faith has turned into the devastating evil of intellectualism. Here the wall of defence has killed the life which it was there to protect, or at least has almost stifled it ; here the wood which was intended to support the tree has used up all the vital sap. . . . This disaster is not due to dogma, the formulated Creed of the Christian Church ; for without dogma the world invades the Church or lays it waste. The disaster is due to the fact that dogma . . . has itself been deified. When dogma has ceased to be a witness pointing to something behind and above itself, then it is fossilized into a concrete ' word ' or fetish. Or, if we say that the ethical meaning of the word of God has been forgotten, we mean the same thing. The Word is no longer a challenge ; it has become an object for consideration, a theory." (*The Mediator*, pp. 595-596.)

This " fossilization " has often taken place, and the meaning of dogma has often been obscured by a neglect of its relation to the Gospel and to worship. Hence there has come—notably in modern liberal Protestantism of the school of Ritschl—a reaction against dogma altogether, and an insistence that Christianity means personal faith in Jesus Christ and moral allegiance to Him, and not assent to metaphysical propositions about Him. This reaction has had salutary results in loosening the rigidities of dogmatism and in recovering the ethical meaning of faith and the figure of Jesus in His human life. Yet this reaction has led easily into the swamping of Christian teaching with subjective and humanistic ideas, and into a presentation of Christ as one who achieves men's values and fosters a man-centred religion rather than one who reveals Truth about God and thus draws men out of themselves in the worship of concrete divine realities. The remedy, both for scholastic fossilization and for the sentimental reaction against it, lies not in a belittling of dogma but in a recovery of its right relation to the Gospel and to the Church's whole structure and worship. In relation to the Gospel, dogma will be seen to spring directly from the fact of Christ crucified and risen : His pre-existence tells of the awful self-emptying of His work for men, and " the Blessed Trinity " means the infinite love which is the ground of the love of Father and Son in the life and death on earth. Used in this right relation, the Creeds bear witness to the Gospel which is before and behind the philosophies of men and to the one historic society, whose *orthodoxy* is not a series of correct propositions about God, but the living out of the Truth through the building up of the one Body of Christ.

If this is the relation between the Creeds and the Gospel, then the fact that human thought progresses and varies enormously is not an argument for abandoning the Creeds, but rather the ground of their existence and their retention. The Gospel can never be expressed adequately in terms of any philosophy or scholasticism ; it must constantly use many modes of human thought and speech, but the Creeds all the while point behind such modes to the Gospel itself. Attempts have often been made to wed Christianity permanently to some system of human thought, and even to call some such system " Christianity." Thus many Eastern Orthodox theologians have spoken as if they believed the thought and language of the Greek Fathers to be permanently valid and indispensable for the Christian faith. Similarly the Roman Church has seemed to ascribe a permanent sanction and sanctity to the philosophy of S. Thomas Aquinas, and it is often maintained that a competent Christian theologian must be a Thomist. Nor is the error very different in the case of the school of thought in the Church of England to-day, which is known as " Modernist." For the thinkers of this school urge that " modern thought " must control Christian theology and its expression, and " modern thought " means but one of a number of conflicting tendencies, namely liberal religious Humanism.[1] The Creeds are thus disliked and the doctrine of the " Two Natures " is held to be obsolete on the ground that such things belong to a scheme of thought which is now superseded.

Now the root error of the English " Modern Churchman " is similar to that of the rigid Greek orthodox or the rigid Thomist. He is taking Creeds and dogma in a scholastic way instead of as a signpost to the Gospel before all scholasticisms, and he is isolating dogma from life and Liturgy. But his real quarrel is not with " ancient thought " but with the Gospel itself. For the characteristic note of " Modernist " theology in England is not its use of Biblical criticism (where it is sometimes a little out of date), nor its attempts to relate Christianity to the fact of Evolution (where notable work has been done by orthodox theologians), nor yet a temper of free inquiry, but its dogmatic assertion of a humanistic axiom, which belittles the theme of sin and redemption. But while the Gospel can use as its handmaid both Platonism and Thomism and modern Humanism, it cannot succumb to the domination of any one of them ; for by thus succumbing the Church limits its authority, mars its universalism and becomes too wedded to the " spirit of this present age " to bear witness to the Gospel which both scandalizes and uses the thought of every age. By a faithless alliance with any partial or limited " rationalism," the Church restricts its widest witness to Truth and to reason as a whole. Hence the Church adheres to the Creeds not with a view to foreclosing thought and inquiry, but because Creeds point away from the

[1] The term " Modernist " is here used solely of the theological position broadly represented by the journal *The Modern Churchman* This position—akin to an extreme liberal Protestantism—must be distinguished from that of the movement in the Roman Church to which the term Modernist was *first* applied. Cf. Vidler, *Modernist Movement in the Roman Church*, pp. 244-247.

dogmatisms of each modern age in its turn to the freedom of the Gospel of God.

The time may yet come when Creeds may be discarded, but it will be a time when the Gospel is so rooted in men's life and worship that words to describe it will be super-fluous. But the meaning of *present* controversy about the Creeds is clear. Behind the issue " Creed or No Creed " there lies not the issue of " modern thought " versus " ancient thought," but the timeless issue of whether Christianity has at its centre the theme of sin and redemption and the work of Christ the Mediator, or whether that theme and that work are to be belittled before a humanistic view of Christ who is called Divine since He is admired as Perfect Man. " In that day," wrote F. D. Maurice, " when the intellect and the will shall be utterly crushed upon the car of the idol which they have set up ; in that day when the poor man shall cry and there shall be no helper ; may God teach his saints to proclaim these words to the sons of men. *He was born of the Virgin, He suffered under Pontius Pilate, He was crucified, dead and buried, and went down into hell. He rose again the third day, He ascended on high, He sitteth at the right hand of God, He shall come to judge the quick and the dead.* May they be enabled to say, This is our God, we have waited for Him." (*The Kingdom of Christ*, II. 13.)

III

The problem of " Creed or No Creed," however, is but a small part of the whole question of the Truth of God. For to this the Church bears witness not only by its recital of Creeds but by its utterance of the Gospel and by its whole life in Christ. The issues of the Truth of God are thus as wide and as varied as are all the issues discussed in Part I of this book ; and it may now be well to ask whither the whole discussion seems to point.

We began with the Bible. The books of the old covenant disclose a Church and a Passion ; Jesus Christ fulfils them both, and in His Passion the Church of the new covenant is born. In the midst of this Church His saving work is known through a new access of men to God. This access is in one Spirit and in one Body, and the outward order of the Church points to the events whence this access has come and to the universal life wherein it is made complete. The Faith of the Bible therefore leads straight to the Catholic Church, but this gets its meaning only from the Gospel of God. Thus the general trend of our earlier chapters is corroborated by the specific study of the phrase ἡ ἀλήθεια τοῦ θεοῦ.

Thus interpreted, Catholicism is not a burden upon the mind of the thoughtful Christian but rather the means whereby he can be free. For it frees him from partial rationalisms, such as have identified Christianity with the Bible or with some scholastic system or with some humanistic shibboleth ; and it delivers him into an orthodoxy which no individual and no group can possess, since it belongs only to the building up of the one Body in love. As he receives the Catholic sacrament and recites the Catholic creed, the Christian is learning that no single movement nor partial experience within Christendom can claim his final obedience, and that a local Church can claim his loyalty only by leading him beyond itself to the universal family which it represents. Hence the Catholic order is not a hierarchical tyranny, but the means of deliverance into the Gospel of God and the timeless Church.

So far, therefore, from foreclosing the activities of the human mind the Catholicism of the Gospel bids men to think as freely and as fearlessly as they can, and by saving them from rationalisms it enables them to use their reason to the full. For " all things were made by Him," and all honest endeavour in science, in philosophy, in art, in history, manifests the Spirit of God. But the key to these mysteries of nature and of man is the Word-made-flesh. Hither alone the Church shall point ; and here men shall know the Truth, and the Truth shall make them free.

PART II

CHAPTER X

The Church of the Fathers

BECAUSE the Catholic doctrine of the Church is rooted in the Gospel of Christ crucified and risen, the history of the Church can never be rightly described in ordinary human terms as the " progress of Christianity." For the Church does not perform its task by an even and discernible process of expansion. The wheat and the tares grow together ; the mystery of iniquity is apparent until the City of God finally descends from heaven.

The bewildering spectacle presented by the history of the Church is intelligible in the light of the New Testament facts upon which the Church is based. Its holiness does not mean the holiness of a sect of men and women conscious of their perfection, but the holiness of a Spirit and a family wherein sinners are trained and from which they may not be excluded unless they renounce the Spirit. Its unity is a unity of race, which can persist beneath all the scandals of outward division. By such scandals both holiness and unity have often seemed entirely hidden. But this disturbing situation is a part of the Passion of Christ, and within it there is the power of God who redeems and who summons the members of the Church to regard its tragedies not in terms of their own pain and loss nor in terms of what the world thinks, but in terms of Christ's death, found in those who " make up what is left behind of the sufferings of Christ for his body's sake which is the church." (Col. I[24].) Here is discerned by faith the Resurrection from the dead, the lives of the saints, and the working of God's sovereign purpose in the history of His people.

In the chapters which follow some attempt will be made
to inquire into one aspect of Christian history. Starting
from the New Testament, where the doctrine of the one
Body and the Gospel of the Cross are inseparable themes,
we shall examine some phases of Christian life and teaching
from the point of view of these two themes. It will be
asked in these chapters, How far has Catholicism borne
witness to the true doctrine of σῶμα Χριστοῦ? When it
has failed has the failure been due to a neglect of the
Gospel of the Cross? How far has Reformed Christianity
borne witness to the Gospel which was its initial impulse?
When it has failed, has the failure been due to a neglect of
the historical doctrine of the Church? The twofold test
supplied by the New Testament may provide a key to the
interpretation of Church history, and to the problems of
reunion or the gathering of the broken fragments of the
one Church of Christ.

.   .   .   .

The first part of this book described how the Gospel of
God created the structure of the one Body whose outward
marks of Scripture, Creeds, Sacraments and Episcopate,
by pointing to the universal Church, bear witness to the
Gospel. The study of the New Testament thus leads on, in
one inescapable movement, to the study of the Patristic
Church. But the importance of the age of the Fathers must
not be misunderstood. It is important, not as a golden
age nor as a model for the imitation of Christians (as the
Tractarians somewhat extravagantly claimed), but as an
age when the whole Gospel found expression in the life and
Liturgy of the one Body, with a balanced use of all the
Church's structure and with a depth and breadth and unity
which contrast strikingly with every subsequent epoch.
In these early centuries the Syrian, the Greek and the
Roman were in one fellowship, with a Eucharistic worship
exhibiting something like a balance of all the elements of
thanksgiving, commemoration, fellowship, sacrifice, mystery.
The Church was world-renouncing, first with its martyrs

and later with its hermits, and also world-redeeming, with its baptism of Greek culture and humanism into the Faith. Amid all these varieties of type and of temper the Body was one ; and the doctrine of the mystical Body retained its inner depth and breadth since the doctrine of redemption still controlled it.[1]

The close relation between the doctrines of the Body and of redemption is apparent in all the important teaching about the Church from S. Paul to S. Augustine. But at an early date there appear differences of emphasis between the East and the West.

The Greek Fathers

There is little variety in the teaching of the Eastern theologians about the mystical Body. They thought and wrote mainly of its place in God's purpose of uniting mankind in Christ, and more of its inner relation to the Incarnation than of its outward order and the practical problems concerning it.

The teaching of the New Testament is echoed in *S. Ignatius* of Antioch. He sees in the Church the continuation of the union between spirit and flesh, between the invisible and the visible, which Christ has begun. He dwells on this dual nature of the Church as expressing the life of the risen Christ.[2] " Thou art fleshly and spiritual," he says to Bishop Polycarp (*ad Polyc.* 2). Further, the Church shares in the Passion. The Christians are " branches of the Cross " (*Eph.* 19, *Philad.* 8), and separation from the Church is separation from the Passion (*Philad.* 3). Unity is thus based upon Jesus in the flesh and the sharing of the Christians in His life and death. Hence, as we saw in Chapter VI, S. Ignatius' insistence upon Episcopacy

---

[1] A full account of the history of this doctrine will be found in Mersch, *Le Corps Mystique du Christ* (Louvain, 1933). Vol. I deals with the New Testament and the Greek Fathers ; Vol. II with the Latin Fathers, the Middle Ages and the Post-Reformation period.

[2] *Smyrn.* 1, *Eph.* 10, *Magn.* 1, *Trall.* 11.

springs from no new theological position but from his sense of the historical and apostolic meaning of the Church in relation to Jesus in the flesh.

Henceforth Greek theology gives its fullest expositions of the Church in the course of its expositions of Christ's work as Redeemer. Very often the Church is dealt with not as a subject in itself, but as an inevitable part of teaching about Christ as the Second Adam and the head of a new humanity. S. Paul's teaching about the " summing up " of the race in Christ is developed and elaborated by *S. Irenaeus*. His main concern is with the Biblical and Christian revelation of God, and in expounding this revelation he shows the importance of the Church as the new humanity in Christ. To refute the Gnostic attempts to separate the God of creation from the God of redemption in a dangerous dualism, S. Irenaeus appeals to Scripture and his teaching is scriptural through and through. The God who redeemed men through Christ is the God of the Old Testament, the creator, who sums up the whole process of creation and history in Christ the Second Adam, in whom is the ἀνακεφαλάιωσις or " recapitulation " of mankind :—

" There is one God the Father, and one Jesus Christ our Lord, who cometh by a universal dispensation and sums up all things unto Himself. Man is in every respect the formation of God, and, therefore, He recapitulates man into Himself, the invisible becoming visible, the incomprehensible becoming comprehensible, the one superior to suffering becoming subject to suffering, and the Word becoming man. Thus He summeth up all things in Himself, that, as the Word of God is supreme in heavenly and spiritual and invisible matters, He may also have the dominion in things visible and material ; and that, by taking to Himself the pre-eminence and constituting Himself Head of the Church, He may draw all things in due course unto Himself." (*Adv. Haer.* III, xvi. 6.)

Spread abroad in the world the Church teaches the same things which the Apostles taught ; and the scriptures and the Episcopate are her links with the primitive truth.

S. Irenaeus emphasizes these outward things since he is concerned with the one historical revelation wherein the true doctrine of God is seen. Thus his emphasis upon Church order springs from his insight into the Christian view of God. The full exposition of God in Christ includes the Church as part of the fact of Christ.

It was left for the later Greek Fathers to work out more fully the doctrines of which S. Irenaeus gave a grand and inspiring outline. The Arian controversy provoked deep reflection about the Church as the redeemed humanity. *S. Athanasius*, in defending the Christian redemption, described the place of the Christians as themselves the humanity of Christ, a truth which is—he urged—impossible but for the underlying fact of His divinity. Had the Arians, he argued, perceived the meaning of churchmanship, they would not have stumbled about the Incarnation.

"The Son of God became man, so that the sons of men . . . might become sons of God." (*De Incarnatione*, 54.)

"Men, now made incorruptible, will be for ever the temples of the Word. If the enemies of Christ had realized this, if they had grasped the point about the Church as the anchor of faith, they would not have made shipwreck concerning the faith." (*Orationes Contra Arianos*, III, 58.)

The unity between Christ and His people is drawn out specially in the discussion of certain passages of scripture, which the Arians used to prove that Christ was a creature, but which S. Athanasius uses to show that the Christians are exalted in Christ. Thus on Phil. 2⁹, "wherefore also God highly exalted him, and gave unto him the name that is above every name," he writes

"God exalted Him, not so as to make Him higher—for He is the most-High, but to sanctify us in Him. For thus we have our entry into heaven, He opens its gates to us, and those who behold us say, Open your doors ; lift up your heads, eternal gates, and the King of glory shall come in." (*Orationes Contra Arianos*, I, 41.)

Similarly on Acts 2³⁶, " God hath made him both Lord and Christ, this Jesus whom ye crucified," he writes

" It is not of the divinity of Jesus that Peter asserts that God has made him Lord and Christ, but of his humanity which is the whole Church." (*Ibid.*, II, 12.)

These are typical of many passages where, while refuting Arianism, S. Athanasius quite incidentally shows the depth of his belief that the Church is verily the humanity of God Incarnate.

S. Hilary lived in Gaul and wrote in Latin. None the less, he may be classed with the Greek Fathers owing to his closeness to S. Athanasius, and his kinship with Greek theological thought. Mersch, indeed, maintains that S. Hilary's teaching on the mystical Body dates from his sojourn in Asia Minor.¹ His teaching is very similar to that of S. Athanasius, but it is marked by a more thorough-going " realism," and both in the Middle Ages and at the Reformation his view of the Church was criticized as bordering upon pantheism. He links together the flesh of Christ Incarnate and the actual bodies of the Christians, and maintains that the mystical Body is continuous with the body of flesh worn by the Son of God upon earth. He uses the word " Assumptio " (whose later associations are with the Blessed Virgin) of the raising of all Christian people to heaven in Christ. And he refers to the seventeenth chapter of S. John to refute the idea that unity amongst Christians is one of feeling and desire, and not one of essence.

" What do you mean when you speak of unanimity, of a unity of soul and heart, reached through agreement of will ? If the Saviour had thought of making us one only in this sense, He would have prayed like this : Father, just as we wish the same thing, so may they also wish the same thing so that, by their agreement, we may all be one." (*De Trinitate*, VIII, 11.)

¹ *Le Corps Mystique du Christ*, Vol. I, pp. 340-346.

Unity is not a state of feeling or desire, but a fact, even as membership in a family or in a race is a fact.

Beyond this point the thought of the Greek Fathers about the Church did not move very far. But two more names must be mentioned. *S. Cyril of Alexandria* thought out and described fully the manner in which the Divine Word, taking to Himself humanity at the Incarnation, enables the sons of men to share in the humanity of Christ, who is μία φύσις τοῦ λόγου σεσαρκωμένη. " All mankind is in Christ, since Christ is man." (*In* 1 *Joh.* 5².) And *S. Chrysostom* especially described the implications of the doctrine for worship and for social life. The taking of manhood by the Son of God involves the Christian at once in the duties of care and reverence for all the brethren and for the poor in whom the image of Christ is seen. This practical teaching is rooted in the Eucharist ; and of all Eastern writers S. Chrysostom is nearest to S. Augustine in his insistence upon the unity between the Eucharistic Body and the Body the Church. Christian worship, he teaches, both lifts men to heaven and points them to earth in loving contact with their fellow men.

" When thou seest the Lord sacrificed and lying as an oblation, and the priest standing by the sacrifice and praying, and all things reddened with that precious blood, dost thou think that thou art still among men, and still standing on earth ? Nay, thou art straightway translated to heaven, so as to cast every carnal thought out of thy soul, and with unimpeded soul and clean mind to behold the things that are in heaven ? " (*De Sacerdotio,* III, 4.)

But the worship which lifts to heaven is mindful of duty upon earth. There are two altars, the one made of stone, the other made of human persons whom the Christians must love.

" This other altar is composed of the very members of Christ, and the very body of the Lord is made thine altar. . . . The one altar is a stone by nature, but becometh holy since it receiveth Christ's body ; but this other altar is holy

L

because it is itself Christ's body. . . . Thou honourest the
one altar because it receiveth Christ's body ; but him that is
himself the body of Christ thou treatest with contumely,
and when he is perishing thou neglectest him. This altar
thou mayest see everywhere lying, both in lanes and in
market-places, and mayest sacrifice upon it every hour. . . .
When thou seest a poor brother, reflect that thou beholdest
an altar." (1 Cor. 9¹⁰ ; *Hom.* XX.)

Indeed, as Mersch says, " John Chrysostom is worthy
to follow Ignatius, Irenaeus, Athanasius, and Hilary.
They fought for the doctrine, he fought for its moral
implications."

These quotations from the Greek Fathers are typical
enough and illustrative enough to show the characteristic
ethos of Greek Catholicism—its conservatism, as these
writers dwell upon the inner meaning of the Pauline teaching
about the Second Adam, the Body, the Fulness, the One
New Man ; its mysticism, as they dwell upon the " divini-
zation " of men by the Son of God and tend towards an
identification of Christ with His people,—a tendency kept
free from danger by the sense of redemption, of ethical
values, and of the difference between creature and Creator,
saved and Saviour. That Greek Catholicism had its dangers
is undeniable, but it bears striking witness to certain
elements of Christianity which are less apparent in Latin
and in modern church-life and doctrine.

Firstly, it is noteworthy that the Greek Fathers gave their
deepest teaching about the Church without treating the
Church as a separate subject in itself. They did not
expound the Church ; they expound Christ the Redeemer,
and in such a way that the Church is included in their
exposition. And indeed the glory of the Church is most
apparent not when it is buttressed and defended as an
institution but when, without any particular " Church-
consciousness," it is seen as the spontaneous glory of the
Christ. καὶ ἐθεασάμεθα τὴν δόξαν αὐτοῦ.

Secondly, the Greek phrase σῶμα Χριστοῦ in itself speaks

a truth which every translation tends to obscure. The Church is not a " corpus " in the sense of a corporation or institution, somewhat external to its members. It is an organism whose members are one with Christ who is its essence. With this truth enshrined in their language and with a certain avoidance of Western legalism, the Greeks were able to keep their thought about the one Body more free from the " externalizing " and " institutionalizing " tendency. Hence the Easterns have insisted that the word " Catholic " describes not only external universality, reaching to every race and land, but also internal whole-ness, whereby every member has his share in τὸ καθ' ὅλου.[1] Church life and the life of the soul are identical.

Thirdly—and this springs from the previous facts—the cultus of the saints in the East is practised as a part of the life of the one Body. It does not mean the elevation of marked individuals to special places of influence and intercessory power, enthroned betwixt God and man. It means rather the giving glory to Christ in His one Body, whose family life (in the seen and in the unseen) is a manifestation of Christ's own life. Hence, in the East, there has never been the rigid distinction, apparent in the West, between " praying to " and " praying for " the saints and the departed; the sense of the one family prevents such rigid conceptions and binds saints and sinners in one ; for the sainthood belongs only to the one Body which is Holy. In reverencing a saint the people reverence the life of Christ who is the life of them all. Hence also the Eastern cultus of the Virgin Mary, the Mother of God, has meant the veneration not of an isolated figure enthroned in heaven but of one who is humanity indwelt by God, herself the first-fruits of the Church, in whom is focused uniquely in history the truth about the whole Body of Christ. In the liturgy of S. Basil the priest prays :—

[1] Cf. Cyril of Jerusalem, *Catech.* xviii. 23, and see G. Florovsky in *The Church of God* (S.P.C.K.), pp. 56-58.

" And all us, who partake of the one bread and the one cup, do Thou unite one to another in the communion of one Holy Spirit : and grant that no one of us may partake of that holy body and blood of thy Christ unto judgment or unto condemnation ; but that we may find mercy and grace, together with all the Saints, who, in all ages, have been acceptable unto Thee. . . . . For the repose and remission of sins of thy servants (n.n.) ; give them rest, O God, in a place of brightness, whence sorrow and sighing have fled away.   And give them rest where the light of thy countenance shall visit them ; especially our most holy, all-undefiled, most blessed and glorious Lady, the birth-giver of God and ever-Virgin-Mary.

" And S. John, the Prophet, Forerunner and Baptist ; the holy, glorious and all-laudable Apostles, Saint N. (the saint of the day), whose memory we commemorate ; and all thy Saints ; through whose prayers visit thou us, O God.   And call to remembrance all those who have fallen asleep before us in the hope of Resurrection unto life eternal.   And give them rest where the light of thy countenance shall visit them."

Fourthly, the ideas of truth and authority in the East have been more free from the legalistic and scholastic tendencies apparent in the West.   Truth, tradition reside in the Body as a whole ; they are not something cleric-ally imposed upon the Body.   Hence truth is very close to life and worship.   Both in Russian and in Slavonic the phrase ἡ ὀρθοδόξια is translated so as to mean not right " opinion " but right " glory " or " worship."   Hence, while the danger of intellectual stagnation and of super-stition is ever present, doctrine is always related to the Body's whole life.   The singing of the Creed in the Liturgy is introduced by the words,

" let us love one another, that with one accord we may confess. . . ."

Indeed the deepest initiation into Eastern Orthodoxy comes not from the texts of the Fathers but from sharing in the Liturgy.   For there the worshipper will find what the textbook can never make articulate, the sense (as prominent in the East as that of the Crucifixion is prominent in the West) of the triumph of Christ who has risen from the dead, and has shattered the gates of Hell, of the Resurrection as the present fact about the Christians who are His Body, of the heavenly host whose praises are shared by the family on earth.

The Western Fathers

While the Greek Fathers dwelt upon the Church's inner relation with the Incarnation, the Latin Fathers were more concerned with thinking out its relation with the men and women from whom it was composed, and with tackling the practical problems of grace and freedom, of sin and guilt, and of Church order. At an early date a legalistic temper is apparent in Latin theology; the Latin mind naturally inclined towards this temper; the great influence of Tertullian accentuated it, and the particular problems faced by the Western Church gave scope for its exercise. The brunt of the conflict caused by the first schisms was borne by the Western Church. Both Novatianism and Donatism were schismatic movements expressing an extreme Puritanical tendency, and insisting that those who had once apostatized under persecution could not be readmitted to Christian fellowship. Both movements claimed to be themselves alone the true Church. And in face of problems such as these, the Western theologians, instead of resting in the contemplation of the Church's inner mystery, were compelled to tackle the question, who are in the Church, and who are not? The dominant ideas about the Church and their application to the practical problems are seen in S. Cyprian and S. Augustine in rather different ways.

In S. Cyprian the place of the Episcopate as an organ of unity, unfolded first in S. Ignatius and S. Irenaeus, finds full and systematic exposition. The Church's unity is unbreakable ; its oneness is of the charity of God, and only in this oneness can the charity of God be known and lived. Hence separation from the Church means separation from God. The Novatianist schismatic is cut off from the Church and from charity and needs re-baptism if he seeks to return to the fold, and re-ordination if he has received Novatianist orders. The mark and the bond of the Church's unity is the Episcopate, an organ in which each Bishop equally shares (" Episcopatus unus est, cuius a singulis in solidum pars tenetur." *De Unitate*, 5), and by which the Body is joined in one (" Ecclesia quae Catholica una est scissa non sit neque divisa, sed sit utique conexa et cohaerentium sibi invicem sacerdotum glutino copulata." *Epistles*, 6, 8.) All Bishops, in S. Cyprian's view, are equal. The commission to S. Peter in Matt. 16 means that the Church was built first " on one man " as a lesson about its unity, but Christ gave " equal power " to all the Apostles (John 20[22]) who share with S. Peter in the one apostleship. The Bishops as a united college succeed the Apostles as the organ of unity, and they exist (*a*) to pray for the flock as priests united to Christ the High Priest, and (*b*) to rule and guide and protect it. But the Bishops are never isolated ; they are organs of the Body wherein the rights and duties of presbyters and people (who chose the Bishops) are emphasized again and again.

" He who holds not this unity of the Church, does he think he holds the faith ? He who strives against and resists the Church, is he assured that he is in the Church ? For the blessed Apostle Paul teaches this same thing, and manifests the sacrament of unity, thus speaking : *There is one body, and one spirit, even as ye are called in one hope of your calling, One Lord, One Faith, one Baptism, one God.* This unity firmly we should hold and maintain, especially we Bishops, presiding in the Church, in order that we may approve the Episcopate itself to be one and undivided. . . . The Episcopate is one ; it is a whole in which each enjoys full possession. The Church is likewise one, though she be spread abroad, and multiplies with the increase of her progeny ; even as the sun has many rays, yet one light ; and the tree many boughs, yet one root ; and as when many streams flow down from one source, though a multiplicity of waters seem to be diffused from the bountifulness of the overflowing abundance, unity is preserved in the source itself. . . . She it is who keeps us for God, and appoints unto the Kingdom the sons whom she has borne. Whosoever parts company from the Church, and joins himself to an adulteress, is estranged from the promises of the Church. He who leaves the Church of Christ, attains not to Christ's reward. He is an alien and outcast and enemy. He can no longer have God for a Father, who has not the Church for a mother." (*De Unitate*, 4 and 5.)

A certain rigidity is apparent here. Novatianist baptisms and orders are invalid, says S. Cyprian. The contemporary Church in Rome would not follow S. Cyprian in this attitude, and the less rigid view in the end prevailed as regards baptisms and orders. How, then, are we to estimate S. Cyprian's own view ? (1) It springs at bottom not from legalism, but from a sense of the Church as the indivisible home of love. The Church *cannot* be divided ; there can be but one Church, inward and outward, and the only sacraments are those which are acts of this one Church. This sense that a divided Church is a monstrous impossibility is indeed the needful basis of all Christian thinking about the Church. (2) While the Episcopate is essential, along with the scriptures and sacraments, to the Church's one and complete life, it may be asked whether it is legitimate to treat the Episcopate as *in itself* the ground and the test of Church unity. There is in Cyprian an attempt to base unity upon Episcopacy as the one and outstanding bond. But Episcopacy cannot bear alone the whole weight of the tensions of controversy ; and the pure Cyprianic theory seems to break when S. Cyprian himself is found in an *impasse* with his brother Bishop Stephen of Rome. (3) While S. Cyprian's denial of the baptism and the orders of schismatics was rejected later in favour of S. Augustine's " wider " view, it was linked with a deeply Catholic sense of the Church which the later view may often miss. To

S. Cyprian validity of orders depended upon their derivation from and their exercise within the one life of the whole Church. The first fact must be the Church's corporate family life ; then come valid orders which are an organ of that whole life. The later view was " broader " ; it recognized the orders of the schismatics, but it opened the way towards the view that valid orders come first, perhaps even as an isolated channel of grace, and that Church life depends solely upon them. A return to the Cyprianic view would enable clearer and more Catholic thinking about the meaning of a valid ministry in a reunited Church.

S. Augustine was confronted with the menace of the Donatist schism, and he faced it with teaching handed down from S. Cyprian, which he now modified and expanded in certain ways. His doctrine of the Church left a deep impact upon the whole subsequent history of the Church, and indeed upon the history of European politics. . It is a teaching as complex as is any part of his many-sided life and character as Bishop, doctor and mystic. Here an attempt will be made to draw out only the main lines of his thinking, and his influence ; and the subject falls into three main parts—(a) his teaching in reaction to Donatism, (b) his teaching which reveals the tension between his otherworldly and his this-worldly views of the Church, and (c) his teaching which has no special controversial interest, but which reproduces with astounding insight and energy of phrase the general Christian belief about the Church.[1]

(a) The Donatist schism in Africa was as vexing a problem as any Bishop can have had to face. It had existed since Constantine's day and was disturbing the

[1] For these three parts of S. Augustine's teaching, cf. (a) Sparrow-Simpson, *S. Augustine and African Church Divisions* ; C. H. Turner, ch. on " Apostolic Succession " in *Essays in the Early History of the Church and the Ministry ;* and a convenient summary in Headlam, *Doctrine of the Church and Reunion*, Ch. IV. (b) The *De Civitate Dei ;* Figgis, *Political Aspects of S. Augustine's City of God ;* Robertson, *Regnum Dei*, Ch. V. (c) Commentaries on the Psalms and on S. John ; Mersch, *Le Corps Mystique du Christ*, Vol. II, pp. 80-131.

peace of many cities by its propaganda and its violence. S. Augustine met the Donatists' insistence upon their own identity with the one pure Church by developing the lines of thought which had already appeared in S. Cyprian. (1) He first appealed to the existence of the one visible Church as the home of charity :—

" The Christian charity can be guarded only in the unity of the Church." (*Contra Litteras Petiliani*, II, 172.)

" He does not possess the charity of God who does not love the unity of the Church." (*De Baptismo*, III, 21.)

In contrast to the charity of the one Church there is the contentiousness of the Donatists, who miss the charity of the whole Body :—

" I do not know who has placed the limits of charity in Africa." [1]

This was the ground of S. Augustine's thought, though his witness to it was marred by his willingness, at one period, to persecute. In 396 he had pleaded for toleration (*Ep.* 34, 93) ; by 401 he was advocating force against the heretics. (*Contra Litteras Petiliani*, II. 431 ; *Ep.* 86.) (2) He next made what was in effect an appeal to the size of the Catholic Church. The witness of the one institution in every part of the world suffices to confound the claims of the sectaries. In one pregnant phrase he voiced his belief—" *securus judicat orbis terrarum* " :—

" Ask, O ye Donatists, if ye know it not, ask how many stopping-places there were in the Apostle's journeys from Jerusalem round about unto Illyricum. Add up the number of the churches, and tell me how they have perished through our African strife. Corinth, Ephesus, Philippi, Thessalonica, Colossae—you have only the letters of the Apostle to read which he addressed to them. We read the letters, we preserve the faith, we are in communion with the churches." (*Epist. ad Catholicos*, XII. 31.)

[1] Cf. *In Psalm* 22[26], Exposition II.

The underlying conviction of S. Augustine was that truth and charity exist only in the one Catholic Body. The sacraments belonged to that Body. Yet God was the author and the agent in them, hence baptism into the Name was real baptism wherever performed. And in his longing for peace S. Augustine abandoned the rigid and Cyprianic view that baptism and orders are invalid outside the Church. By delicately and reverently challenging the authority of the greatest African doctor then known he insisted that baptism and ordination are valid wherever carried out. Their full effect could only be realized by restoration into the one Church; none the less the rites were real rites, God being their agent, and neither re-baptism nor reordination was necessary. Amid all the variety of thought and statement, which makes single quotations from the anti-Donatist letters so meaningless, this practical policy emerges as S. Augustine's own contribution. He urged the laxer view, and the laxer view prevailed.

But if this new view was " broader," it contained the seeds of much perversity in later history. For while the Cyprianic view makes orders utterly dependent upon the Church and validity a part of the Church's single life in grace, the Augustinian view leaves room for thinking of orders as valid apart from the Church's corporate life and for the idea of succession by orders as a single and isolated channel of grace. S. Augustine has " broadened " Church theory; but he has opened the way for a line of thought which glories in the name of Catholic but which severs the doctrine of orders from the doctrine of the Body of Christ.

(b) From the existing traditions of the Latin Church S. Augustine inherited the sense of the visible Church as an institution expressing divine rule upon earth and the tendency, congenial to the Latin mind, to equate the Church with the Kingdom of God itself. Yet another and very different tendency was also present in his mind. Partly through his neo-Platonism, and partly through his doctrine of predestination, he thought of the Church as an invisible Body, the company of the elect, a reality of which the Church's visible order can be only a faint copy. The two conceptions cross one another in his writings. (i) As the practical statesman and Bishop, anxious to guide his fellow Christians in their distress and in the crises of world upheaval through which they were passing (Rome was sacked by the Goths in 410), he wrote of the City of God, within whose earthly structure and order upon earth men shall find solace and security while the ancient political order is shaken so as never to survive. The *De Civitate Dei* certainly gives the impression that the Kingdom of God is identified with the Church on earth. (ii) Yet the other conception appears in the same work. For the *De Civitate* was written during the years when the predestinationist idea was gripping Augustine's mind more and more, and as the argument proceeds the reader is not allowed to forget that the visible Church is but a fragment of a Kingdom which includes the departed and the angels and the elect who are yet unborn, the *ecclesia qualis tunc erit* contrasted with the *ecclesia qualis nunc est*. And while there are passages in which the Kingdom of Christ and the Church are identified, it is important to notice that both " Kingdom " and " Church " are used in two senses, and in the crucial passage (XX, 9, 10) the variety of usage is clearly present.[1] The earthly city is a shadow of the " superna sancta civitas."

[1] " When the devil is bound, the saints reign with Christ during the same thousand years, understood in the same way, that is, of the time of His first coming. For, leaving out of account that Kingdom concerning which He shall say in the end, ' Come, ye blessed of my Father ' . . . the Church could not now be called His Kingdom, or the Kingdom of heaven, unless His saints to whom He says, ' lo, I am with you always ' were even now reigning with him, though in another and far different way. . . . Accordingly, the Kingdom of heaven is to be taken in two senses. In one sense it contains both him who hears what He (Christ) teaches, and him who keeps it— the one is least and the other great (in the Kingdom). In the other sense there is the Kingdom of heaven into which he only enters who

But even if—as many scholars claim—the identification of the Kingdom and the visible Church is made, there is nowhere an identification of the Kingdom with the visible Church's temporal and political power. S. Augustine says that from the earliest days the Church manifested God's Kingdom, which means that it manifested it *under persecution and humiliation.* This was an important safeguard. But, neglecting this safeguard and neglecting also the transcendental element in S. Augustine's thought of the Church, some of his successors in the West developed the doctrine of an ecclesiastical theocracy as the visible Kingdom of God. This doctrine arose through men following one side of his teaching, and almost ignoring the other. And it fell to the Reformers, reacting against the misuse of his ecclesiastical teaching, to revive in extreme forms his doctrines of grace and predestination.

(c) Apart, however, from all controversial issues, there stands the teaching of S. Augustine about the inner mystery of the Church as Corpus Christi. The Pauline and Johannine sense of the Church had eaten its way into his soul. His teaching here is saturated in scripture, and three parts of scripture especially inspire his thinking —the text "Saul, Saul, why persecutest thou me?", the seventeenth chapter of S. John, and the Psalter. The "Saul, Saul" passage he quotes again and again to show that Saul is converted to no solitary Christ but to a Christ who suffers with His people. The seventeenth chapter of S. John is the basis of S. Augustine's oft-repeated phrase,

keeps the commandments. The Kingdom which contains both is the Church as it now is. The other is the Church as it shall be, when no wicked man shall be in it. Therefore the Church even now is the Kingdom of Christ, and the Kingdom of heaven. Accordingly His saints even now reign with Him, yet not indeed in the same way as they will reign then. The tares do not reign with Him, although they grow in the Church along with the wheat. For those reign with Him . . . whose conversation is in heaven. They reign with Him who are so in His Kingdom that they themselves are His Kingdom " (XX, 9). For a full discussion of the passage, cf. Newton Flew, *Idea of Perfection*, pp. 201 ff.

" quia et ipsi sunt ego." And the Psalter is interpreted as the voice of Christ Himself, identified with the sins and sorrows and prayers of His Church. On the passage " O my God, I cry unto thee in the daytime, and thou answerest me not " (Psalm 22³) S. Augustine comments :—

" Truly He says this of me, of thee, of this man too. He bears his Body which is the Church. Perhaps you will not believe, my brothers, that when he says ' My father, if it be possible let this cup pass from me ' the Saviour is afraid of death ? . . . And Paul, too, desires death so as to be with Christ. What then, the apostle desired death so as to be with Christ, and Christ Himself feared death ? What does this mean except that He bore in himself our weakness, and that for those who still fear death and are a part of his body He said these things ? See now, whence came this cry. It was the cry of the members, not of the head." (*In Psalm* 21.)[1]

The Psalter is the utterance of the life and pain of the whole Church since it is the utterance of Christ to whom belong both the Old Testament and the New :—

" He prays for us, as our priest ; He prays in us, as our head ; He is prayed to by us, as our God. Let us recognize then our words in Him, and His words in us." (*In Psalm* 37.)

His meditations on scripture led S. Augustine to revel in the language of actual identification. These phrases recur, as descriptions of the Church, " universus Christus, caput et corpus," " Christus totus plenusque," " totus filius, caput et corpus," " plenitudo Christi, caput et membra," " nos sumus Christus." In the Church the Passion of Jesus is a present fact :—

" Jesus Christ is but one Man, who has head and body ; the Saviour of the body and the members of the body are

[1] Cf. " Vocem de cruce dixit non suam sed nostram " (Mk. 15⁴²), *in Psalm* 43. S. Augustine's comments on the Psalms of the Passion are of striking interest, since in them he sees not only the Church's mystical life but the Donatist problem also in close relation to the sufferings of Christ. Cf. especially the expositions of Psalms 22 and 40 (21 and 39 in Latin editions).

both in one single flesh, and one single voice, and one single passion, and—when sin shall pass away—one single rest."
—(*In Psalm* 61.)

The meaning of Corpus Christi in the Eucharist was mentioned in a previous chapter ; the haunting words may here be repeated :—

" the mystery of yourselves is laid upon the table of the Lord ; the mystery of yourselves ye receive." (*Sermon* 272.)

And as with S. Paul and S. John, so also with S. Augustine the meaning of unity springs from the oneness of God alone. The love of the Blessed Trinity is the ground of the love which is the Church :—

" Love is of someone who loves, and with love something is loved. So here are three things : he who loves, and that which is loved, and love." (*De Trinitate*, VIII, x. 14.)

" We must not say that His unity places itself beside our multiplicity, but that we, the many, are one in Him who is one." (*In Psalm* 127.)

" In loving the members of Christ thou lovest the Christ, in loving the Christ thou lovest the Son of God, in loving the Son of God thou lovest the Father. Impossible is it then to divide charity." (*ad Parthos*, X.)

From the one God, through the many who are made one in Christ, and thence to the one God again—thus moves the thought both of S. John and of S. Augustine. The people of God share in the mutual love of the Father and the Son,

" et erit unus Christus amans se ipsum."

The depth and the complexity of S. Augustine's teaching make him a figure in history which defies analysis. Indeed, he himself defied the claims of consistency. Into him there flow many of the currents of thought and experience within and without the Church of the Fathers. And from him there have been deduced theories, which, when isolated from his other teaching, have destroyed the balance of

Catholic truth. He stands thus on the brink of the division between Catholicism and its later perversions. Isolate his statements about the validity of orders apart from the life of the Church, and there is the " clericalist " view of Apostolic succession. Isolate his lapse into persecution and his language about the Kingdom of God on earth, and there is a basis for the mediæval Church-theocracy. Isolate his teaching about grace and sin and predestination, and there is the cruder element in the theology of the Reformation. Such is the complexity of S. Augustine, himself a creative chapter in the history of mankind.

S. Augustine thus appears to the historian as the creative religious genius moulding the movement of some of the greatest forces in human life and thought. But he was creative because he had himself been created by Christ in His Church. He became what he became through the Christ who converted him and through the one Body in which he learned and prayed, and, in the Pauline sense, died and lived. In him was focused in full measure the life of the Church of God, in all its rich variety. And the Church of the Fathers had a unity and a life which was one. For all the differences between the East, with its mysticism, its conservatism, its concern with the Church's inner relation to the Incarnation, its liturgical emphasis upon the Resurrection, and the West, with its practical bent, its concern with problems of order, its sense of personal guilt, its tendency towards legalism—it is still true to speak of the one Church of the Fathers. For the balanced doctrine of " unum corpus ", $\dot{\epsilon}\nu$ $\sigma\hat{\omega}\mu\alpha$, is taught, and this doctrine is dominated by the doctrine of redemption. The structure of Scripture, Creed, Episcopate, Sacraments is still intact as one whole ; no element in this structure fails to have its due attention. If the See of Rome is advancing in prestige and beginning to press its claims unduly, the sense of the Episcopate as the organ of unity is still powerful. If the idea of an isolated clerical priesthood is threatening, there is still the teaching of an Augustine and a Chrysostom about the truly Eucharistic meaning of the Corpus Christi or $\sigma\hat{\omega}\mu\alpha$ $X\rho\iota\sigma\tauо\hat{\upsilon}$.

If the dogmatic debates are sometimes tedious, the theme which dominates them is still the redemptive work of Christ. If there is talk of an earthly kingdom which is the Church, there is still the New Testament sense of the " not yet " and of the ecclesia " qualis tunc erit." There is, in other words, a doctrine of the mystical Body with its Pauline and its Johannine features still manifest. The phrase τὸ καθ' ὅλου has a meaning for the centuries between S. Paul and the fall of the Western Empire. The study of the Gospel in the New Testament forces us to study the Church of the Fathers; the Church of the Fathers still shows us Christ crucified and risen, and a Body which is one.

ADDITIONAL NOTE

To the literature on the doctrine of the Church in Cyprian and Augustine must now be added S. L. Greenslade *Schism in the Early Church*.

CHAPTER XI

DEVELOPMENTS IN CATHOLICISM

I

THE history of mediæval Catholicism and of the Reformation is so fraught with controversy that it would be a hopeless task to trace in a short compass the movements of cause and effect. Our task, therefore, is a restricted one—to see the main stages in the story of the doctrine of the Corpus Christi and to ask, in the light of the New Testament, whether and in what ways the Catholic Church has failed to bear witness to the καθ' ὅλου and to the Gospel whereon that Catholicity is based. Our theme is still the inter-relation of the Gospel and the Church.

In the year of S. Augustine's death the Vandals had overrun Africa and the Western Empire was plunged into turmoil. "The mind shudders," S. Jerome had written, "when it dwells upon the ruin of the day. For twenty years or more Roman blood has been flowing ceaselessly on the broad countries between Constantinople and the Julian Alps, where the Goths and the Huns and the Vandals spread ruin and death. How many Roman nobles have been their prey! How many matrons have fallen victims to their lust! Bishops live in prison, priests and clerics fall by the sword, churches are plundered, Christ's altars are turned into feeding troughs, the remains of martyrs are thrown out of their coffins. On every side sorrow, on every side lamentation, everywhere the image of death." (*Epistle* 60.) And this passage well summarizes the mood not only of a passing crisis but of an epoch. "For more than three centuries," wrote Dean Church, " it seems as if the world and human society had been hopelessly wrecked, without prospect or hope of escape."

Yet, out of the dying Latin Empire and the barbarians who were moving into her territories, there was slowly created the new Europe with its nations and its culture and its unity. For the Church was able to conserve much of the form and the spirit of old Rome and to pass it on to the Gothic peoples, so that the sense of the one Empire haunted their mind and gripped their imagination. Thus the period between S. Augustine and Charlemagne, known as the Dark Ages on account of its historical obscurity and its lack of moral enlightenment, is a time when the Church was quietly moulding the life of many peoples and giving them an order and a unity, leavened with Christianity, and supplying almost the only link of continuity in a topsy-turvy world. It is plain from purely secular narratives of the story, such as Dill's *Roman Society in Gaul in the Merovingian Age*, that the Church was a creative and unifying force which preserved such elements of culture from the old world as could blend with the Gothic character so as to forge new nations. In this work of integration in law and culture and religion, the leadership was taken by the Papacy, which used the Frankish kingdom for its political support and the monastic orders as its servants in education and evangelism. If Christianity exists to unite, to stabilize, to mould order and progress, the Dark Ages testify to its power. Perhaps the quieter work of the Church in the Dark Ages was—for all the corruptions within it—of greater Christian significance than the more conspicuous triumphs of the days of Hildebrand or of Innocent III.

Yet the story of the rise and the achievement of Western Catholicism contains within itself elements which pervert its witness to the Body and which bring it near to contradictions of the very meaning of Catholicism.

(1) First of all, the unity and efficiency and spiritual and intellectual fruits of the Western Church were obtained at

the expense of the deeper meaning of Catholicism. The temptation was to secure efficiency by the centralized Papacy at the expense of the Episcopate as an organ of unity. It may well be argued that a primacy of a certain kind is implied from early Church history and is ultimately necessary to Christian unity [1]; but there is all the difference between a primacy which focuses the organic unity of all the parts of the Body, and a primacy which tends to crush the effective working of the other parts. Now the Roman See had in the second century been important on account of its representative character; S. Irenaeus had reverenced it as a See of special authority since its contacts with other Churches and with their traditions made it a trustworthy teacher of the truth.[2] But gradually there came a view of primacy totally different. Partly through an interpretation of Matthew 16[18] which by far the greater number of the Fathers had not accepted, partly through political alliances, partly through the acquisition of temporal power in Italy, partly through Forged Decretals, partly through a sincere spiritual leadership in education, evangelism, and reform, the Papacy grew in such a way that the idea of unity in terms of government took the place of the idea of unity in terms of race, and the Christian conception of sovereignty was crossed by a worldly conception.

The climax was reached in the claims of Pope Hildebrand, to be the universal Pontiff, to have the sole right to depose Bishops, to call General Councils, and to depose the Emperor. As regards the idea of sovereignty, this final Papal claim involved the Church in a dilemma. Either it means a supremacy inherently destructive of the sovereignty of kings and rulers, or else it means that their sovereignty has over against it the Church as a rival State, politically

---

[1] See the Appendix.

[2] " For to this Church the rest of the Churches—that is, believers from all quarters—cannot help coming together, because of its powerful pre-eminence; and in it the tradition which springs from the Apostles has always been preserved by these believers from all quarters." (*Adv. Haer.*, III, iii, 1.)

strong enough to hold the balance of power. In either case the view of Church sovereignty has travelled far both from the New Testament and from S. Augustine's *City of God*. And as regards Catholic structure the result is no less drastic. " The proper development of an institution should keep the utmost freedom and greatest vigour in all its parts. The growth of the mediæval Papacy meant ultimately the destruction of the primitive episcopate, the loss of its controlling power over national life. The Papacy did magnificent service to the world·; it bore witness to unity and it fostered religion. In the Middle Ages it did all this. But, in basing its claim to do it upon its own power alone, it destroyed the freedom, the growth of much that lay beneath its power. Feudalism was to pass into tyranny, and tyranny foreshadowed revolution." [1]

(2) The Church's witness to the καθ' ὅλου was also maimed by the severance of the East from the West. It is more important to realize the meaning of the schism as a state of affairs which came and which lasted, than to trace its many causes and to attach blame to one side or the other. The growing divergence culminated in the formal schism of 1054, a schism of which the pretexts were the rivalry of the Sees of Rome and Constantinople, and the addition of the *filioque* to the Creed in the West, but the causes of which had long existed in the difference between the two types of Christianity—the West practical, legalistic, centred in the Papacy and bent upon enforcing Canon Law upon the whole Church ; the East, mystical, conservative, still regarding the Episcopate as the organ of unity and bent upon the enforcement of its own mystical and liturgical traditions. The schism meant, in large measure, an isolation. The isolation must not be exaggerated, since the mediæval West still fed upon the Greek Fathers through translations. None the less the one Body was severed. The significance of all ministries and sacraments, as organs

[1] Whitney, *Our Place in Christendom*, p. 74.

of a universal family, was maimed. The West, which spoke of " Corpus Christi," needed and lacked the deeper sense of the inner unity of priests and people which the phrase σῶμα Χριστοῦ expressed ; and it missed also the sense that orthodoxy is not only correct doctrine asserted from without but the " glory " and the worship within the whole Body. Behind all subsequent schisms there stands this Great Schism, the parent of them all. A sundered Christendom can unite and integrate and make saints ; it can never make men *whole* in the inner and outer unity of the one Church.

(3) A further factor in the maiming of Western Catholicism was its legalism. This was an inevitable and in many ways a beneficial development. When the Church's attitude of antagonism towards the Roman Empire as the enemy and the persecutor subsided, the Church was faced with the problem of making some synthesis between the doctrine of God's sovereignty within the redeemed society and His sovereignty manifested in the world's culture and political and social order. To meet this problem theologians borrowed from Stoicism the idea of Natural Law, and this conception enabled them to work out a philosophy of history and a doctrine of God, related to creation and to politics as well as to redemption and the Church. The idea of Law so dominated certain parts of Christian thought, that it lasted far into post-Reformation theology, and is nowhere more apparent than in Luther and in Calvin and in Hooker. Its value to the Church is undeniable ; it enabled S. Thomas Aquinas, through the union of the supernatural and the law of nature in one scheme of thought, to work out the profoundest Christian sociology yet known. Hence the mere decrying of " legalism " is futile and unhistorical. Yet legalism treading where it ought not is the abomination of desolation ; and in the West legalism invaded the Church's thought and teaching about our Lord's work as Redeemer, about God's love in redemption, about sin and forgiveness, and the mystical Body the Church. It encroached upon those intensely personal aspects of the Gospel and the

Church's life where the whole idea of law is meaningless. As witnesses to the effects of legalism on theology, two writers of very different interests will suffice, a jurist and a Roman Catholic theologian :—

" Almost anybody," writes Sir Henry Maine, " who has enough knowledge of Roman Law to appreciate the Roman penal system, the Roman theory of the obligations established by contract or delict, the Roman view of debts and of the modes of incurring, extinguishing and transmitting them, the Roman notion of the continuance of individual existence by universal succession, may be trusted to say whence arose the frame of mind to which the problems of Western theology proved so congenial, whence came the phraseology in which these problems were stated, and whence the description of reasoning employed in their solution." [1]

And Fr. Mersch, the historian of the doctrine of the Mystical Body, writes :—

" We must dare to say that, in principle, a legalistic way of understanding the Gospel, on condition that it keeps itself within reasonable limits, is perfectly defensible and that it is also a means of progress. Only, we must also say, it is palpable that between the Christian religion and law the correspondence is far from being complete, and all the verities of our doctrine are not equally susceptible of finding, in law, the kind of exposition which suits them. Our union with Christ in particular, pregnant with charity and piety, differs to the point of contrast from the rigidities with which the codes deal, and the legalistic spirit does not tend to speak of that union with fulness and force." [2]

Thus the legalistic temper is specially fatal to the doctrine of the organic Body, and to the Gospel which that Body mediates. But Latin legalism did not spare these sacred regions of the Church's life. The ministry of reconciliation became legalized. The Confessor, whose true function is to blend the offices of Father, Physician and Judge, and to

---

[1] *Ancient Law*, p. 318 (tenth edition).
[2] *Le Corps Mystique du Christ*, II, 152.

subordinate law to the Gospel, became primarily the Judge, trying cases and assigning penances. Sin came to be measured as a series of quantitative acts rather than as an attitude of the soul. The merits of Jesus and of the saints and of the penitent were treated as quantities which can be added and subtracted. Apart altogether from the system of indulgences and the accompanying abuses, upon which controversialists have dwelt, the normal working of Latin Catholicism has had a legalistic tinge which often obscures the meaning of divine redemption, and of the mystical Body of Christ.

(4) Of legalism one inevitable fruit is a diminished sense of the oneness of the Body, wherein all the members, clerical and lay, share in one single priesthood in Christ. The Church becomes viewed as an institution to which men submit and within whose world-wide structure men say their prayers and live their lives, rather than as a Body which *is* its members themselves. Similarly, Truth becomes viewed as correct beliefs imposed from above by the teaching clergy, rather than something which dwells in the Body and all its members, themselves the shrine of Truth. Karl Adam has contrasted the primitive view of the Church as an organism with the later Latin view of the Church as something " external " :—

" The more one-sidedly Christ is considered, the more attention is concentrated upon His divinity, and the less he is regarded as the first-born among many brethren, and the new head of mankind, so much the more do the great truths of His priesthood and of His mystical Body retire into the background of the devout consciousness. . . . The Christian isolates himself from the Head, and from his fellow-members in the Body of Christ. He has no feeling of union and solidarity with Christ and His members but a consciousness rather of separation and individuality. That unity which S. Paul, Ignatius, Cyprian, and Augustine celebrate over and over again with enthusiasm as the blessed gift of our salvation, that *vinculum pacis, spiritus unitatis, unitas caritatis*, is no longer, or at least in no sufficient measure, a regular constituent of Christian sentiment. And so also the average believer regards the Church from without rather than from within. He sees rather its outward hierarchial structure and imagines that the whole essence of our holy Church is exhausted in the activities of the priestly and pastoral ministry." [1]

This defective sense of the one Body, to which all Christians are liable through their human frailty, was fostered by many of the tendencies of mediæval piety. Eucharistic developments explain much of it. Here the greatest emphasis was placed upon the propitiatory sacrifice of Christ in the Mass (sacrifice being commonly identified with death rather than with the offering of life) and upon the adoration of Christ's presence in the Host. Communion became infrequent, the note of " fellowship " in the Eucharist was hardly recognized in popular piety. The use of Latin in the rite made it difficult for the laity to participate intelligently. And the phrase " Corpus Christi " came to mean the presence to be adored, and a Feast in honour of that presence, rather than the Body of Christ which includes both the Eucharist and the whole Church. The deepest expression of the sacramental piety of the Middle Ages, the " *Imitatio Christi*," reveals a religion of devotion and self-sacrifice inspiring to men of every age, but individualistic through and through. Mediæval prayer and practice have travelled very far from the " one bread, one body " of S. Paul, and from S. Augustine's teaching about the mystery of the Christians placed upon the table of the Lord.

(5) Beneath perversions in the doctrine of the mystical Body there always lie perversions in the Gospel of God. From the beginning of Christianity the two are interdependent, and the corruption of the one means the corruption of the other. The piety of the Middle Ages knew that " if any man sin, we have an advocate with the Father, Jesus Christ the righteous ; and he is the propitiation for our sins " ; it knew that " Christ our Passover is sacrificed for us." It failed, however, to see these truths about pro-

---

[1] *Christ our Brother*, pp. 42-43.

pitiation and sacrifice sufficiently in the context of the loving work of God's own initiative—" God is in Christ reconciling the world unto himself," and " God commendeth his own love towards us, in that while we were yet sinners Christ died for us." Thus the Mass came to be regarded popularly as man's method of propitiating God without due thought of God's own declaration to men of His own sacrifice in which the initiative is His. The Confessional was thought of as the meeting-place of the grace of God and the merits of man, each with its contribution to make, rather than as the place where God's word of forgiveness and judgment eliminates all idea of human merit. The Passion was known as the object for the devotion of Christians and as the impulse to penitence and humility ; it was known too little as the means of God's sovereignty over the world—a sovereignty to which the Church can add nothing but which the Church can share and interpret by accepting the Cross as its own way of power in human life. Beneath the issues concerning the Church there lie the issues concerning the Gospel.

The sense of a deeper Catholicism, wherein the whole Body shares and of which the Episcopate is the organ of unity, never became extinct. The Conciliar Movement strove to revive this ideal, by asserting that authority resides with the whole Church, that the Pope is one who administers under the authority of the whole Church, and that a General Council can make and restrict and depose a Pope. The movement failed, and other efforts at internal reform failed also, because the issue was deeper than reform and administration, and deeper than the doctrine of the Church. The issue was the Gospel of God, whereon the meaning of Catholicity rests ; and instead of peaceful and painless reorganization there came the convulsions of the Reformation which shook the structure of European society. The moment of crisis was the moment when Luther pinned the Ninety-Five Theses to the door of the church at Wittenberg. There men could read not only the criticism of practical abuses, but this assertion :—

" The true treasure of the Church is the Holy Gospel of the glory and grace of God." (*Thesis* 62.)

And they could read also of the storms and stress through which alone a lost Gospel can be recovered :—

" Away then with all those prophets who say to the people of Christ, ' Peace, Peace,' and there is no Peace.

" Blessed be all those prophets who say to the people of Christ, ' The Cross, the Cross,' and there is no Cross.

" Christians should be exhorted to strive to follow Christ their Head through pains, deaths and hells,

" And thus trust to enter heaven through many tribulations, rather than in the security of peace." (*Theses* 92-95.)

This was an obscure saying, " ' The Cross, the Cross,' and there is no Cross." A letter of Luther, written on June 22, 1516, to a prior of the Augustinian order, makes it plain :—

" You are seeking and craving for peace, but in the wrong order. For you are seeking it as the world giveth, not as Christ giveth. Know you not that God is ' wonderful among His saints ' for this reason : that He establishes His peace in the midst of no peace, that is of all temptations and afflictions ? It is said, ' Thou shalt dwell in the midst of thine enemies.' The man who possesses peace is not the man whom no one disturbs—that is the peace of the world ; he is the man whom all men and all things disturb, but who bears all patiently and with joy. You are saying with Israel, ' Peace, Peace,' and there is no peace. Learn to say rather with Christ, ' The Cross, the Cross,' and there is no Cross. For the Cross at once ceases to be the Cross as soon as you have joyfully exclaimed, in the language of the hymn—

> ' Blessed Cross, above all other,
> One and only noble tree.' "

—(*Letters*, De Wette, I, 27.)

Only through a deep disturbance could the recovery of Catholicism take place.

.   .   .   .

The revolt of Luther—symbolized both by the Ninety-Five Theses and by the burning of the " Corpus Juris Canonici " —was a revival of the Gospel of God, and also a revival of many vital elements in the doctrine of the one Body which springs from the Gospel. It meant the recovery of truths about the Church which are central in the teaching of S. Paul and S. Augustine and in the inner meaning of Catholicism.[1] The revolt was soon perverted by negative and individualistic conceptions ; but meanwhile the official Church had lost its chance. It met the revolt with the voice of authority, it failed to see the inner meaning of Luther's demands, and it set about to reform itself along lines of efficiency and deep spirituality, yet with the crisis of the Gospel still unfaced. Hence the counter-Reformation, with its stirring story of piety and heroism and its witness to the supernatural, failed to recover τὸ καθ' ὅλου and the real meaning of the word " Catholic." To read of S. Ignatius Loyola or of S. Philip Neri or of S. Francis de Sales is to be aware that the Roman Church was possessed by a zeal for spiritual and moral reform as great as that of the Protestants of Northern Europe, and by a vocation to prayer and holiness which the Protestants barely understood. Yet some of the uncatholic tendencies of the Middle Ages were continued and even deepened in the revival which was led and organized by the Council of Trent.

(1) The Council of Trent gave order and stability to the new Catholicism. It tackled vigorously some of the worst abuses of Church life ; it rejected the extreme Augustinian doctrines of sin and grace which had gripped the Reformers. But it did nothing to recover the organic conception of the Church and its worship. It tolerated—if it did not actually assert—the view that the priest is an individual with sacrificial powers unrelated to the priestly Body. (Session 23, Canon 1.) And it was ambiguous with regard to the most important issue connected with Church order and Catholicity—the relation between the Bishops and the Pope. After a long struggle between those who insisted

[1] See later, Chapter XII.

on the primitive and Catholic rights of Bishops and those who regarded the Bishops as delegates of the Pope, the Council defined the matter (cf. Session 23, Canon 8) in a way which both sides could claim in their own favour. The path was thus opened for further growth in the Papal power, and the centralizing tendency so took root that it could never be effectively resisted. Gallicanism withstood it in vain, and it reached its climax at the Vatican Council in 1870, where the Pope was decreed supreme and infallible. Döllinger's words are worth quoting :—

" The new Vatican doctrine confers on the Pope the attribute of the whole fulness of power over the whole Church as well as over every individual layman. As every student of history and of the Fathers will admit, the Episcopate of the ancient Church is thus dissolved in its inmost being, and an Apostolic institution to which, according to the judgement of the Church Fathers, the greatest significance in the Church belongs, fades into an insignificant shadow." [1]

The climax of Papal supremacy marks the climax of the distortion of genuine Catholic order. For the unity of the one race there has been substituted the governmental unity of the Roman See with the unchurching of those who do not submit to it. For the authority of the Spirit in the one Body there has been substituted the external authority of the ruler " ex cathedra." The institutional has triumphed over the organic, and the institution represents something narrower than the Body of Christ.

(2) The inner piety of the Counter-Reformation—no less than its outer polity—failed to recover the doctrine of Corpus Christi. It emphasized the soul of the individual rather than the mystical Body, and its spiritual achievements are mainly of an individual type of prayer and sanctity. The Corpus Christi figures little in the piety of the French and Spanish schools. In contrast with the older piety of the Benedictines which centres in the Liturgy where priests and people take their part in a corporate act and are taught

[1] *Declarations and Letters on the Vatican Decrees*, pp. 91-92.

to relate their prayers to that corporate act, the piety
of the Jesuits is mainly concerned with the training of the
individual. The Church is indeed the school where the
training is done, and the institution wherein the soul is
fed and grows ; but the soul's own acts of prayer are not regarded as part of the one liturgical action of Corpus Christi.
And if individualism is thus prominent in the spiritual
teachers of the Counter-Reformation, what of its presence
in popular piety and parochial life ? The meaning of the
Mass as the act of the one Body, with its interwoven elements of sacrifice and communion and fellowship, was often
neither taught nor heard of. The Liturgy sometimes becomes
regarded as the offering of a sacrifice, in which the people
assist not by entering into the various stages of the rite
but by private devotions of their own ; communion becomes
a private act often quite separated from the Liturgy ;
and adoration may be equally private and focused upon
the presence of our Lord in the Blessed Sacrament reserved
in the tabernacle. Now non-communicating attendance,
communion from the tabernacle, extra-liturgical adoration,
—all these may be legitimate developments of proven
efficacy in the training of souls, and all these may find
their place in the Church's whole life and worship.   But
when these become the centre and the norm ; and when
communion, isolated from the corporate worship in the
Liturgy, becomes regarded as " une visite "[1] or as " une
simple nourriture "[1]; and when the true liturgical unity
and centre of worship is *never* made articulate, then it is
hardly an exaggeration to say that the Pauline and
Augustinian sense of " Corpus Christi " is lost from sight.
And it has thus been lost for thousands of devout Christians,
for whom the term " Corpus Christi " means neither the

[1] These two phrases are used by Dom Laporta, *Piété Eucharistique*
(Louvain, 1928), to describe what has often been the popular idea of
communion as a solitary gift of food to the individual soul. He
pleads that the true idea of the Church is only realized when it is
remembered that " cette vie n'est pas seulement une ' vie eucharistique,' elle est aussi une ' vie baptismale ' " (p. 12).

Church the Body, nor the Eucharist as a whole, but one isolated aspect of the latter. Through all these tendencies —both in spiritual teaching and in popular piety—the religion of the Counter-Reformation failed to answer Protestant individualism with an effective witness to the Body of Christ.

II

Is Christ divided ? In all these ways Catholicism has appeared in broken fragments of what it is meant to be. It is severed into at least three main elements, the Latin, the Eastern Orthodox and the Anglican. Its historic Church order is obscured by these divisions ; the place of the Episcopate as the organ of the Church's universal life and the meaning of the sacraments as the acts of the one Body are sometimes hidden from sight. The name " Catholic " is often linked to piety which is individualistic, and to systems which are sectarian and incomplete. A cry is forced from the Christian's lips, " is Christ divided ? "

Yet, if the rent in the robe of Christ has been a part of His Passion, there has been in the midst of it the power whereby saints are made, and whereby civilizations are moulded. Hence the broken history of the Catholic Church is not a mere parody of Catholicism, but a manifestation in flesh and blood of the Way, the Truth, and the Life. Not only in the saints whose names the Church commemorates, but in men and women whose lives have been secret, a love and a humility have been seen whose roots are in heaven. Such men and women, and countless others also, are ever less conscious of what the Church had failed to do than of what the Church has done and is doing within them, and its name spells only thankfulness and praise. The quest of ideal Catholicism must not seem to deny the actual. If the partial character of every presentation of Catholicism in history seems to say " It doth not yet appear what we shall be," the testimony is sure which says " Beloved, *now* are we sons of God."

For the essence of Catholicism all through the ages has consisted not in partial systems—such as Papal government or Greek theology—which have been both its servants and its dividers, but in the unbreakable life to which the sacraments, scriptures, creeds and ministry have never ceased to bear witness. Unity, therefore, exists already, not in what the Christians say or think, but in what God is doing in the one race day by day. And the outward recovery of unity comes not from improvised policies, but from faith in the treasure which is in the Church already.

But recovery is hindered whenever Catholicism is identified with something less than itself, and whenever the definition of it is based upon what is really local, temporary, partial. Hence the opportunity is great for Anglican Catholics—in view of their greater freedom and their contact with many phases of Catholicism—to teach the richest and deepest meaning of the word Catholic and to find the *essence* of Catholicism not in particular systems of government or thought or devotion (Anglican or Latin) but in the organic, corporate idea of the Body in life and worship. They do this not by looking exclusively to developments of modern Romanism and equating them with Catholicism, nor yet by looking to their own or any partial standards. They will indeed look and learn in both these ways, but they will search behind and within for the fact of the Corpus Christi, the σῶμα Χριστοῦ. Recovery along these lines is indeed already taking place.

(1) The Liturgy itself utters the truth of Corpus Christi. Recovery is there ; and in the deeper realization of the meaning of the Liturgy the power of Catholicism is found. Here the liturgical movement in the Roman Communion is pointing the way. This movement has its roots in the nineteenth century, but its fruits have been specially visible since the first world war. Its work owes much to two Benedictine houses, the one at Mt.-César in Louvain, and the other at Maria Laach in the Rhineland; and it is looking behind the individualism of mediaeval and post-reformation piety to the corporate meaning of worship.

which was more in evidence at an earlier stage of liturgical history, and which the Liturgy still proclaims to those who have ears to hear. If the movement is little discussed this is because it works not as a self-conscious party, but quietly and unobtrusively with the blessing of Roman Catholic Bishops, and because it seeks not to discover something new but to live afresh the old truth, " This is my body—ye are the body of Christ."

In many parishes the impact of this movement is being felt. Lay folk are being taught to follow the rite in their missals instead of using it mainly as an occasion for individual prayer. The offertory is being emphasized by appropriate ceremonial, which brings out its meaning as the people's own gift to God of the bread and wine representing their own common life. The modern cults, which detract from the Liturgy as the centre of worship, give place to the Parish Mass, where sacrifice and communion are seen once more as the inseparable parts of the one action. And at the Parish Mass the people are taught to join in the singing of the people's parts of the service. Thus, both in doctrine and in parochial practice, the truth is revived that the sacrifice of the Mass includes the sacrifice of all the members of the Body. The Bishop of Liège wrote, in a Pastoral letter preceding a " semaine liturgique " held in that city in 1934, " My brothers, the Mass can be thought of under many aspects. We set ourselves to show it to you as the sacrifice of the Church and your own sacrifice for yourselves. . . . Consider that the Church is the mystical Body of Christ. . . . When therefore the Saviour is present as victim on the altar and offers Himself to His Father, His presence and His action are not isolated from His mystical Body, for this is joined to its Head in one and the same act of offering. . . . You see how, after the consecration, the priest, leaning on the altar with hands joined, signifies the unity of priest and people with the sacrifice of Christ, and prays ' O God Almighty, we pray Thee to command that these things be carried to Thy heavenly altar into the presence of Thy Divine Majesty.' The things in question are verily the body and the blood of Jesus, but they are the body and blood together with ourselves and our prayers; and all these form one single offering." [1]

The movement clearly goes deeper than matters of cultus; it involves a revival of the Pauline doctrine of τὸ σῶμα and the Pauline doctrine of redemption through Christ, the victor over sin and death. The Mass is thus seen in relation to Christ risen and glorified and as the worship offered through Him to God the Father. [2]

Hence the Liturgy is being discovered, not as a mere exercise in piety, but as the basis of a Christian sociology. "The Liturgy," writes Abbot Herwegen, "was of old a formative life-force; it was the impress of the spirit, which at once inspired and gave form to the young and vigorous life of the early centuries. . . . As the embodied expression of the Christian spirit it must again become a formative life-force for us Christians of to-day." [3]

"I see but one road to renewal," writes Karl Adam, "and that is the road which both dogma and Liturgy point out to us, and of which we shall be daily reminded as often as we pray ' through Jesus Christ our Lord.' " [4]

In Anglo-Catholicism also the liturgical idea is reviving. Many parish priests are convinced that the arrangement whereby Mass is said at an early hour with communion, and sung later in the day as an act of worship and thanksgiving with few or no communicants, is far from the ideal. And they are moving towards the custom of a Parish Mass at some intermediate hour, where all the elements of sacrifice and worship and communion are set forth in one, and where the Body of Christ, as S. Paul and S. Augustine spoke of it, is the centre of Church life. Practical difficulties are many, and practical arrangements must vary.

---

[1] *Les Questions Liturgiques*, April, 1934, pp. 95-99.

[2] For instances of Pauline doctrine, cf. Abbot Capelle, " Le Chrétien offert avec le Christ," *Les Questions*, Dec. 1934, and Feb. 1935; and Abbot Vonier, " La Victoire du Christ," op. cit., April, 1935.

[3] *Alte Quellen neuer Kraft*, p. 77.   [4] *Christ our Brother*, p. 76.

But apart from all the special problems of the Anglican or Roman parish, the Liturgy itself is teaching the unity wherein Christians are one, and the Gospel which is in their midst.[1]

(2) While many are finding in the Liturgy a new vision of the Corpus Christi, there are others who are finding it in the renewal of contact with the Christians of the East. The drawing together of East and West in the movement of Anglicans and Eastern Orthodox towards unity has an importance for every member of the entire Christian Church. For the schism of East and West was the parent of later schisms. It caused the witness of both parts of Christendom to be a maimed witness, and, while it is for the East to confess its own deficiencies, the West may admit that many of its own corruptions and divisions were caused by the lack of those notes of Church life which the East had particularly fostered. It is customary to say that the East is static and conservative and that it is merely reactionary for Englishmen to seek unity with her. Now while there is an element of advanced and adventurous thinking amongst some of the Russian exiles in France and in England, it remains true that the Eastern Church is in large measure conservative ; it clings tenaciously to the language and to the atmosphere of the Greek Fathers. But what if the East has *conserved* elements of faith and life and worship which the West sorely needs for the

[1] For an account of the Liturgical movement see A. G. Hebert, *Liturgy and Society* (1935), espec. pp. 125-138. The Roman Catholic literature is considerable. (i) From Maria Laach there is the " Ecclesia Orans " series, including Abbot Herwegen's *Kirche und Seele* and *Christliche Kunst und Mysterium*. One of the series, R. Guardini, *The Spirit of the Liturgy*, has been translated into English. (ii) From Mt.-César there is the small but classical work of Dom Beauduin, *La Piété de l'église* (1914), and Dom Laporta, *Piété Eucharistique*. The work of the movement in Belgium is chronicled in *Les Questions Liturgiques et Paroissiales* (Mt.-César, quarterly) ; the No. for Oct., 1934, dedicated to Dom Beauduin, contains a retrospect of the whole movement. (iii) From Klòsterneuburg in Austria there have been many tracts, including the fortnightly booklet, *Lebe mit dem Kirche*. See, however, note on p. 180.

realizing of her own inner Catholicity—elements of the mystery of worship, of the communion of saints, of the Church as a family described better by τὸ σῶμα than by "Corpus Christi," of the close relation between doctrine and life expressed in the Eastern idea of "orthodoxy," of the Resurrection as the centre of the Church's being? It is difficult to witness the Eastern observance of some of the great Christian feasts—such as the Epiphany or the Transfiguration—without realizing that the Easterns have much to teach their Western brethren concerning the meaning of the central Christian mysteries. Hence the presence in the West of the dispersion from Russia, where faith has been sealed with martyrdom and where Christianity has had its closest contact with its Communist enemies, has an importance as great as that of any of the central events in Christian history. The growing unity between East and West goes behind and brings deliverance from the failings of the centuries of isolation. It does not hinder but help the healing of the divisions in the West.

(3) In these and in similar ways the Pauline doctrine is returning. The liturgical movement is bearing witness to the Corpus Christi; and the contact between East and West is recovering the sense of the σῶμα Χριστοῦ and of the truth which the Greek phrase tells about Christ and the Church. But the full recovery of the doctrine of the Church is bound up with the return of the Gospel of God. Catholicism, created by the Gospel, finds its power in terms of the Gospel alone. Neither the massive polity of the Church, nor its devotional life, nor its traditions in order and worship can in themselves ever serve to define Catholicism; for all these things have their meaning in the Gospel, wherein the true definition of Catholicism is found. Its order has its deepest significance not in terms of legal validity but in terms of the Body and the Cross; its Eucharist proclaims God creator and redeemer; its confessional is the place where men see that in wounding Christ sin wounds His Body, and where by learning of the Body they learn of Christ; its reverence for the saints is a part

of its worship of the risen Lord. The claim of Catholicism is that it shows to men the whole meaning of the death and resurrection of Jesus.

And if Catholicism is thus closely related to the Gospel, the Catholic is again and again driven back to the scriptures, and is compelled to face very seriously the questions raised by the Reformers of the sixteenth century and by the revived Reformation teaching on the Continent to-day. Formal Protestant systems he rejects, but the initial and creative impulses both of the Reformation and of the Barthian revival—" The Word of God," " sola fide," " sola gratia," " soli Deo gloria "—he again and again pauses to ponder. For these are Catholicism's own themes, and out of them it was born. But they are themes learnt and re-learnt in humiliation, and Catholicism always stands before the Church door at Wittenberg to read the truth by which she is created and by which also she is judged.

" The true treasure of the Church is the Holy Gospel of the glory and the grace of God."

ADDITIONAL NOTE

In the last twenty years the liturgical movement has made striking progress and parallel movements have been seen in different parts of Christendom. The present chapter gives an impression of the movement when its impact and freshness were first being felt in England.

CHAPTER XII

THE REFORMERS AND THE CHURCH

IN the story of Luther and Calvin, not only was the Gospel of God uttered afresh, but, springing from that Gospel, some vital parts of the doctrine of the Church were recovered. The positive witness of the Reformation to the meaning of churchmanship must not be belittled. Yet this witness was incomplete because the Reformers' return to S. Paul was incomplete. Whereas the New Testament shows us the importance of the Church's structure (the parts depending upon the whole and the Apostolate expressing this dependence), the Reformers omitted from their view of Christianity that element which the Apostolate represented by its place in the Body. Luther did not believe that Church order in this sense mattered; in this he differed from S. Paul. Calvin believed intensely that Church order mattered, but he blurred the difference between the Bishop and the presbyter. Hence, while the Reformation recalled men to the fact of the Church as the Body of Christ, its omissions led to the maiming of its witness both to the Church and to the Gospel.

I. *Luther* [1]

In the life of Luther there is seen re-enacted the deliverance from the law to the Gospel which S. Paul had

[1] The main lines of Luther's thought may be studied most conveniently in his *Primary Works* (English translation, edited by Wace and Buchheim). The fullest account of his life in English is Mackinnon, *Luther and the Reformation*, 4 vols.; Vol. I is a very

experienced, and, as a result, the discovery of the social meaning of the Christian life to which S. Paul's experience had led. As a conscientious Augustinian monk, Luther struggled to become right with God by the observance of law and by the penitential practice bound up with the later-mediæval doctrine of grace and human merit. He wrestled for a forgiveness and a union with God which was regarded as in part God's gift but in part something earned by a man's own practice of virtue. As with S. Paul, Luther's sensitiveness to the moral meaning of God's righteousness and his awareness of the entire incapacity of man to possess merit before God led him to the agony of despair over " what the law could not do." Deliverance (foreshadowed by his studies of S. Augustine and of the mysticism of Staupitz) came through the pondering of Romans 1^{17} :—

" a righteousness of God from faith unto faith."

The righteousness of God is there seen in a flash to be not the righteousness which judges and punishes sinners, but the righteousness which accepts already as sons those whose faith is fixed on Jesus Christ, treating them not as the sinners that they are, but as the just men that God can and will make them through the root of faith within them. " Therefore," wrote Luther, " just as I had previously hated the phrase ' justice of God,' so now I extolled it with equal love as the sweetest of words. And so to me that passage in Paul was the true gate of Paradise." (*Documente* 17.)

That the view of religion which springs from such experiences should contain a tendency towards antinomianism seems inevitable. And Luther's critics have dwelt on this antinomian strain, seen for example, in the well-known

readable and inspiring account of his theological development, and takes full note of recent research. For his view of the Church, see Mackinnon, Vol. III, pp. 280-297 ; Grisar, *Luther*, Vol. VI, pp. 290-325 (very critical) ; Troeltsch, *Social Teaching of the Christian Churches*, Vol. II, pp. 461-576. For the Confession of Augsburg, see Kidd, *Documents of the Continental Reformation*, No. 116.

passage " Pecca fortiter." [1] Yet it must be insisted that Luther's systematic teaching leads on, like S. Paul's, from the experience of justification to the life of discipline through the Spirit of God, and to practical brotherhood in Christ. The treatise *Concerning Christian Liberty* suggests at first that morals may not matter. " One thing, and one alone is necessary for life—justification and Christian liberty " (p. 257). Yet, when once the centrality of justification by faith has been asserted, Luther passes on to the fruits of justification in the ethical life. Christ indwells the soul through His promises :—

" Now, since these promises of God are words of holiness, truth, righteousness, liberty and peace and are full of universal goodness, the soul which cleaves to them with a firm faith, is so united to them, nay thoroughly absorbed by them, that it not only partakes in, but is penetrated and saturated by all their virtues. For if the touch of Christ was healing, how much more does that most tender and spoken touch, nay, absorption of the word communicate to the soul all that belongs to the word. In this way therefore the soul, through faith alone without works, is endued with peace and liberty, and filled full with every good thing, and is truly made the child of God, as it is said ' To them gave he power to become sons of God, even to them that believe on his name ' " (*ib.*, p. 261).

Thus Faith receives Christ and is alive with the works of Christ. In the Preface to his *Romans* Luther had written :—

" Faith is a divine work in us, through which we are changed and regenerated by God. . . . Oh, it is a living, busy, active, powerful thing faith, so that it is impossible for it not to do good continually. It never asks whether good works are to be done ; it has done them before there is time to ask the question, and it is doing them always."

[1] " esto peccator et pecca fortiter, sed fortius fide et gaude in Christo . . . sufficit quod agnovimus, per divitias gloriae Dei, Agnum qui tollit peccata mundi ; ab hoc non avellet nos peccatum, etiamsi millies millies uno die fornicemur aut occidamus." Letter to Melancthon, 1 Aug., 1521.

And in *Christian Liberty* he reiterated this teaching :—

" It is not from works that we are set free by the faith of Christ, but from the belief in works, that is from foolishly presuming to seek justification through works " (p. 288).[1]

Faith therefore issues in a new attitude towards the world and towards one's neighbour. Towards the world the Christian will look without fear ; God is sovereign over it, and the Christian shares in this sovereignty, as a king and as a priest :—

" First as regards kingship, every Christian is by faith so exalted above all things that, in spiritual power, he is completely lord of all things, so that nothing whatever can do him any hurt. Yea, all things are subject to him, and are compelled to be subservient to his salvation. Thus Paul says, ' all things work together for good even to them who are the called ' (Rom. 8[28]), and also ' Whether life, or death or things present, or things to come; all are yours, and ye are Christ's.' (1 Cor. 3[22, 23].)

" Not that in the sense of corporeal power has any one of the Christians been appointed to possess and rule all things, according to the mad and senseless idea of certain ecclesiastics. That is the office of kings, princes and men upon earth. In the experience of life we see that we are subjected to all things, and suffer many things, even death. Yea, the more of a Christian any man is, to so many the more evils, sufferings and deaths is he subject, as we see in the first place in Christ the First-born, and in all His holy brethren.

" This is a spiritual power, which rules in the midst of enemies, and is powerful in the midst of distresses. . . . This is the inestimable power and liberty of Christians.

" Nor are we only kings and the freest of all men, but also priests for ever, a dignity far higher than kingship, because by this priesthood we are worthy to appear before God, to pray for others, and to teach one another mutually the things which are of God. . . . Who then can comprehend the lofti-

[1] Cf. Luther on Gal. 2[19]. " Then being possessed by the Holy Spirit, you do works accordingly. The Holy Spirit does not keep holiday ; He is not slothful but will bear the Cross and exercise works in all."

ness of that Christian dignity which, by its royal power, rules over all things, even over death, life, and sin, and, by its priestly glory, is all-powerful with God, since God does what He Himself seeks and wishes, as it is written ' He will fulfil the desire of them that fear Him ; He also will hear their cry and will save them ' (Psalm 145[19]). This glory certainly cannot be attained by any works, but by Faith only " (pp. 267-269).

Here is foreshadowed the " expansive optimism, the keynote of Luther's piety, lending a power to the will and a spring to the heart, such as, in dependence on and trust in God, rings out in his spiritual battle hymns, " Nun freut euch lieben Christen gemein," and " Ein feste Burg ist unser Gott," challenging, triumphing over a world of enemies, taking God at His Word and daring all for Him and for righteousness, possessing all things in Christ, supreme over sin and death." [1] Here also is foreshadowed the Lutheran sense of God's sovereignty in common life, which calls men not to flee from the world and become monks, but to serve God in the world. Characteristic of Lutheranism is this idea of " *vocation*," brought from the cloister and applied to the market-place and the home.

Fearless towards the world, the Christian will, through the purging of selfishness by faith, be loving to his neighbour :—

" Here is the truly Christian life, here is a faith really working by love, when a man applies himself with joy and love to the works of that freest servitude in which he serves others voluntarily and for nought, himself abundantly satisfied in the fulness and riches of his own faith " (p. 280).

" We conclude therefore that a Christian man does not live in himself, but in Christ and in his neighbour, or else he is no Christian : in Christ by faith ; in his neighbour by love. By faith he is carried upwards above himself to God, and by love he sinks back below himself to his neighbour, still always abiding in God and in His love, as Christ says, ' Verily, I say unto you, Hereafter ye shall see heaven open, and the angels of God ascending and descending upon the Son of Man ' (John 1[51])" (p. 287).

[1] Mackinnon, Vol. IV, p. 257.

S. Paul has here come into his own—and in a deep and wide sense; not only the S. Paul of Romans 3, but the S. Paul of Romans 6 and Romans 8 also. And still more significant is the fact that as soon as the Pauline Gospel comes back, the Pauline sense of the Church *inevitably* comes back with it. Hence the *Primary Works* disclose again and again a passion for the Church as the one fellowship of Christians, with protests against the Papacy and contemporary Church order as obscuring the true meaning of the Church. Yet the tension in Luther between old and new, between the positive and the negative is always great, and his own statements contain elements liable to be destructive of the truths which he is recovering.

The Church is invisible, Luther taught; it is the multitude of those who have faith in Jesus Christ, and who in virtue of that faith are " the Holy Catholic Church, the Communion of Saints," the " congregatio (or communio) fidelium," the " Volk der Glaübigen." But the Church is visible also, and the visible Church is the expression of the invisible and is found on earth wherever the Word of God is preached and the sacraments, which are an utterance of the Word, rightly administered. The preaching of the Word constitutes the Church :—

" But you will ask what is this Word and by what means it is to be read, since there are so many words of God. I answer, the apostle Paul explains what it is, namely the Gospel of God, concerning His Son, Incarnate, suffering, risen, glorified, through the Spirit the sanctifier. To preach Christ is to feed the soul, to justify it, to set it free, and to save it if it believes the preaching."

Wherever this Word is preached, there is the Church of God, and (as we shall see) Baptism and the Eucharist are actions of that Word. And the belief that the Church is thus constituted took deep root in Protestant thought. Its classic expression is in the Confession of Augsburg :—

" Est enim ecclesia congregatio sanctorum, in qua evangelium recte docetur, et recte administrantur sacramenta. Et ad veram unitatem ecclesiae satis est consentire de doctrina evangelii et administratione sacramentorum." (*Aug. Conf.*, VII.)

This view of the fundamentals of the Church recurs in Protestant Confessions, and it appears in Article XIX of the Church of England. It shows the Lutheran insistence that the chief question about a Church is not "How is it organized?" but "Is the Christian Gospel taught?" That is the test of Church life.

It is no vague fellowship but a real community that the Word creates, and, like S. Paul, Luther sees this community interpreted and sustained by the Eucharist. He revives some of the deepest teaching of S. Augustine :—

"Therefore it is commonly called *Synaxis* or *Communio* that is fellowship, and the Latin ' communicare ' means to receive this fellowship, where we speak in German of going to the sacrament. And the point is this, that Christ with all His saints is one spiritual Body, just as the people in a city are a community and a body, and every citizen is related as a member to his neighbour and to the city.

"So are all saints members in Christ and in the Church, which is a spiritual, eternal, city of God ; and when one is received into this city he is said to be received into the fellowship of the saints and is drawn into and made a member of Christ's spiritual Body. Thus to receive the sacramental bread and wine is nought else than to receive a sign of this fellowship, and to be incorporated into Christ with all His saints." (*Werke*, II, 743. Weimar edition.) [1]

It is hard to speak readily of "Protestant individualism." The Corpus Christi is taught once again by Luther with the same forcefulness with which S. Augustine had taught it in his sermons.

But Luther's teaching on the Church is not thought out quietly and systematically ; rather it is fought out amid the desperate struggle that the evangelical teaching shall exist, and amid the tensions of a turbulent mind

[1] Quoted, together with other important passages, in Brilioth, *Eucharistic Faith and Practice*, pp. 96 ff.

drawn both towards conserving as much of the old order as can be reconciled with his cardinal doctrines, and towards denouncing the old order with all his powers of invective and of satire. Hence come contradictions. Rome is Anti-Christ; but elsewhere we find that Rome is within the true Church of the Word and can be reformed by the German nobility. Yet, despite all inconsistencies, there is in Luther a deep churchmanship, and the striking fact is its presence and persistence amid the storms within him and around him. Its presence is seen in a number of specific ways.

(1) First and foremost, there is Luther's revival of the teaching of S. Peter, S. Paul, and S. Augustine about the priesthood of all Christians—a teaching which is yet fraught with dangers. He sometimes seems not to be describing the share of the people in the priesthood of the one Body, but the independent rights of the laity in a manner that is easily "politicized" and "individualized." The *Address to the German Nobility* both recalls the meaning of the Church in a truly Catholic sense, and suggests tendencies which might soon lead to its denial.

(2) His teaching upon Baptism is emphatic. As it appears in the *Greater Catechism* its Catholic forcefulness is striking :—

"Mark then this distinction; the baptismal water is a very different thing from other water, not because of the natural element, but because something nobler is added to it, since God Himself has bestowed upon it His mercy and given it His strength and power. Therefore it is not merely natural water, but a divine, heavenly, holy and blessed water; and whatever else can be said in its praise, all is for the sake of the Word, which is a heavenly, divine Word, which none can glorify enough, for it is and can accomplish all that is of God. For thence also it derives its nature, and is called a sacrament, as S. Augustine teaches 'Accedit verbum ad elementum, et fit sacramentum '." (*Primary Works*, p. 132.)

"Faith does not make the Baptism, but receives the Baptism " (p. 138).

After a stout defence of the Baptism of infants Luther explains that the Christian life is one continuous response to the act of grace once wrought by God in Baptism :—

" Therefore everyone should regard Baptism as a garment for everyday use, which he should always have on, that he may ever be in the midst of faith and its fruits, in order to be able to subdue the old Adam and go forward in the new man. For if we would be Christians, we must adhere to the work which makes us Christians " (p. 142).

(3) Equally remote from a merely destructive Protestantism is Luther's adherence to sacramental Confession and Absolution, when once he sees it apart from its association with the doctrines of merit, satisfaction and indulgences. Amongst the *Ninety-Five Theses* there is this assertion :—

" God never remits any man's guilt, without at the same time subjecting him, humbled in all things, to the authority of his representative the priest." (*Thesis* 7.)

Thus Luther's main quarrel was not with the ministry of reconciliation through the Church, but with the corruption of that ministry by legalistic ideas of guilt and merit. Within his *Shorter Catechism* there is the section " How simple folks should be taught to confess." The section opens—" Confession consists of two parts : first, to confess our sins, and secondly to receive the absolution or forgiveness bestowed by the Confessor, as from God Himself, and not to doubt thereof, but firmly to believe that our sins are thereby forgiven in the sight of God in heaven." And passing thence to consider " what sins should be confessed," Luther stresses specially the *social* sins ; and the social significance of Confession and Absolution is strikingly taught. Hence Luther was unwilling to join in the reckless denial of five of the traditional sacraments ; he clung to the belief that there were three sacraments : Baptism, Eucharist, Absolution, although he would not name the last as a sacrament since he regarded it as a sort of continuation of the work of Baptism. Lacking a doctrine of a priesthood acting on behalf of the whole body, Luther could not preserve his view of Confession from becoming very vague ; any Christian may absolve his brother. None the less he shows us a use of Penance which is rooted in the Gospel of God and in the social conception of the Church, and is free from ideas of human merit, while it involves the use of human agencies by the Word of God.[1]

(4) More successful was Luther's adherence to the essence of traditional belief in the Lord's presence in the Eucharist. For " transubstantiation " he substituted " consubstantiation." His doctrine of the " ubiquity of Christ's risen body " involved him in crudities and difficulties ; but the Luther who wrote on the table at the Marburg Conference, " hoc est corpus meum," and would not move an inch from the literal interpretation of these words, belongs to the history of positive sacramentalism.

These illustrations suffice only to point to the main lines of Luther's teaching. But they show one plain fact and they force upon us one plain question. The *fact* is that in Luther the sense of the Pauline Gospel leads on to the sense of the Church ; the Cross leads on to the Corpus Christi, and Luther shows a very deep insight into both. The *question* forced upon us is, why is this all ? and why does not the Reformation create a full, permanent, unshakeable doctrine of the Body, instead of succumbing later to the tendencies to individualism and subjectivism ? That is our problem.

The answer is at once apparent, for it lies not in an analysis of historical and psychological causes, but in a plain contrast between Luther and the New Testament. His return to it had been incomplete. (1) He dwelt upon the initial experience of justification to such an extent

[1] Cf. Luther's work on Confession. *Werke*, VIII, 140 f., summarized in Mackinnon, III, 13-16. Cf. also the Augsburg Confession, Chs. XI and XII ; Melanchthon, *Loci*, XIII.

that he failed to recognize aright the discipline and struggle and order by which the soul, once justified, is led along the road of sanctification. And he was therefore ensnared by a false antithesis between the inward and the outward. His reaction against contemporary Romanism intensified this false antithesis in his mind. (2) Hence he failed to see that in Apostolic Christianity the order of the Church matters supremely, expressing the dependence by which every group and individual learns the full meaning of the life-in-Christ. In failing to understand this, Luther missed an element in S. Paul, in the New Testament, and in the Gospel of God.

It is no doubt impossible to blame Luther for this. If he looked around him he could see Church order only in distorted and perverted forms ; nowhere could he see the Episcopate as the organ of the one Body, deriving its character from the Body's one life ; nowhere could he see the priesthood as a ministry acting for the priestly Body— it seemed to him only an isolated order possessing sacrificial powers. The genuine article was not to be found. He saw the contrast between the Pauline Church and the contemporary idea of a sacrificing priesthood ; and the latter seemed to be a hopeless perversion. What was Luther to say ? As the Word constitutes the Church, so also, in his view, the Word constitutes the ministry. It exists to proclaim the Word, and not, like the Roman priesthood and its Levitical prototype, to offer propitiatory sacrifices.

This Lutheran ministry of the Word was nothing vague, but a regular " ministerium verbi et sacramentorum " [1]—the sacramental work being included as a part of the Word. Yet how was this ministry to be ordered ? The only necessary organization seemed to be some protection and safeguard, that the work of preaching and sacrament might be done. And who better than the Prince or the State— if such be found willing—to provide this protection and

---

[1] Cf. *Conf. Aug.*, Part II, ch. vii.

to order the due ministrations of religion? And was not this the Prince's privilege as a priest, through baptism, in the Church of God? So reasoned Luther; and while the Bishop was sometimes omitted, sometimes retained as a superintendent, the idea of the local Church's dependence upon one visible and continuous order was missed. Thus the control of the churches passed largely to the States. In the struggle to enable evangelical teaching to live and breathe, Luther leaned on the State. He was rewarded, both in his own lifetime and after his death, by the failure of Lutheranism to avoid continual subjection to the State and alliance with nationalism. The "cujus regio, ejus religio" of the Peace of Augsburg marks the inability of Lutheranism to preserve the meaning of Church order. It became the handmaid of religious nationalism, and its submission to prevailing political systems bears witness to the defect in Luther's thinking and statesmanship.[1]

There was thus something missing in Luther's return to the primitive Church. He omitted the fact of the one visible Church as historical, apostolic, and continuous in its ordered life, with an Apostolate expressing the dependence of the parts upon the whole. Lutheranism in fact tended to represent the Pauline communities *without* the Church order behind them and without S. Paul in his office as Apostle. The Corinthians, to whom S. Paul wrote, were no doubt justified, sanctified, full of gifts and of the assurance of faith; but they needed to know their continual dependence upon the one historic society, and to own that their life in Christ was but a fragment of the life of the historic Church. To be justified is to depend upon no solitary Christ; it is to depend upon One whose people, the continuous race of God, are His own humanity. Omitting the meaning of the Apostolate, Luther weakened for his people the Gospel which that order expresses; and so the tendencies to individualism and subjectivism

---

[1] For the nationalistic tendency in Lutheranism, see Troeltsch, op. cit., Vol. II, pp. 489-494, 520-521, 574.

(already present and threatening in the *Primary Works*) could not but increase. In Luther the Gospel is heard again ; the Church as the Body is known again. Yet the witness to both is incomplete.

II. *Calvin*

Unlike Luther, Calvin worked and taught when the first convulsions of Reform were passed. Before he wrote, much water had flowed beneath the bridges ; and he set himself calmly to think out a logical system of Christian theology, and to consolidate the Protestant Christians into an ordered Church life. He was as zealous and as efficient in Church organization as Luther was indifferent and casual. But for the doctrinal intransigence of Lutheranism and the national isolation of the English Church, Calvin might possibly have welded all the children of the Reformation into one united force. He was above all things the Churchman ; and at times when Lutherans, Anglicans and Catholics have succumbed to State domination, Calvinists—both of Presbyterian and of Congregationalist order—have upheld the " Crown Rights of the Lord Jesus " in a free Christian society. Calvin and Hildebrand have at least this one conviction in common.

Like Luther, Calvin started with the Church as invisible, his doctrine of predestination making this view of the Church more prominent. Almost at the beginning of his systematic exposition of the Church, which forms the Fourth Book of the *Institutes*, we read :—

" When in the Creed we profess to believe the Church, reference is made not only to the visible Church of which we are now treating, but also to all the elect of God, including in the number even those who have departed this life. . . . But as they (the elect) are a small and despised number, concealed in an immense crowd, like a few grains of wheat buried among a heap of chaff, to God alone must be left the knowledge of His Church, of which His secret election forms the foundation." (IV, i. 2.)

Yet the Church is also visible, known and seen wherever the Word is preached and the sacraments administered :—

"Hence the form of the Church appears and stands forth to our view. Wherever we see the Word of God sincerely preached and heard, wherever we see the sacraments administered according to the institution of Christ, there we cannot have any doubt that the Church of God has some existence, since His promise cannot fail, 'Where two or three are gathered together in my name, there am I in the midst of them' (Matt. 18²⁰)." (IV, i. 9.)

Churchmanship is therefore essential to Christianity :—

"For such is the value which the Lord sets on the communion of His Church, that all who contumaciously alienate themselves from any Christian society, in which the true ministry of His Word and sacraments is maintained, He regards as deserters of religion. So highly does He recommend her authority, that when it is violated He considers that His own authority is impaired. . . . Whence it follows that revolt from the Church is denial of God and of Christ." (IV, 1. 10.)

Already it is clear that order and discipline are very prominent in Calvin's mind. He is emphatic about the ministry ; and (in striking contrast with Luther !) he insists that laymen must not be allowed to administer baptism (IV, xv. 20). The note of discipline in morals and worship and order is one of the most characteristic notes of Calvinism. A Lutheran Church has its "Confession"; a Calvinistic Church has its "Confession" and its "Book of Discipline" as well.

The ministry is prescribed and depicted with great solemnity. It represents Christ in a special sense, and rules the Christian society on His behalf :—

"For though it is right that He alone should rule and reign in the Church, that He should preside and be conspicuous in it, and that its government should be exercised and administered solely by His word ; yet as He does not dwell among us in visible presence, so as to declare His will by His own lips, He in this (as we have said) uses the ministry of men, by making them, as it were, His substitutes, by transferring His right and honour to them, but only doing His own work by their lips, just as an artificer uses a tool for any purpose." (IV, iii. 1.)

And, after quoting 2 Cor. 4[7] and Eph. 4[4-16], Calvin shows that the ministry is needed for the unity and order of the Church :—

" By these words he (S. Paul) shows that the ministry of men, which God employs in governing the Church, is a principal bond by which believers are kept together in one Body. He also intimates, that the Church cannot be kept safe, unless supported by those guards to which the Lord has been pleased to commit its safety. . . . Whoever, therefore, studies to abolish this order and kind of government of which we speak, or disparages it as of minor importance, plots the devastation, or rather the ruin and destruction of the Church. For neither are the light and the heat of the sun, nor meat nor drink, so necessary to sustain and cherish the present life, as is the apostolical and pastoral office to preserve a Church on the earth." (IV, iii. 2.)

The ministry, clearly, is of the " esse " of the Church. But of what officers is it composed ? Calvin goes back to Scripture ; there alone will he look for the true Church order :—

" Those who preside over the government of the Church, according to the institution of Christ, are named by Paul, first *Apostles*, secondly *Prophets*, thirdly *Evangelists*, fourthly *Pastors*, and lastly *Teachers* (Eph. 4[11]). Of these, only the two last have an ordinary office in the Church. The Lord raised up the other three at the beginning of his kingdom and still occasionally raises them up when the necessity of the times requires." (IV, iii. 4.)

This passage is second to none in importance for the whole history of Protestantism. Calvin here asserts that the prophets and the Apostles (with whom he groups evangelists, IV, iii. 5) were temporary only ; they belonged to the apostolic age ; they are not an abiding part of the Church and have no successors. Pastors and teachers alone remain as the permanent part of Christ's instituted ministry. And this passage is the parent of Presbyterianism; there is to be one ministry throughout the Church, its position is exalted, its succession is maintained, and yet the Bishop and the presbyter are " levelled " into a parity.

Certainly Calvin was scriptural in his thinking. In Scripture the Bishop and the presbyter are almost certainly the same. And certainly Calvin could claim phrases of S. Jerome in his favour. But he was using Scripture in the archæological way. He failed to perceive in the New Testament the organic relation of the local community to the whole Church, the place of the Apostles as representing this relation, the permanent character of this relation in Church life, the need for an Apostolate (other than the presbyterate) to represent this relation in every age. The answer to Calvin is to appeal to Scripture, not archæologically but " organically," and to study the growing organism, and the Apostles' unique place in it, and thence to see the later Episcopate filling the same place. But meanwhile from Calvinism there grew two kinds of Church order, (1) the *Presbyterian*, with a genuine emphasis upon order, succession, the unique status of ministers, (2) the *Congregational*, with its belief in the one Church of all believers, visible and invisible, and in the autonomous local community which is in itself the Church, existing wherever two or three are gathered together in Christ's name, the seat of authority for itself, choosing and authorizing its own ministers. Both traditions have upheld a robust Churchmanship at times when the Episcopalians have failed to do so. Both traditions can appeal to elements in the New Testament. But both lack one note of the primitive Church—the note of a continuous, visible, historical society, upon which the local community depends, inwardly and outwardly, in all its sacramental acts. Both omit from their picture " Paul the Apostle" and Ignatius the Bishop representing the universal Church; and both have thus borne incomplete witness to the " One Holy Catholic and Apostolic Church."

Calvinism is second to no form of Christianity in its emphasis on order and discipline. It misses, however, a great deal of the inner spirit of Churchmanship. While Luther ignores outward order he has a warm sense of the Church's mystical meaning in his view of Christ and the Christians. " Ye are the Body " rings through his writings. For Calvin, however, the Church is rather utilitarian. It is not perceived as the glow of Christ's Incarnate presence ; it is the policeman sent to protect the Christian life by commands and prohibitions. Here is discipline, without the sense of union with the death and life of Christ which gives discipline its meaning ; here is order, without the sense of the wondrous historical and apostolic race which gives order its meaning. Yet both Luther and Calvin bid the Christian historian bow his head in thankfulness for the Gospel revived, and for the Church revived also, before he can dare to speak of the incompleteness of their work.

III

These illustrations of the history of Luther and Calvin are all too scanty. They will suffice, however, to show where and how the Reformation recovered the primitive Gospel and Church, and where and how it particularly failed. The same main characteristics belong to the Protestantism of the succeeding centuries. It has uttered the Gospel of God, it has nourished the Christian fellowship, and it has at the same time lacked the notes of the historical and apostolic structure in its Church life. It has had a varied history, at times declining into extreme individualism and subjectivism, at times recovering, with the *sola fide* and the *soli Deo gloria* sounding afresh. But all the while, both in the times of its poverty and in the times of its wealth, it has lacked one definite element in Christian truth ; and this lack may perhaps account for its liability to decline into tendencies so far removed from its initial supernaturalism. Here are some results.

(1) With the lack of the historical structure, the sense

of worship as the act of the one historic society has been lost. In essential Catholicism, worship is the act of the Christ showing forth His own eternal sacrifice through the Liturgy of His one Body on earth and in heaven. In this one action both the individual Christian and the local community of worshippers share by merging themselves into the one liturgical movement. Thus the service in any Christian building is not the act of the local group of Christians; it is, in inward reality and in outward ritual, the act of the timeless Church, and the worshippers are pointed beyond their topical needs and feelings and interests to the one sacrifice of Christ and to the universal Church of God. The topical and congregational elements are needed, but in true worship these elements subserve the Corpus Christi and the one sacrifice of Christ. " Reality " in worship will not, therefore, mean that the worshipper expresses warmly his own *feelings* and needs; it will mean that he identifies himself by his *will* with the Name and the Glory of God in the one divine action.

But Protestantism, lacking the universal Church order and the liturgical structure, has made central in worship what really belongs to the circumference. The congregation expresses " its own worship," the " reality " of which is often tested by its correspondence with the *feelings* of the worshippers. Thus, for all the power of the Gospel in its midst and for all the true supernaturalism of the austere Calvinist tradition of worship, Protestant worship has seldom protected itself from the perils of the man-centred and the sentimental. Worship is not something to be devised by groups of Christians; it is something *there* already in the continuous liturgical action of God in His Church. Worship is not primarily " Our Approach to God," but God's utterance of His own sacrifice in heaven and on the Cross and in the Corpus Christi wherein men die and rise again. It is hard to see how Christians can recover the meaning of worship in this liturgical and Catholic and yet utterly Evangelical sense except in the atmosphere of the historic Church order.

(2) With the defective sense of worship as the act of the historic society, there grows easily a false emphasis on the place of human feelings in worship and in religion generally. Emil Brunner has described how the God-centred idea of justification by faith has often declined into a man-centred feeling. " Melanchthon, in his first edition of the *Loci*, enunciated the following statement: ' . . . *hoc est Christum cognoscere, beneficia ejus cognoscere.*' Certainly this statement is right, and it is important in so far as it is directed against scholastic casuistries, against the metaphysical perversion of the doctrine of Christ. In this sense we might render it thus : It does not matter how the divine and the human natures in Christ are united with each other, or how they can coexist, but what does matter is *what we have* in this Christ; how Christ speaks to us, not what we think about Him, is the problem for faith. This is evidently the real purport of the statement of Melanchthon. His formula, however, has a shade of meaning which could easily lead men astray, and has actually done so. It contains the germ of the whole anthropocentric point of view of later Lutheranism, and this simply means religious egoism. It is man with his need for salvation, not God and His glory, His revelation, that occupies the centre of the picture. Thus God becomes one who satisfies the needs of man. Not in vain has Ritschlian pragmatism so often appealed to these words. Christ is needful in order that we may be helped ; God is the guarantee of the value of human life." [1]

Thus the experience of justification can decline into the comfort of " feeling justified." But this is only one instance of the misplaced emphasis upon feeling, where the true ethos of Corpus Christi is absent. Warm feelings are often made the test of reality in prayer and worship ; Holy Communion comes to be regarded as the supreme moment when the Christian *feels* the Lord's presence,

---

[1] *The Mediator*, pp. 407-408. Cf. the very similar discussion in Newman, *Lectures on Justification*, pp. 324-325, and in Maurice, *Theological Essays*, pp. 205 ff.

rather than an act of God's grace to be received by faith as a movement of the will, without any concern about warm feelings. With this perversion continually besetting it, Protestantism has seemed unable to understand the worshipful meaning of historic Christianity and some of the treasures of the spiritual life. Just as it has never made sense of Monasticism (whose roots are in our Lord's own words in the Gospels), so it has hardly made sense of the truth expressed in Von Hügel's saying, " Religion is Adoration."

(3) With defect in life and worship there is defect in the presentation of truth. By its attempt to make a " nude " appeal to Scripture, Protestantism has failed to find a centre of unity and authority in doctrine. Luther turned to the Bible as the sole authority. But how is the Bible to be interpreted ? It was not enough to say, as Luther did in 1519, " scriptura sacra sui ipsius interpres." He had to assert further that Scripture must be interpreted through the Gospel, or the fact of Christ.[1] This was finely said ; but too ofteñ the Gospel was taken to mean " justification by faith," and the Lutherans tended to judge Scripture by this one doctrine. Hence came Luther's arbitrary remark that the Epistle of S. James was a " letter of straw," and hence the way was open for private doctrinal standards to control the interpretation of Scripture. Complications increased ; and from Luther's " simple gospel " there grew up the Protestant dogmatic " Confessions," expressing theologies and controversies as complex as the old scholasticism, far more complex than the Catholic definitions, and too ephemeral to provide a basis for doctrinal unity. Then came the reactions against Reformed dogma, and the attempts to return to the " simple gospel " found in the Bible, with the many confusing conflicts between the Biblicism of the fundamentalists and the arbitrary and eclectic religion of those who extract from Scripture their own view of the historical Jesus.

---

[1] " Quod si adversarii scripturam urgent contra Christum, urgemus Christum contra scripturam." " Non res verbis, sed verba rebus subjecta sint et cedant." (W.A., V, 637.)

Thus the method of the Reformers has often prevented the real voice of Scripture from sounding with its rightful power. For their appeal to the Truth of Christ was incomplete ; the right appeal is to the Truth as found in Scripture and as witnessed and interpreted by the one primitive organism of sacraments, ministry, and tradition. Here alone is a doctrinal basis which rises behind and above all partial and ephemeral " isms " and controversies and points men to the one Christ in His one family on earth.

These defects have beset Protestantism at every stage of its history. They seem to be derived from a defect in the initial stages of the Reformation, and they point to the incompleteness of a Christianity which lacks the sense of the one historical and ordered structure in worship and Church life. Hence while Catholicism must face the issues of the Gospel and examine itself as to its Pelagianism, Protestantism must ask whether, after all, the historic Church order has not something to do with the Gospel of God. It need not deny its own experience nor the power of its own ministries ; it needs to own, in common with all Christendom, the need for the one Apostolate, as the organ of unity and of continuity, to be made universal for all Christians. At present all are incomplete : " In him ye are all made full."

IV

The weakening of dogmatic Protestantism opened the way for the very subjective and humanistic types of religion manifested in the schools of Schleiermacher and Ritschl and culminating in the modern type of liberal Christianity, which has belittled the fact of sin and the meaning of redemption and, in its extreme forms, has identified the Kingdom of God with ethical progress and social morality. To many this type of religion has the appearance of pointing the way towards Christian unity. It claims to possess the secret of fellowship and brotherhood through the insistence that dogma and Church order matter little and divide Christians ; but, in its belittling of dogma and Church order, it often tacitly dilutes the Gospel of God which gives dogma and order their meaning, and substitutes an ideal of humanistic fellowship for unity in the Cross of Christ. The parent of this line of approach is Ritschl's teaching on the Church. Ritschl certainly drew out the corporate character of Christian life in an inspiring way; but he so diluted the Gospel, upon which the Church rests, and the idea of worship, which is the centre of the Church's life, that his teaching is full of the most subtle dangers.[1]

Liberalism of this kind has offered attractive pictures of unity, but its promises are illusory since it tries to hide the depth of man's spiritual crisis before God. In contrast to liberalism there has been, in the work of Karl Barth and Emil Brunner, a recovery of the supernatural Gospel and a return to the classic themes of the Reformers. This revival is concerned with the doctrine of the Church no less than with the other parts of theology, for, while there is little room in Barthian thinking for any attention to the Church's form and structure, the Barthians have forced upon their readers and listeners the issue of the Church's function. It exists, they have said, to be a witness to the Gospel through its emptiness of any significance or beauty in its own right. Thus witnessing, it is full of tribulation since, whether it be faithful or faithless, it is always the meeting-place between sinful man and the love and judgment of God. " The Church suffers from many well-known human failings, which are not difficult to discover and expose. . . . And yet it is unprofitable for us even to speak of these exposures, except in the context of the veritable tribulation of the Church—a tribulation lying far deeper than this or that corruption, however corrupt it be, which men suppose they can remove. . . .

[1] For Ritschl's insight into the meaning of the Church, cf. his *Justification and Reconciliation* (1900 edn.), pp. 130-139 ; for criticism of the weaknesses of his position, see Flew, *The Idea of Perfection*, Ch. XXI.

The tribulation of the Church is simply the expression in time of His glory, of His righteousness, of His will to help all men." (Barth, *Romans*, Eng. tr., pp. 340, 401.)

It may be urged that, as the Reformers failed to sustain their supernatural message through their failure to see the structure of the Church as a part of that message, so also the neo-Reformers may fail unless they work out a fuller doctrine of the Church. In one striking passage, Dr. Barth, in expounding 1 Cor. 12, has shown the connexion between membership in the Body and humility before the Cross (cf. *The Resurrection of the Dead*, Eng. tr., pp. 81-83), and has thus stood on the verge of the scriptural meaning of the Catholic Church. Yet the differences remain vast, since the Barthian teaching on man's depravity seems to the Catholic to deny the doctrine of creation, and the Catholic sacramental theory seems to the Barthian to make too great a surrender to "natural religion."

Both Catholic and Protestant, however, returning to their roots in the Liturgy and in the Word, are proclaiming a supernatural faith in the face of modern paganism. And theologians of both traditions have been finding new ways of contact with one another, through being driven back to the divine facts which underlie both the Mass and the preaching of the Word.

ADDITIONAL NOTE

In recent years much has been written by English Scholars to advance the study of Luther and his theology: of P. S. Watson *Let God be God* and Gordon Rupp *The Righteousness of God*. I have, however, allowed pp. 181-190 above to stand unaltered in the belief that they do not misrepresent the cardinal features of Luther's doctrine.

CHAPTER XIII

ECCLESIA ANGLICANA

I

AMID the convulsions of religion in Europe in the sixteenth century the English church had a character and a story which are hard to fit into the conventional categories of Continental Christianity. The Anglican was and is a bad Lutheran, a bad Calvinist, and certainly no Papist. His church grew into its distinctive position under the shelter of the supremacy of the English King, and, its story is bound up with the greed and the intrigues of Tudor statesmen. " Thus saith the Lord " sounds but faintly in the language of the Tudor settlements; while such phrases as " over all causes and all persons within his dominions, King, supreme, defender of the Faith " and " the pure and reformed part of it established in this kingdom " sound more loudly. Yet this church of England cannot be explained in terms of politics alone. It bore a spiritual witness, if only by linking together what Christians elsewhere had torn asunder—the Gospel of God, which had made the Reformers what they were, and the old historical structure which the Reformers as a whole had rejected but without which the Gospel itself lacks its full and proper expression. The impact of Luther and Calvin was felt in the Anglicanism of the latter half of the sixteenth century, and is seen not only in the Thirty-nine Articles but in the general return to the scriptures as the ruling element in faith and piety. The Bible was put once more into the hands of the people. Yet the Anglican church appealed to the Bible along lines very different from those of the Lutherans and the Calvinists ; for it appealed also to the primitive Church with its structure and tradition, and thus interpreted the Bible in its true context.[1] By refraining from the Lutheran error of giving particular statements in Scripture a domination over the rest, and from the Calvinistic error of pressing the use of Scripture into a self-contained logical system, it saw that Scripture centres simply in the fact of Christ Himself, and that this fact is to be apprehended with the aid of the whole structure and tradition of the Church. Here, therefore, was an appeal to antiquity, coherent and complete, and a faithfulness to lessons of history which the Reformers on the Continent were missing.

Prominent in the old structure which the Anglicans retained was the Episcopate. The reasons given for this ministry varied; for the stress and the strain of controversy were intense, and the Anglican position had to be defended, often self-consciously, against Rome or the Puritans without and the pressure of the more extreme Reformers within. Hence the English church did not always perceive the meaning of its own order in its deepest relation to the Gospel and the universal Church. For some churchmen, Episcopacy was of a divine law found in Scripture ; for others, it was the best way of imitating antiquity ; for others, it was well suited as a buttress to the doctrine

[1] The Anglican attitude to Scripture is well expressed by Francis White, *A Treatise of the Sabbath Day* (1635), p. 11 :—

" The Holy Scripture is the fountain and lively spring, containing in all sufficiency and abundance the pure water of life, and whatsoever is necessary to make God's people wise unto salvation.

" The consentient and unanimous testimony of the true Church of God, in the Primitive ages thereof, is Canalis, a conduit pipe, to derive and convey to succeeding generations the celestial water contained in Holy Scripture.

" The first of these, namely the Scripture, is the sovereign authority and for itself worthy of all acceptation. The latter, namely the voice and testimony of the Primitive Church, is a ministerial and subordinate rule and guide, to preserve and direct us in the right understanding of the Scriptures."

of the Divine Right of Kings ; for others, it happened to be the order of the national church, and it was thought legitimate for other Reformed churches to use other orders. But what matters most is not the opinions of English divines about Episcopacy, but the fact of its existence in the English church, just as what mattered in the first century was not the Corinthians' language nor even S. Paul's language about his Apostleship, but the fact that, under God, it existed. For its existence declared the truth that the church in England was not a new foundation nor a local realization of the invisible Church, but the expression on English soil of the one historical and continuous visible Church of God. It meant that, in spite of the pressure of Erastianism and even the frequent acceptance of Erastianism by the church's leaders, the English church was reminded by its own shape and structure that it was not merely an English institution but the utterance in England of the universal Church.

This *fact* about the Anglican church coloured the thought of the Caroline divines. Their theology was anti-papal, but was opposed also to the new scholasticisms of the Reformers. It appealed to the Bible as the test of doctrine and also to the Fathers and to the continuous tradition of Church life, *semper et ubique et ab omnibus*, both in West and East alike. The study of Greek theology gave to the churchmanship of these seventeenth-century divines a breadth which reached beyond the West and its con-troversies ; and their idea of the Church is summed up by Bishop Lancelot Andrewes when, in his *Preces Privatae*, he prays

> " for the whole Church Catholic
> Eastern
> Western
> our own."

This sense of the English church as the representative of the Church universal was checked by the Puritan supremacy under Cromwell ; it was revived at the Restoration in a narrower and more self-conscious form, when order was stressed but the sense of the universal meaning of order was largely lost. It was obscured throughout most of the church's life in the eighteenth century; and it was revived by the Tractarians early in the nineteenth. The issue before the Tractarians was, what essentially is the church of England? Very widely it was held to be simply a State department; to contemporary liberalism it was an English society formed by the confluence of various schools of English religious thought; but to the Tractarians it was the expression in England of the one historic and universal Church. " I saw," said Newman, " that Reformation principles were powerless to save her. I kept ever before me that there was something greater than the Established Church, and that was the Church Catholic and Apostolic set up from the beginning, of which she was the local presence and organ. She was nothing unless she was this." Hence the Tractarian emphasis upon the Apostolic succession. Printed in large type in the first number of the *Tracts for the Times* were the words " OUR APOSTOLIC DESCENT "; and these words did not express merely a doctrine about the status of the clergy, a revived clericalism, but a belief that the rites in English churches are not only acts wrought between Christ and Englishmen, but acts of Christ in His one universal Church in which Englishmen share through its representatives on English soil.

This aspect of the English church—its historic order, its sacramental life, its kinship with the pre-Reformation church and with the Catholic elements still existing in Rome—has always appealed specially to one part of the English clergy and laity. Others have been more concerned with the church's kinship with the Reformers, with the preaching of the Gospel, with the conversion of the individual, and have been indifferent to Church order or have regarded it as something valuable only because it is ancient and because it is useful. Both these schools of thought have existed side by side in the English church;

both have had their times of poverty and their times of wealth and revival; and it has become customary to rejoice in the church's comprehensiveness and to stress the need for balance and for the due recognition of these two elements, besides the element which has kept alive the humanism of the Renaissance and has been known as Broad or Liberal. But, if our reading of the New Testament and especially of the Pauline Epistles is correct, these two truths—the Evangelical and the Catholic—are utterly one. To understand the Catholic Church and its life and order is to see it as the utterance of the Gospel of God; to understand the Gospel of God is to share with all the saints in the building up of the one Body of Christ. Hence these two aspects of Anglicanism cannot really be separated. It possesses a full Catholicity, only if it is faithful to the Gospel of God; and it is fully Evangelical in so far as it upholds the Church order wherein an important aspect of the Gospel is set forth. To belittle the witness of the Reformers and the English church's debt to the Reformers is to miss something of the meaning of the Church of God; to belittle Church order and to regard it as indifferent is to fail in Evangelical insight since Church order is of the Gospel. Hence " Catholicism " and " Evangelicalism " are not two separate things which the church of England must hold together by a great feat of compromise. Rightly understood, they are both facts which lie behind the church of England and, as the New Testament shows, they are one fact. A church's witness to the one Church of the ages is a part of its witness to the Gospel of God.

Varieties of thought and of apprehension of course exist. There are always those to whom certain aspects of truth appeal more than others. There may always be those who dwell chiefly upon the one Body, the Church, as the pillar and ground of the truth; and there may always be those whose minds are more filled with the thought of Christ and the individual, " He loved me and gave Himself for me." But there is a true and a false way of thinking of the comprehensiveness of the Anglican church. It can

never be rightly expressed in terms of Victorian latitudin-
arianism or broad-mindedness, or by saying " Here are
two very different conceptions and theologies, but with
a broad common-sense humanism we combine them both."
Rather can the meaning of the church of England be stated
thus: " Here is the one Gospel of God ; inevitably it includes the scriptures and the salvation of the individual ;
as inevitably the order and the sacramental life of the
Body of Christ, and the freedom of thought wherewith
Christ has made men free." Translated into practice this
means that the parish priest has a heavy responsibility ;
he must preach the Gospel and expound the scriptures,
and he must also proclaim the corporate life of the Church
and the spiritual meaning of its order. In every parish
the Prayer-Book entitles the laity to hear the Gospel
preached, and the scriptures expounded, and also to receive
the full sacramental teaching of the historic Church including the ministry of Confession and Absolution for those
who desire it. For the Anglican church is committed not
to a vague position wherein the Evangelical and the
Catholic views are alternatives, but to the scriptural faith
wherein both elements are of one. It is her duty to train
all her clergy in both these elements. Her Bishops are
called to be not the judicious holders of a balance between
two or three schools, but, without any consciousness of
party, to be the servants of the Gospel of God and of the
universal Church.

II

If the meaning of the Anglican church is thus sought
in terms of the Church of the New Testament, then none
of the cries of partisans can ever interpret it aright. To
be faithful to the Gospel, to foster freedom of thought
and inquiry, to uphold the Apostolic succession, are not
sectional loyalties ; they concern the one call of the Church
as a whole. And since false antitheses are sometimes
drawn, and since Apostolic succession is sometimes isolated

and misinterpreted, it may be well to see how this last fact was expounded by one who was certainly no Tractarian, but believed fervently in Episcopacy just because he believed in the Gospel of God, and who combined these beliefs with the rôle of a leader of critical thought.

Frederick Denison Maurice lived from 1805-1872, a period when the conflict was very apparent between the old Evangelicalism, the Tractarian movement and the rising liberal school of Arnold and Stanley. Maurice was one of those rare teachers who do not fit into the categories of any party. Tractarians and Evangelicals bitterly opposed him ; and in the popular mind he was an advanced and heretical thinker, notorious through his deprivation from office at King's College, London, for alleged disbelief in hell, and through his habitual championing of critical thought and of natural science. Yet he had little in common with the Broad Church party of his day. His liberalism was not born of any indifference to dogma ; rather was it the freedom of mind which can come to those, whom genuine orthodoxy lifts above the partial conceptions of a particular age and above the partizanship into which the orthodox so often fall :—

" Every hope I had for human culture, for the reconciliation of opposing schools, for blessings to mankind, was based on theology. What sympathy, then, could I have with the Liberal party which was emphatically anti-theological, which was ready to tolerate all opinions in theology, only because people knew nothing about it, and because other studies were much better pursued without reference to it." (*Life*, I, 183.)

" But that which seems to me to be the greatest disease of our time, that we talk about God and about our religion, and do not confess him as a living God, Himself the redeemer of men in His Son . . . is characteristic of no school so much as of this." (*Life*, II, 359.)

The theology of Maurice had its roots in S. John and in the Greek Fathers. " He was in the world, and the world was made by him " pervades Maurice's thinking ; the world to him was not a mass of perdition but the scene of the continuous life-giving activity of the divine Word manifested in all life and in mankind. Yet this divine Word, Maurice insists, cannot be fully known except through the Gospel of the Cross, because sin is a reality. Hence there recurs in Maurice's letters an almost " Barthian " sense of the difference between revelation as God's self-disclosure and religion as man's attempt to feel after God. It is remarkable to find an English writer of Victorian times using the word " religion " almost with disparagement :—

" The one thought which possesses me most at this time, and, I may say, has always possessed me, is that we have been dosing our people with religion when what they want is not this but the living God." (*Life*, I. 369.)

This living God is active in redemption through the Crucifixion of Jesus Christ. Maurice insists upon the Gospel :—

" Every year and day convinces me that our preaching will be good for nothing if the main subject for it is not the atonement of God with man in Christ ; if we may not proclaim His sacrifice as a finished work ; if we may not ground all our sacrifices upon it ; if we stop short of the Eucharistic proclamation that God of His tender mercy hath given us His Son to be a full, perfect and sufficient, sacrifice, oblation and satisfaction for the sins of the whole world. Any notion, theories, practices which interfere with the fulness of this Gospel deprive men, it seems to me, of a blessing which has been bestowed upon them and to which they have a right—deprive them of the only effectual foundation for social and individual reformation." (*Life*, II, 365.)

Further, the Liturgy is the proclamation of this Gospel :—

" What I say of preaching, I say also of prayers. If they are separated from the confession and presentation of the perfect sacrifice, once made,—if they are not petitions that the will which is expressed in that sacrifice may be done on earth as it is in heaven, if they are not presented through the High Priest and Mediator within the veil,—they are, in my judgement, not Christian prayers. I say not that they are ineffectual; for it is He who makes prayers effectual which are very dark and ignorant, (otherwise what would become of us ?) ; but I say that they are anticipations of a Gospel,—attempts to reach an unknown, unrevealed God— not derived from the Gospel of God, from the revelation of the perfectly righteous and loving Being in the perfect Mediator." (*Life*, II, 365.)

" The Liturgy has been to me a great theological teacher ; a perpetual testimony that the Father, the Son and the Spirit, the one God blessed for ever, is the author of all life, freedom, unity to men ; that our prayers are nothing but responses to His voice speaking to us and in us. (*Life*, II, 359.)

The God who is thus revealed is one. Here Maurice clings to the truth he has learnt in his Unitarian home. Yet the Unity is that of Father, Son and Spirit, whose Oneness is the only perfect oneness revealed or imaginable. Only in this way can Maurice think of the Divine Unity :—

" I was bred a Unitarian. To realize the meaning of the name of Father, the meaning of the Unity of God, is my calling and name. I believe there cannot be a Father without an only-begotten-Son, of the same substance with Himself, that there cannot be unity, but the Unity of the eternal Father with the Eternal Son in the Eternal Spirit."

And this Divine Unity is the only source of unity amongst men. Hence the doctrine of the Trinity is no bare metaphysic, it is the activity of love which creates the unity of the Church and which is the hope of the unity of all mankind :—

" I not only believe in the Trinity in Unity, but I find in it the centre of all my beliefs, the rest of my spirit, when I contemplate myself or mankind."

" The Name into which we were baptized, the Name which was to bind together all nations, comes to me more and more as that which must at last break the fetters of oppression. I can find none of my liberal friends to whom that language does not sound utterly wild and incomprehensible ; while the orthodox would give me for the eternal Name the dry dogma of the Trinity. . . . I am sure the Name is the all-embracing charity, which I may proclaim to publicans and harlots as that in which they are living and moving and having their being" (quoted in Masterman, *F. D. Maurice*, p. 228).

Thus the Divine Unity has entered into mankind. And to share in it is not to admire Jesus Christ and to follow Him as one who has " the value of God." It is to *die* :—

" The death of Christ is actually, literally, the death of you and me." " To believe that we have any self of our own is the Devil's lie ; and when he has tempted us to believe and to act as if we had a life out of Christ, he then mocks us, and shows us that this life is a very death."

" Let us believe that we have each a life, one only life, not of you nor me, but a universal life in Him " (op. cit., p. 18).

Maurice has led our thoughts deeply into the New Testament. His theme is the unity of God, the Father, Son and Spirit—the unity uttered through Christ—the death of the Mediator—the unity of men through death in Him. And he continues the line of thought from the inward to the outward. Unity means the dependence of all individuals, parties, movements, experiences, upon the one historic family founded by Christ. The historic structure bears witness to this family, and Baptism, Eucharist, Creeds, Episcopate, Scripture are the " signs of the spiritual constitution," things not Anglican, nor Roman, nor Greek, nor Lutheran, nor Calvinist, but things belonging to the one people of God :—

" It is to the divine constitution of the Church that I have always turned, especially as a deliverance from systems. The Church . . . is represented in scripture as a Kingdom, . . . On this ground I have always loved Episcopacy as expressing the fatherly and Catholic character of the Church, and have maintained that when it is lost the Church of necessity becomes hard, narrow, formal." (*Life*, I, 524.) [1]

[1] Cf. *Life*, i, 248 ; ii, 318.

This conviction recurs in Maurice's letters. But it finds fullest expression in his work, *The Kingdom of Christ, or Hints on the Principles, Ordinances, and Constitution of the Catholic Church, in letters to a member of the Society of Friends*. Here the meaning of the divine order is fully worked out. Generous in his understanding of Quaker, Lutheran, Calvinist and Anglican, Maurice sees that the witness of each of them fails through becoming an isolated "ism," and he asks what are the signs of the universal family beneath and behind them all :—

"These systems, Protestant, Romanist, English, seem to me each to bear witness to the existence of a *Divine Order;* each to be a miserable partial, human substitute for it. In every country, therefore, I should desire to see men emancipated from the chains which they have made for themselves, and entering into the freedom of God's Church." (*Kingdom of Christ*, II, 314.)

Here is a theologian whose emphasis upon Church order springs directly from his sense of the Gospel of God. A thinker with the widest interests, in reinterpretation, in natural science, in social democracy, in all that is modern,— he does not conclude that Christianity is so big and so progressive that enlightened men can move ahead of the old Church order. Rather does he devote one of his largest systematic works to expounding that order. But his exposition differed from many of those which preceded him ; for while others often appealed to Church order as part of an appeal to " antiquity," Maurice appealed to it rather as to something timeless, and symbolic of a universal family. He felt that while the Tractarians were sometimes led to contend for Episcopacy as a party issue, the true contention was for its universal meaning :—

"I do not fancy that you will get much satisfaction from the Oxford Tracts, but I cannot tell. To me they are, for the most part, more unpleasant than I quite like to acknowledge to myself and to others. Their error, I think, consists in opposing to τὸ πνεῦμα τοῦ αἰῶνος τούτου the spirit of a former

age, instead of the ever-living and active Spirit of God, of which the spirit of each age is at once the adversary and the parody."
—(*Life*, I, 226.)

The turn of events—and perhaps a sad misunderstanding—threw Maurice in opposition to the Tractarians, and the Tractarians in opposition to him. Yet his message and theirs are similar. They were fighting for the recovery of a principle, and had sometimes to express that principle in a static and partisan way. Maurice, looking beyond and behind the issues of momentary controversy, saw the same principle in its universal significance, and perceived that the " ever-living and active Spirit of God " is the source of all good life and thought only because He is the Spirit of the Mediator calling men into the one divine family, whose constitution points to its universality and to the redemptive acts of Christ.

In a teacher, therefore, who was mistrusted both by Catholics and by Evangelicals, the underlying unity of the English church's history finds striking expression. For self-conscious Catholicism can miss the deeper meaning of the Catholic church; self-conscious Evangelicalism can miss the strength of the Gospel; and self-conscious Liberalism can foster intolerance of temper and rigidity of thought. And while the assertions of the Evangelical, the Tractarian and the genuine Liberal are utterly true, the moment their assertions become "isms," falsehood ensues. Maurice himself cannot altogether be acquitted of self-consciousness, yet his freedom from the dominant party-cries enabled him to see the great facts of the Gospel and the Church and the Spirit of Truth before and behind all partial theories about them. Upon these facts, and upon no theoretical compromises, the English church is based.

And if Maurice thus interprets the past position of the Anglican church, he is equally a guide for some of its future tasks. For conspicuous amongst these tasks to-day are the reinterpretation of doctrine in the widening realms of science and thought, and the expression of Christian life in the new and complex social and economic order. In both these fields Maurice was a pioneer, through his influence on Hort and the Cambridge school, through his refusal to join in the condemnation of Darwin, and through his fostering of "Christian Socialism". But he was able to be a pioneer precisely because he refused to succumb to the modernisms of his time,[1] and because he drank deeply from a theology learnt from the Greek Fathers, from the Catholic order, from St. John, and from the Gospel of God. He enabled others to build because he chose himself to "dig."[2] And the English church can again lead the way in the problems which confront it only if it digs down to its own foundations, which are the Gospel of God, the sacramental life, and the soundest learning that its clergy and laity can possess.

III

If one who has been hailed as a father of modern theology could think thus of the historic Church order, then the modern Anglican can dare to cherish it without the reproach of partisanship or obscurantism. In so cherishing it he will baffle many of his fellow-Christians with whom he has close affinity in the Gospel. The Lutherans have marvelled at the Anglican's interest in order combined with what seems to be his indifference to deep issues of faith.[3] But the

[1] Cf. his appeal to the 39 Articles as enshrining an orthodoxy which delivers men from the false type of dogmatism, *Life*, Vol. I, pp. 339, 530 ; Vol. II, pp. 214, 600-604. Cf. also his attitude to the Prayer Book, II, 169, and the Creeds, II, 457 and *passim*.

[2] Cf. *Life*, II, 136-138, a striking passage.

[3] Cf. the reply of the Church of Sweden to the Lambeth Appeal of 1920 (Bell, *Documents on Christian Unity*, Vol. I, pp. 185-195) ; and Brilioth, *The Anglican Revival*, pp. 180-210, 329-330. Dr. Brilioth criticizes the Tractarians' emphasis on Apostolic succession as being a narrowing obstacle to the growth of their sacramental piety. The fact is that this emphasis (however narrowly it was at first expressed) was the means whereby sacramentalism was taught as *historical*, and linked with the one historical redemption. Apart from this link, their intense sacramental mysticism might easily have grown unevangelical and immanentist. Curiously, Dr. Brilioth makes no reference to Maurice's teaching.

Anglican can fairly reply that, though he may have spoken little of justification by faith and often failed greviously in his preaching of the " Word," yet all the while the Church order, linked with the Liturgy, has been quietly expressing to English people the " givenness " of Christianity, the " donum Dei." None the less, the Lutheran criticism is salutary, for it is the issues of faith that are fundamental, and only in their context does Church order find its meaning. The further the question of reunion advances, the greater is the need for the Anglicans so to expound Church order and so to *live* it, that its relation to the Gospel is plain. This need is fulfilled less by discussions of Church order in isolation, than by the growth of that whole inner life of the Body wherein Bishop, presbyters and people have their evangelical place.

As this corporate life grows, there comes with it an escape from certain tendencies which have obscured the meaning of the Church's ministry. The test is whether Apostolic succession is used as a means of commending ourselves, as if it were an Anglican possession of our own, or whether it is used as a symbol of our nothingness *qua* ourselves and of our dependence upon the universal Church and upon Jesus in the flesh.

The atmosphere of controversy has sometimes prevented the universal significance of Church order from being clearly seen, for controversy begets self-consciousness, and self-consciousness and Catholicity go ill together. In several ways the Catholic meaning of Church order has been obscured.

(1) It was obscured by the old-fashioned " Three Branch theory " held by some of the earlier High Churchmen. This theory, classically expressed in William Palmer's *Treatise on the Christian Church*, is that the Church is one, yet represented by three great Branches, Greek, Roman, and Anglican, which constitute the Church in different areas, of which each Branch is the rightful possessor. Thus the claim of unity is made, while the fact of schism is acquiesced in and rationalized by a theory. Church order is used

defensively to buttress the Church's claims, but the crucial corollary, that the meaning of Church order is maimed by disunity, is never faced. The " Branch theory " seems, in fact, to be an unconscious attempt to make the best both of unity and of schism, and the relation between Church order and the Gospel is obscured.

(2) Again, the meaning of Church order is obscured by an Erastianism or nationalism which treats the Bishops as an English institution. There have been Bishops who in their domestic style, their political position, the method of their appointment, their theology and their ecclesiastical ideals, have represented English society or a part of it, rather than the Catholic church. Sometimes they have acted as prelates claiming an utterly unconstitutional power, and have seemed unconscious that their office has its meaning as an organ of the Body in close connexion with the presbyters and the laity. The Bishop has often appeared as the English ruler of an English society for English people, and disasters have happened as a result of this perversion. The attempt to force Episcopacy on Scotland in the reign of Charles I failed, because the Bishops appeared to the Scots not as the Fathers of the one family, nor as the organs of Catholicity, but as English dignitaries representing an English system. And henceforth the word " Bishop " suggested to the Scottish mind a merely English institution.

(3) In the face of Erastian perversions of the ministry the Anglo-Catholic revival has borne witness to the fact of "Our Apostolic Descent." But it has sometimes obscured its witness by expounding the ministry as if it were a channel of grace isolated from the life of the Body. Whereas in the more primitive view, seen both in S. Cyprian and in the Eastern church, validity of orders depends upon the life of the Church, some of the Tractarians and their successors were led into a view which is Augustinian and " clericalist " rather than Catholic, and which treats validity of orders as in itself the first basis of the Church's life, and even as the sole test of membership in the Church of God. Expositions of the ministry have been common in which the doctrine of

the organic Body has been ignored. Thus a churchman's manual,[1] which was widely used in the early years of this century, begins with a treatment of the validity of Anglican orders, and only when this is complete does it pass on to the one Body and its faith. S. Cyprian would have been ill-at-ease amid teaching of this kind, and it has hindered many from understanding the meaning of Catholicism.

A whole-hearted return to the Cyprianic view will enable, and does enable, Apostolic succession to be understood more widely. This view insists that valid orders depend upon the Church's life, and that authorization by the whole Church is an integral part of their validity. And a corollary of this view is that, while the orders of the Protestant bodies are gravely deficient, the meaning of the historic orders themselves is obscured by the divisions in historic Christendom, and the restoration of outward unity is needed in order that the full meaning of orders may be seen.[2]

But if mistaken uses of the doctrine of succession have obscured the Anglican witness to the Corpus Christi, a certain modern tendency to be indifferent to questions of order, to harp upon the distinction between the *esse* and the *bene esse* of the Church, and to blur the distinction between Episcopal and other ministries, can obscure not only the Corpus Christi but the Gospel as well. For while the Church of the future needs the historic Apostolate, and the elements represented by Congregationalism and Presbyterianism and by the prophetic ministries of the Reformed bodies, it needs them precisely because they are *not* identical. To blur the distinction between Bishop, presbyter and prophet is to blur a distinction which from the first concerns the Gospel of God. Hence the Anglican church prepares the way for reunion not by indifference to the historic order, but by restoring a truer presentation of it in the context of the Gospel and of the universal Church. It

---

[1] *The Catholic Religion,* by Vernon Staley.
[2] A return to the Cyprianic view is urged by O. C. Quick, *Christian Sacraments,* pp. 134-154 ; and by L. Hodgson, *Essays in Christian Philosophy,* pp. 145-148. But see Appendix II.

does this as it preaches that Gospel; as it lives the life of Christ's Body; as it recovers the true place of Bishop, presbyters and people in the Body's life of Liturgy; and as it points to a reunited Church wherein the truths seen in every section of Christendom must be preserved in full measure, wherein there will be variety of type and form, but wherein the organ of unity will be the one Episcopate, *never* because it is Anglican, *always* because it belongs to the universal family of God.

For while the Anglican church is vindicated by its place in history, with a strikingly balanced witness to Gospel and Church and sound learning, its greater vindication lies in its pointing through its own history to something of which it is a fragment. Its credentials are its incompleteness, with the tension and the travail in its soul. It is clumsy and untidy, it baffles neatness and logic. For it is sent not to commend itself as " the best type of Christianity," but by its very brokenness to point to the universal Church wherein all have died. Hence its story can never differ from the story of the Corinth to which the Apostle wrote. Like Corinth, it has those of Paul, of Peter, of Apollos; like Corinth, it has nothing that it has not received; like Corinth, it learns of unity through its nothingness before the Cross of Christ; and, like Corinth, it sees in the Apostolate its dependence upon the one people of God, and the death by which every member and every Church bears witness to the Body which is one.

CHAPTER XIV

REUNION, DEATH AND RESURRECTION

IF the work of the theologian is, as Maurice once wrote, to dig rather than to build, this distinction applies specially to the problems of Christian reunion :—

"This is what I call digging, this is what I oppose to building. And the more I read the Epistle to the Corinthians, the more I am convinced that this was S. Paul's work, the one by which he helped to undermine and to unite the members of the Apollos, Cephas, Pauline and Christian (for those who said 'we are of Christ' were the worst canters and dividers of all) schools. Christ the actual foundation of the universe ; not Christ a Messiah to those who received Him and shaped Him according to some notion of theirs ; the head of a Body, not the teacher of a religion, was the Christ of S. Paul. And such is a Christ I desire to preach, and to live in, and die in. Only let us each work in the calling whereto God has called us, and ask Him to teach us what it is, and we shall understand one another and work together." (*Life*, II, 138.)

In his search for the unity of the Church the theologian digs in the fields of Christian origins and of the Church's history. This book has attempted to share in the work of digging, and the process has revealed some plain lessons. From Christian *origins* the lesson is clear that the visible Church and its order is an integral part of man's knowledge of Christ crucified. From *history* the lesson is clear that institutionalism fails, unless it is mindful of the Gospel which gives it its meaning ; and that the faith of the Gospel can wither and fade, unless it is mindful of the one historic Church. But the digging discloses not only lessons but the fact of the divine foundation; for, as the débris of old controversies and one-sided systems is cleared away, there appears the pattern of a structure, whose maker and builder is God.

The return of all Christians to this divine structure is not a movement backwards to something ancient and venerable, nor a submission on the part of some to what especially belongs to others. It is the recognition by all of the truth about themselves as members of the one people of God, whose origin is the historical life of Jesus and whose completeness will be known only in the building up of the one Body. For every part of Christendom this recognition means not only the recovery of the one Church order, but the experience of the Passion of Jesus wherein that order has its meaning. Hence the movement towards reunion consists not only or even primarily in the discussions between churches or in their schemes of readjustment, imperative though these may be. It consists rather in the growth within every part of the Church of the truths of the Body and the Passion, no less than of the " outward marks " which express those truths. The unification of outer order can never move faster than the recovery of inward life.

It is in this theological context that the complex problems concerning orders and intercommunion may find their solution. There are many who fear that to insist on Episcopacy is to deny the experience of many Christians and to blaspheme the Holy Ghost; and there are many who feel that intercommunion on a wide scale would hasten reunion. Perhaps, however, in both these cases the view which pays heed to order is also the view which takes us deeper into the truth about the Body and the Passion.

No " unchurching," and no denials of the experience of any Christians need accompany the firmest insistence upon Episcopacy, so long as the insistence is made in terms of the universal Church. The truth manifested in Congregational fellowship, in Presbyterian order, in every section of Christendom will be preserved as parts, but only as parts of the whole. The Episcopate expresses another factor in the truth, namely the one historic family wherein all sections, including those now possessing Episcopacy, shall be made full. No Christian shall deny his Christian experience, but all Christians shall grow more fully into the one experience in all its parts.

The Episcopate succeeded the Apostolate as the organ of unity and continuity. Its meaning is seen in the rites of ordination and in the ordering of the Eucharist. Every ordination and every Eucharist is the act of Christ in His one Body, and the Episcopate expresses this fact in outward order. The Eucharist celebrated in any place is the act of the one family as represented in that place ; and the validity of the ministry and of the rite is bound up with its meaning as the act of the universal Church. Hence, when historic Christendom is divided, the meaning of its orders and of its Eucharist is maimed ; no longer are they performed with the authority and the outward commission of the *whole* visible Church. Thus while the Protestant ministries are something very different from the Apostolate or Episcopate of the historic Church, it is equally true that the meaning of the historic orders is obscured by disunity. Hence all Christians need the restoration of the one Episcopate. It must be restored to its due place in the lives of all Christian people, that all may share in one Eucharist which is, both inwardly and outwardly, the act of the one Church of God.

The task of this book, however, is not to speak of policies for the Church, but only to say what the Church is. It is the people of God, whose unity of race continues despite the scandal of outward division ; and this unity of race has been known to men in every Christian age, and has brought them, through the Passion, a peace which the world has failed to give them. When, through the same Passion, the outward unity is restored, then the world itself shall know that the Father sent the Son. Meanwhile the broken Church is closer to the needs of men than men can ever know, for it is the Body of Christ, who died and rose again. Its order, its worship, its history, its problems of unity and disunity mean the Passion of Jesus. So we end where we began. The Messiah chose to die, Himself the Israel of God.

Many of the deeds of the Messiah's earthly life have their counterpart in the life of His Body. His proclaiming of the Kingdom, His healing and feeding of men, His hours spent apart in prayer to His Father, His desolation on the Cross—all these have been seen in His people,—in those who preach His Word, in the men of philanthropy and compassion, in the men of quiet and contemplation, in the men who have gone into the desert lonely for His sake. As the Messiah rejoiced in nature and in the common life of men, so His Church has entered the world to claim its common things for God ; and as the Messiah faced the nothingness of the world and the end of time, His Church has borne witness to the coming of the end and to the transitoriness of the things of earth. Its history bears witness to Him, and He has borne witness to its history : " the works that I do ye shall do, and greater works than these shall ye do, because I go to my Father."

But, in the midst of His works for men, the Messiah was moving towards death ; and the meaning of His Messiahship was in the obedience whereby He chose to die. Rabbi—He had spoken with authority ; prophet—a great one was amongst us ; philanthropist—He went about doing good ; but all this wealth of human activity He laid aside, and of every conceivable human possibility He stripped Himself, when of His own will He went forth to die. And as He went to die, He embodied in His own flesh the whole meaning of the Church of God ; for its Baptism, its Eucharist, its order, the truth which it teaches to men, the unity which it offers to them, all these mean simply—" ye died, and your life is hid with Christ in God."

The body of Jesus hung lifeless on the Cross to which they had nailed it, and this was the last that the world knew of its Christ. But it was of this body that He spake when He told the Jews that He would raise up the temple of God. " When therefore he was raised from the dead, the disciples remembered that he spake thus ; and they believed the scripture, and the word which Jesus had said."

(THE END)

THE SEE OF ROME AND UNITY

IT was stated in Chapter V that a Papacy which acted as an organ of the Church's general consciousness and authority in doctrine, and which focused the unity of the one Episcopate might claim to fulfil the tests of true development. And it was further stated in Chapter XI that at certain times in history the Papacy conspicuously failed to do this and has thereby been the means of perverting the real meaning of Catholicism. But this historical fact cannot justify a wholesale refusal to consider the Petrine claims. Other organs in the one Body have had their times of failure and of self-aggrandisement, and we do not therefore conclude that they must be discarded. Hence it seems possible that in the reunited Church of the future there may be a special place for a "*primus-inter-pares*" as an organ of unity and authority. Peter will be needed as well as Paul and Apollos, and like them he will be chastened and repentant.

But it is very difficult to define the functions and limits of such a primacy. (1) The New Testament allows us to affirm only that the commission to Peter does not override the commission to the other Apostles, and that the " foundation " includes the Apostles generally. (2) The consensus of the undivided Church allows us to affirm only that the See of Rome has a certain leadership as the Apostolic See of the West, and that this leadership must not override the organic conception of the Church's life and authority. If the claims of Pope Damasus, of the mediæval Popes, of the Vatican Council of 1870 seem intolerable, it is none the less hard to state precisely the limits of a legitimate primacy. The cautious conclusions of Dr. Kidd, in a paper contributed to *The Malines Conversations* (pp. 123-133), are worth quoting :—

" (1) That the Roman Church was founded by S. Peter and S. Paul the two chief Apostles, of the circumcision and of the Gentiles, and is thus the only See in Christendom known to have *two* Apostles for its founders.

" (2) That the Roman See is the only known Apostolic See in the West.

" (3) That the bishop of Rome is the Patriarch of the West ; or, as Augustine said of Pope Innocent I. ' president of the Western Church.' (*Contra Iul. Pelag.* I, 13.)

" (4) That he has a primacy among all the bishops of Christendom ; so that, without communion with him, there is no prospect of a reunited Christendom.

" (5) That to the Roman See the Churches of the English owe their Christianity through ' Gregory our father ' (Council of Clovesho, A.D. 747, c. xvii.) . . . who ' sent us baptism.' " (*Anglo-Saxon Chronicle, Anno* 565.)

Reference should also be made to the brief memorandum prepared by the Anglican delegation at Malines (*Report*, pp. 289-290), which states frankly that it is impossible to define precisely the relation of Pope and Bishops.

This conclusion may seem so vague as to be worthless, but this is surely not the case. For a primacy should depend upon and express the organic authority of the Body ; and the discovery of its precise functions will come not by discussion of the Petrine claims in isolation but by the recovery everywhere of the Body's organic life, with its Bishops, presbyters and people. In this Body Peter will find his due place, and ultimate reunion is hastened not by the pursuit of ' the Papal controversy ' but by the quiet growth of the organic life of every part of Christendom.

APPENDIX II

IN several places in this book I have expressed the belief that when the Church on earth is divided the meaning of the historic orders is obscured. I cannot, however, ally myself to the theory that in a divided Church all orders are relatively invalid and need to be validated by receiving authority from this and that portion of Christendom. The whole Church does not mean the totality of the Christians of a particular generation who confer authority like a democracy: it is a Body reaching across the generations, and it possesses the organs whereby authority is given to its ministers within the context of its common life.

I quote some words of the late Archbishop Temple spoken to the Convocation of Canterbury on 25th May, 1943: " When we go back to the first records of the Church we find neither a Ministry which called people into association with it, nor an undifferentiated fellowship which delegated powers to a Ministry: but we find a complete Church, with the Apostolate accepted as its focus of administration and authority. When the Lord's earthly ministry was ended there was found in the world as its fruit and as means of its continuance this Body, in which the distinction of Ministry and laity is already established. The Apostles were in no sense ministers of the laity; they were ministers of Christ to the laity, and to the world waiting to be won. They took steps for the perpetuation of the ministry, and it has descended to ourselves. *So when I consecrate a godly and well learned man to the office and work of a Bishop in the Church of God, I do not act as a representative of the Church, if by that is meant the whole number of contemporary Christians; but I do act as the ministerial instrument of Christ in His Body the Church. The authority by which I act is His, transmitted to me through His apostles and those to whom they committed it; I hold it neither from the Church nor apart from the Church, but from Christ in the Church.* I was myself admitted to the Episcopate by the twofold succession—succession in office and succession of consecration. The two streams of succession are different from the point where they converged upon me; but as we trace them back they meet again at some point previous to Gregory who sent Augustine and Vergilius who consecrated him; and so the double line runs back to apostolic times.

This authority to consecrate and ordain is itself witness to the continuity of the life of the Church in its unceasing dependence on its Head, Jesus Christ, who is the same yesterday and today and for ever. Every priest who by virtue of his Ordination celebrates the Holy Communion acts not for the congregation there present nor for all Christian people then living on the earth, but as the organ of the Body of Christ, the ministerial instrument of Christ active in and through His Body; so that though no more than two or three persons be actually assembled, yet the congregation at that Holy Communion service is the Communion of Saints, with which the persons present, be they few or many, are there conjoined. Here therefore, as in the Incarnation itself, we find the eternal in the midst of time, the secret of a fellowship against which the gates of death cannot prevail. (*The Church Looks Forward*, pp. 24-25; the italics are mine.)

INDEX OF SUBJECTS

231

INDEX OF NAMES

233